POSTCARD HISTORY SERIES

Augusta

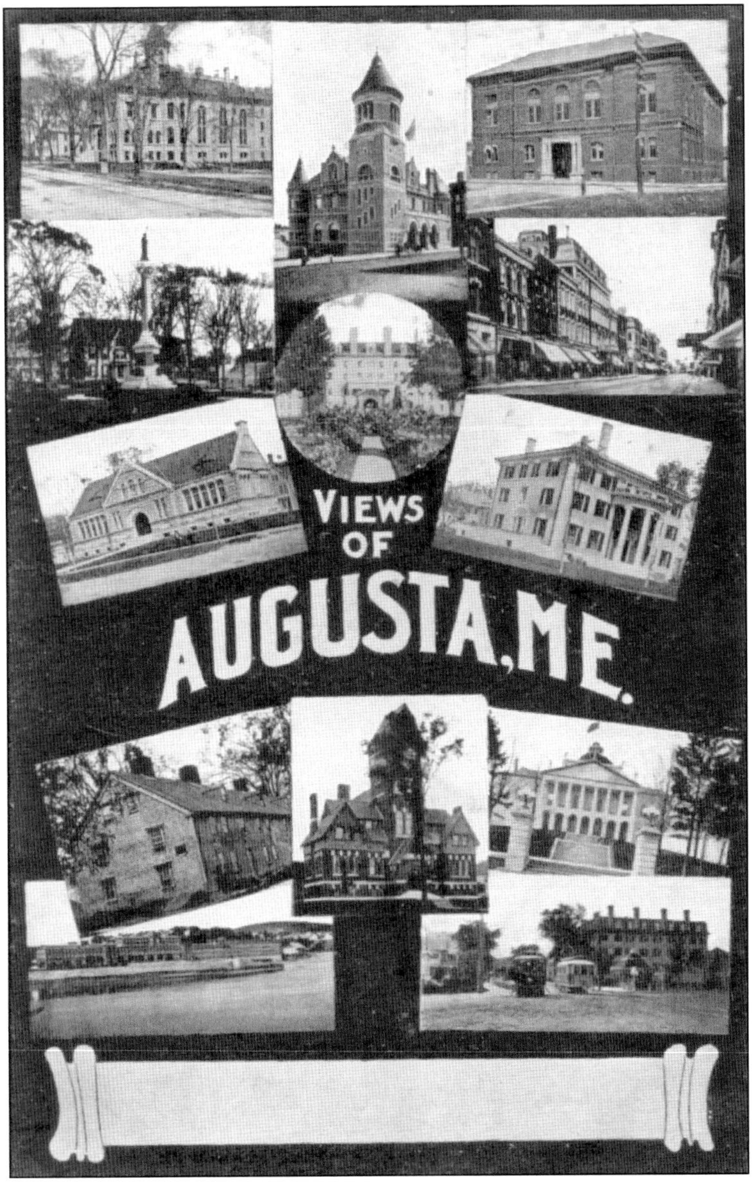

This 1906 postcard provides just a small flavor of the rich history and landmarks that Augusta had to offer at the turn of the century. From left to right are (top row) the Kennebec County Jail, the post office, and city hall; (second row) Monument Park, Maine Insane Asylum, and the bustle of Water Street; (third row) Lithgow Library and Governor Hill's residence; (fourth row) Fort Western, Cony High School, and the State House; (bottom row) Edwards Mill along the waterfront and the Augusta House. (Author's collection.)

On the Front Cover: The trustees of the late judge Daniel Cony completed the Cony Free High School at the junction of Cony and Stone Streets in 1881. The inscription on the memorial fountain, installed in 1897, reads, "In memory of Daniel A. Cony erected by the wish of his sister Susan Cony Manley." Daniel and Susan were the children of Gov. Samuel Cony and the great-grandchildren of Judge Cony. (Author's collection.)

On the Back Cover: After the Great Fire of 1865 had consumed 81 buildings on both sides of Water Street, the rebuilding of the downtown area using brick and stone began the following year. Many of these buildings are from that reconstruction period. In the foreground, a boy can be seen boarding the No. 43 trolley bound for Gardiner. This view is from the balcony of the now gone Hotel North. (Author's collection.)

POSTCARD HISTORY SERIES

Augusta

Roger A. Madore

ARCADIA
PUBLISHING

ISBN 978-1-4671-2271-9

Published by Arcadia Publishing
Charleston, South Carolina

Printed in the United States of America

Library of Congress Control Number: 2014942344

For all general information contact Arcadia Publishing at:
Telephone 843-853-2070
Fax 843-853-0044
E-mail sales@arcadiapublishing.com
For customer service and orders:
Toll-Free 1-888-313-2665

Visit us on the Internet at www.arcadiapublishing.com

To all the Augustans who came before, and to those of today who give them pause and remembrance, this book is dedicated to you.

Contents

Acknowledgments

I do not recall the day or even the year that I was first fascinated by history, but I do remember the exact moment. While walking to the school bus stop in the mid-1970s, I happened upon a tiny piece of paper lying in the street, which I promptly grabbed and stuffed into my pocket. Later that evening, I retrieved the wrinkled scrap and announced to my parents that I wanted to collect stamps, proudly displaying my very first acquisition. It turned out that my first stamp was really just a sticker, but no matter—the seeds had been sown and the collecting bug bit hard. For the next several years, my parents would bring home stamps from their offices, chaperone me to stamp shows, and help me learn the proper care and preservation of these little works of art. They nurtured my love for history and the appreciation of the significance of not just the small bits of paper, but also for the subjects for which they portray. And for that, I will always be eternally grateful to my parents, Robert Madore and Gloria Hills.

I wish to thank Zachary Violette for his insight regarding some of Augusta's most important architectural subjects, and applaud his comprehensive research on Water Street, Winthrop Street, and Sand Hill. The patient folks at the Maine State Library and Lithgow Library who went above and beyond are to be lauded for all their efforts. I also wish to thank the Kennebec Historical Society and Maine Historical Society for their amazing work and collections. And, of course, thanks to my editor, Caitrin Cunningham, for keeping me focused, motivated, and inspired.

The articles of the 19th century *Daily Kennebec Journal* and *Lewiston Evening Journal* were instrumental in much of the text of this book. And any research of Augusta would not be complete without the inclusion of James W. North's *History of Augusta* (1870), *Leading Business Men of Lewiston, Augusta and Vicinity* (1889), *Illustrated History of Kennebec County, Maine* (1892), and the *Augusta Centennial Souvenir* (1897), published by the *Daily Kennebec Journal.*

Unless otherwise noted, all images are from the author's collection.

INTRODUCTION

From the very beginning, the people who built Augusta have had an unshakable resolve. With the first explorers establishing the Cushnoc Trading Post in 1628 and, later, the settlers founding the permanent encampment of Fort Western in 1754, early Augustans understood the importance and value of the valley and its resources along the river, and they were determined to make this area their home, no matter what the obstacles. Even the mighty Kennebec River could not dull their spirit. Beginning in the early 1800s, floods and fires damaged or destroyed the dam many times over, but each time, it was rebuilt better and stronger. And with the dam came great industries. Lumber mills, textile mills, and gristmills heavily populated both sides of the river, and soon, ice harvesting, manufacturing, and publishing grew into big business for Augusta. Thousands of workers, many of them French American, migrated to the area with the ambition to toil in the workshops and mills, never shying from a hard day's labor. Innovations in printing, marketing, and sales made the publications of E.C. Allen, Gannett & Morse, and Vickery & Hill some of the most popular in the world during the late 18th century and beyond. The very essence of the tenacious spirit, inspired ingenuity, and hard work that built Augusta's structures, streets, monuments, and the city itself can be seen within the postcards of a century ago.

Although having been in use for well over 100 years, the golden age of postcards occurred during the 20-year period from 1898 to 1918, with the majority of the images in this book dated after 1905. Subjects portrayed often included historic buildings and sites, along with other items of local interest. Some were used as early advertisements, while others were quite personal, depicting private homes or people. A popular collectible even early on, postcards were more than just pretty keepsakes. They were used to send daily messages, such as notifying relatives of a safe arrival in town or canceling a piano lesson scheduled for the following day. For the cost of a postcard and one cent, one could send a message anywhere in the country. In essence, the postcard was the equivalent of the text message or e-mail of today. As the telephone became more widespread, the functionality of postcards began to decline, which led to their delegation as a colorful souvenir.

Downtown Augusta was once the center of the city's business, shopping, and entertainment venues. Restaurants, bakeries, candy shops, millineries, shoe stores, and department stores—all lined Water Street under the many brick and stone edifices of the hotels and other blocks. Transportation was available from the Maine Central Railroad station or the local trolley, or even horses could be rented from the local livery stables, if so desired. Many publishers could be found downtown, as could the banks and post office that supported them. Virtually everything the early city dweller would want could be found here. And on more than one occasion, parades would occupy the entire length and breadth of Water Street, adding even more to the sights and sounds, and occasional smells, of the already bustling downtown. From Rines Hill to Bridge Street, chapter one gives a taste of this busy district.

Chapter two showcases several of the splendid and unique public buildings that Augusta has offered to residents of the city and to all of Maine over the years. From its construction in 1832, the State House has blossomed, both inside and out, into the grand edifice that it is today. Many county and city government structures, such as the county jail, courthouse, city hall, and fire stations, have evolved accordingly to meet the needs of its people and, in some cases, have been rebuilt several times. The local resources of the Lithgow Library and YMCA are also recognized for their contributions to Augusta, as are the many schools, including Cony High School and several grade schools. The Augusta General Hospital and the Maine State Asylum have cared for thousands of people and have grown and expanded over the years, just as the city has. And no text regarding Augusta would ever be complete without including the landmark that is the core of the city—Old Fort Western.

The churches of Augusta are some of the oldest and most recognized sites of the city, and chapter three contains many of these places of worship. Though most are built from granite, a few of the churches were initially constructed of wood, the transformation of which is seen through these images. There is a wide variety of residential architecture in the city, as seen in chapter four. The Colonial style was quite popular, but other eclectic designs also found their place in the city and the rural communities. From the late 1800s into the early 20th century, many of the wealthy owned expansive estates, often the topics of postcards. John F. Hill and his son Percy V. Hill both had magnificent homes on State Street, but the largest estate, Ganneston Park, was owned by William H. Gannett.

Chapter five contains many of Augusta's industries, including publishing firms, shoe and textile manufacturers, lumber mills, and gristmills, many of which would not have been possible without the Kennebec Dam. The modes and means of transportation, depicted in chapter six, were the lifeblood of the city. While the bridges tied the halves of Augusta together and contributed much of its character, it was the roadways, railways, trolleys, and shipping lanes upon the Kennebec River that produced motive power for trade and the commute of travelers.

There were many hotels throughout Augusta, but sadly, not many were subjects of postcards. The few that were depicted, such as the Augusta House and its growth throughout the years, as well as the Hotel North, appear in chapter seven. Chapter eight shows many of the parks, public grounds, and monuments that honor Augustans whose contributions made the city what it is today. Although not depicted in this book, the memorial in Monument Park honoring the fallen of the later conflicts has special significance to me, as my grandfather Harvey J. Madore gave his life for his country in World War II.

Many of the streets presented in chapter nine are just as old as the city itself. From the tree-lined avenues to the dirt country roads, every area took on the character of the people who lived there, and the street views of these postcards bring to life the spirit of each neighborhood. Chapter ten introduces the Kennebec River and Bond Brook, along with some of the industries and activities that occur upon them. Though commercial transportation and manufacturing contributed much to life on the water, there were other aspects, some a bit more subtle, that made the river unique and enjoyable.

I have often wondered what life would have been like in Augusta 100 years ago. With postcards being a window into the past and painting more than 1,000 words per picture, I can see what my grandparents and great-grandparents saw and understand the city in which I live a little better. Please enjoy this journey back into Augusta's history, and I hope you can make just as many personal connections as I have.

One

Downtown

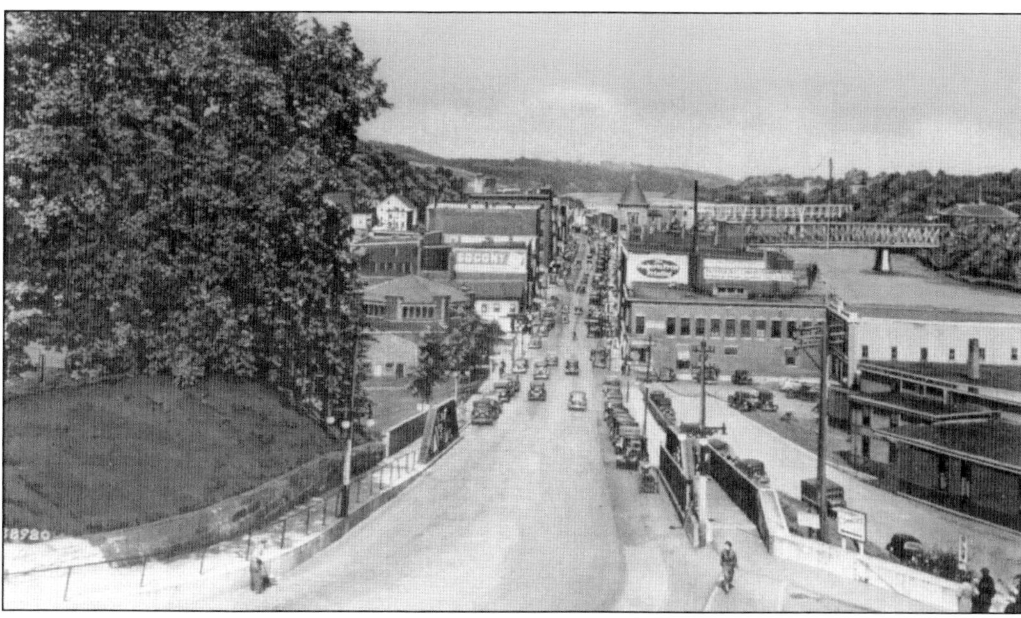

Many of Augusta's landmarks are visible when viewed from atop the Hartford Fire Station. At the bottom of Rines Hill, the octagonal seating room of the train station is clearly visible. Across the street is the tower of the post office. The trusses of the Kennebec River Bridge are seen with the railroad bridge directly behind it. To the far right is the roof of city hall.

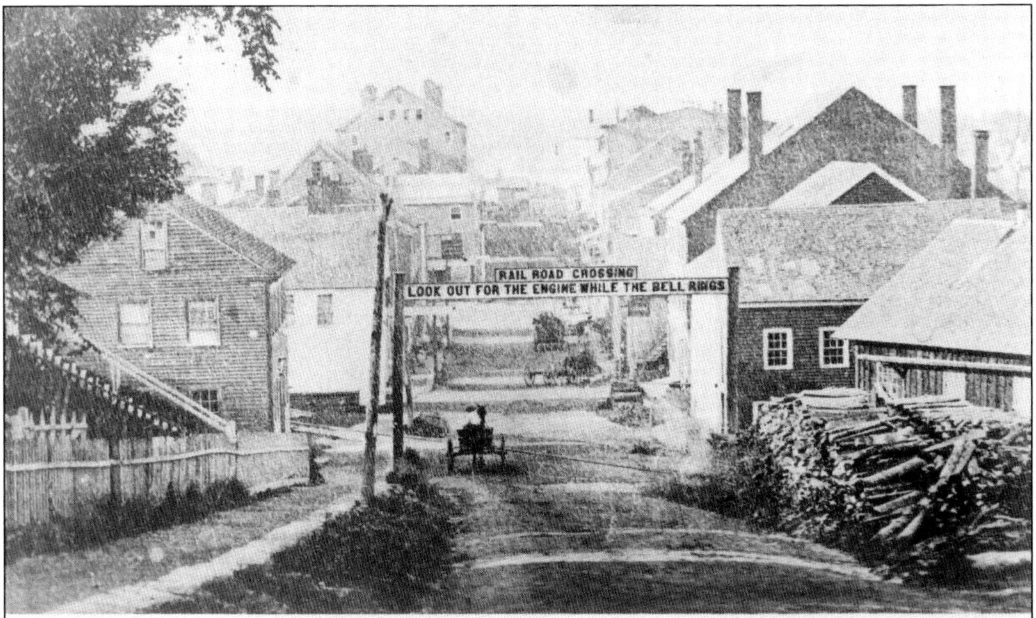

WATER STREET, AUGUSTA, MAINE, from Rines Hill, previous to big fire in September, 1865

On the morning of September 17, 1865, fire swept through the city, destroying 81 buildings between Bridge and Winthrop Streets. Virtually every structure seen above the top of the railroad crossing sign had burned; only the four nearest the bridge remained standing. George W. Jones was convicted of starting the blaze in a newly constructed wooden building on the east side, near the base of Oak Street.

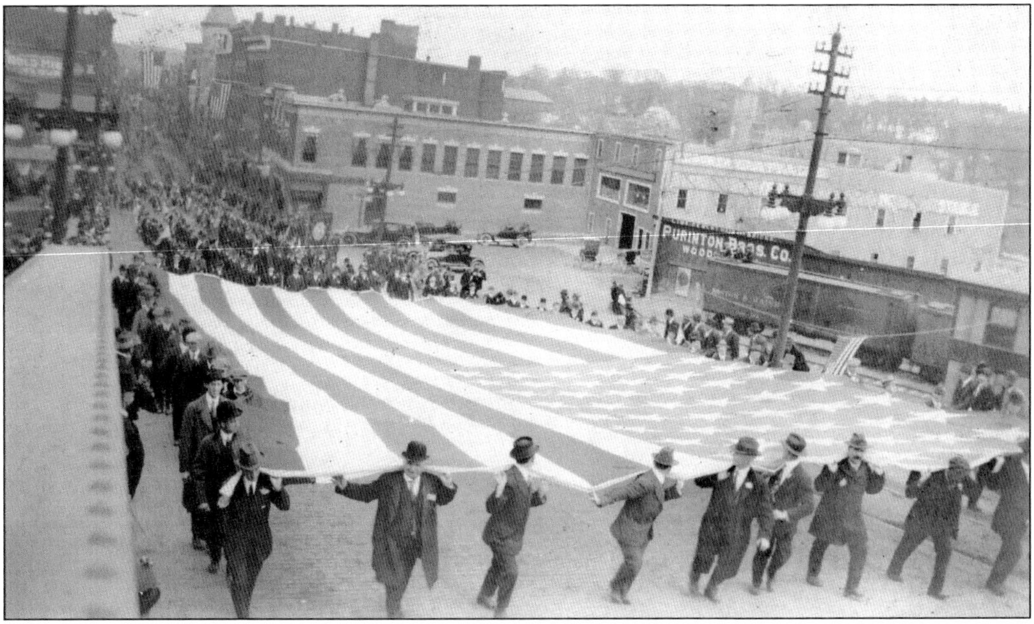

Though this postcard is undated, it was most likely created between 1916 and 1918. In a marching parade, a local chapter of one of the fraternal organizations carries the huge 48-star American flag up Rines Hill. A combination livery stable and garage is located behind Purinton Brothers coal and wood shed, with a variety of automobiles and carriages parked in front.

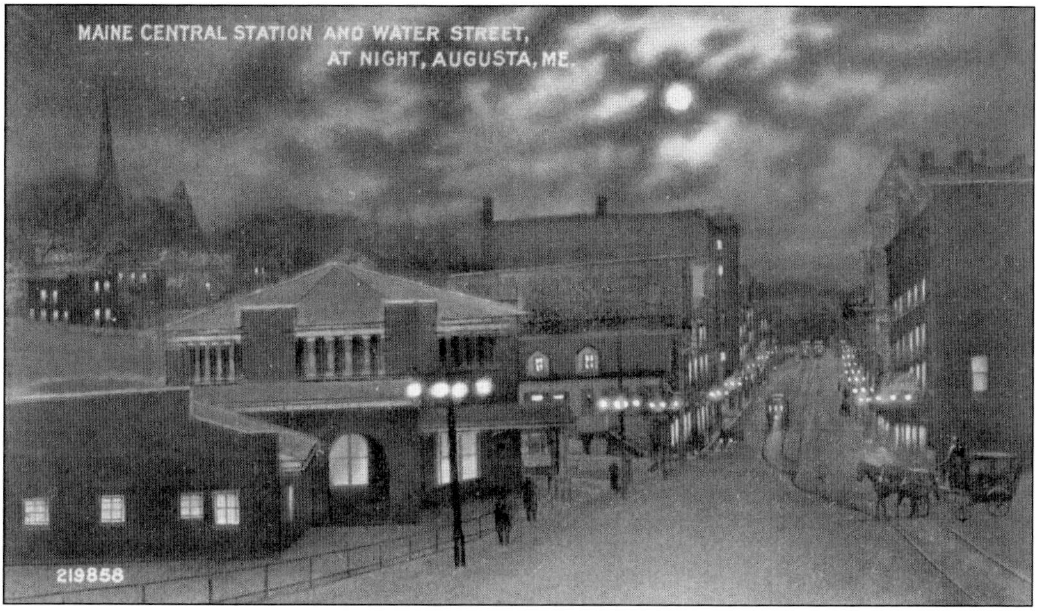

The city's nights were pulled out of darkness when the first streetlamps of the Augusta Gas Light Company were lit in 1859. But it was not until October 1888 that Augusta really began to shine, with the installation of 54 electric arc lights on the street corners by the Kennebec Light and Heat Company. Capable of producing 2,000 candlepower each, they were as bright as 270 gaslights.

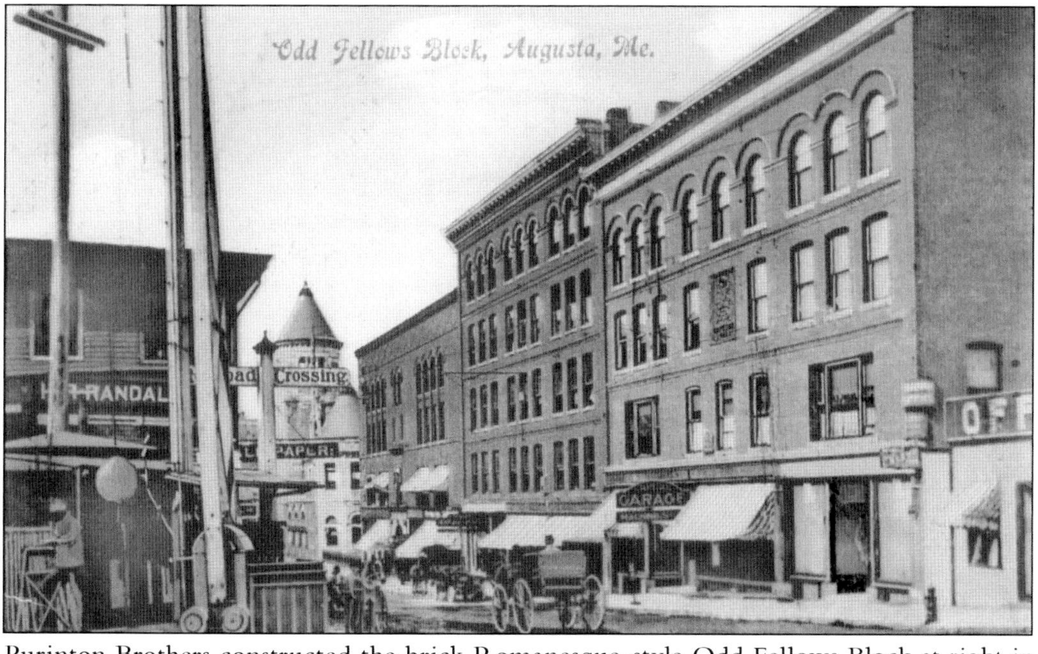

Purinton Brothers constructed the brick Romanesque-style Odd Fellows Block at right in 1898. Farther north is the Gannett Building, built in the Renaissance Revival in 1899 to house the newspaper concerns of the *Kennebec Journal*. Soon after its completion, Gannett purchased the building, where he began publishing *Comfort* magazine. The Masonic Hall, a Romanesque Revival edifice built by Bostonian John C. Spofford in 1894, is just beyond.

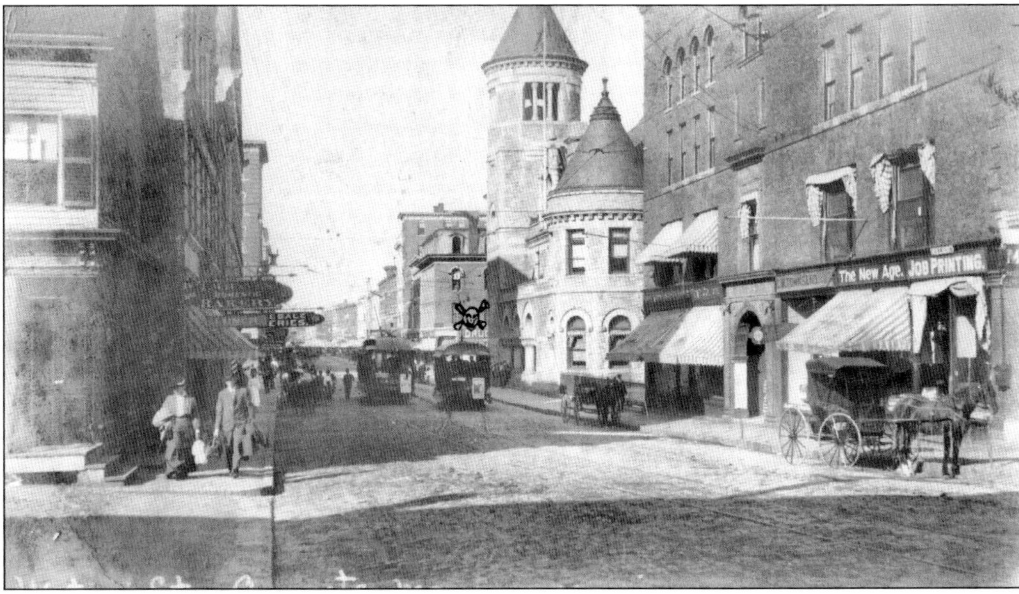

The *Age* was established in 1831 and soon became Maine's most influential Democratic journal, although it did not come without controversy. The editor, Frank Smith, had accused a Belgrade man of being a deserter of the War of 1812, and was subsequently sued for libel. Smith's charges were sustained, which boosted circulation. The paper was bought in 1881, and the name changed to the *New Age*, seen here at the Masonic Hall.

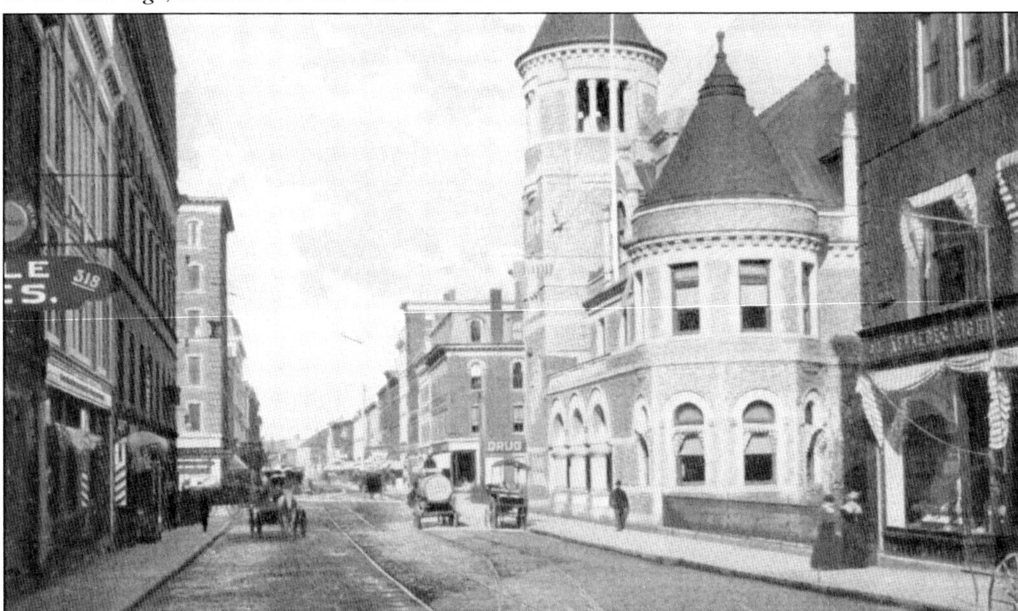

The Kennebec Light and Heat Company was organized in 1887, and by the turn of the century, they had established their business offices at 313 Water Street, in the Masonic Hall. Central Maine Power Company (CMP) purchased Kennebec Light and Heat in 1911 and moved into the latter's Water Street offices the following year. In 1916, CMP opened their first retail electric appliance store at the same location.

Ezekiel Holmes began the *Maine Farmer* in Winthrop as a paper catering to the interests of agriculture and livestock in 1832. Russell Eaton purchased the newspaper in 1843 and moved it to the Granite Bank in Augusta. After relocating twice more on Water Street, current owners Holman and Badger erected the Maine Farmer building in 1904 to house their newspaper business. Woolworth's occupied the ground floor prior to 1913.

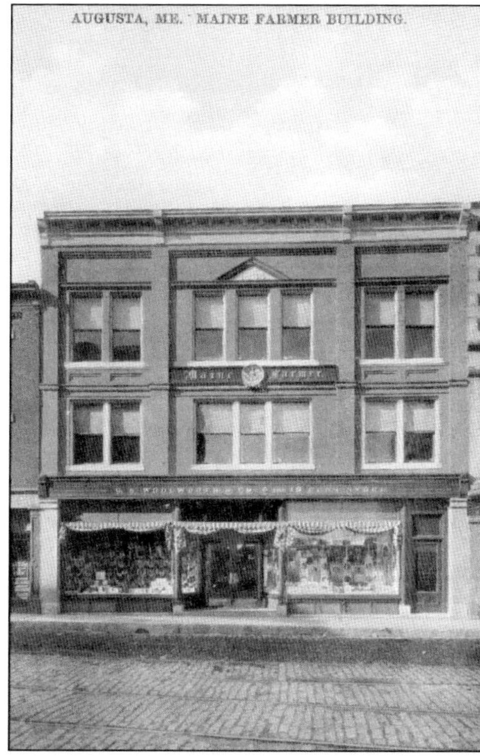

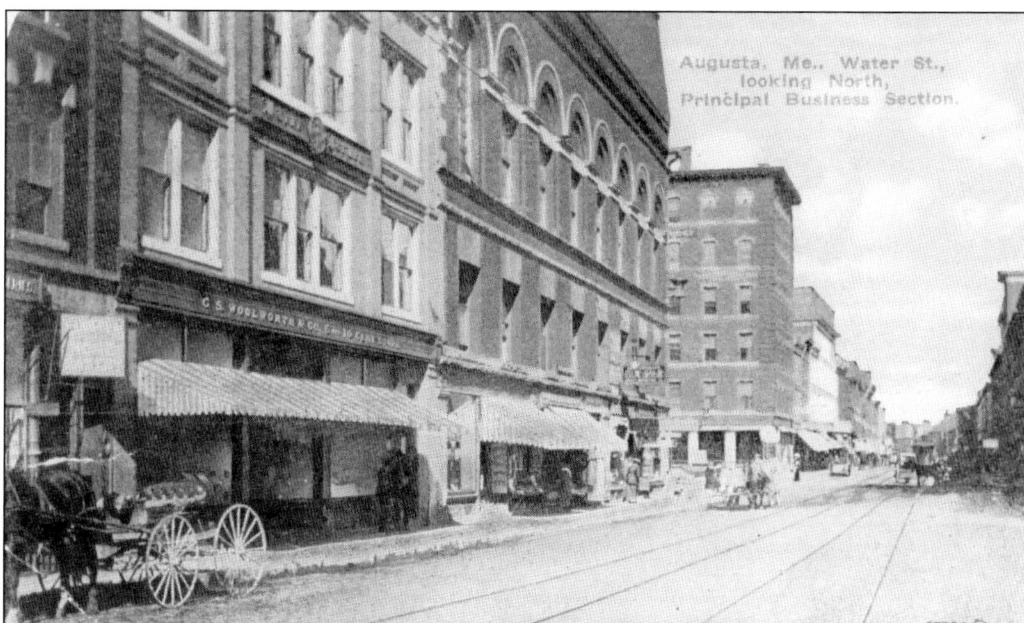

Many of downtown's structures contained storefronts on the first floor, with office spaces or other establishments on the upper floors. C.S. Woolworth's was located in the Farmer Building at left, and at various times, Charles K. Partridge's drugstore, Perry's Restaurant, and Kennebec Savings Bank all occupied spaces under Granite Hall. The Augusta Trust Company and the Hotel North, which also housed retail spaces, can be seen farther up Water Street.

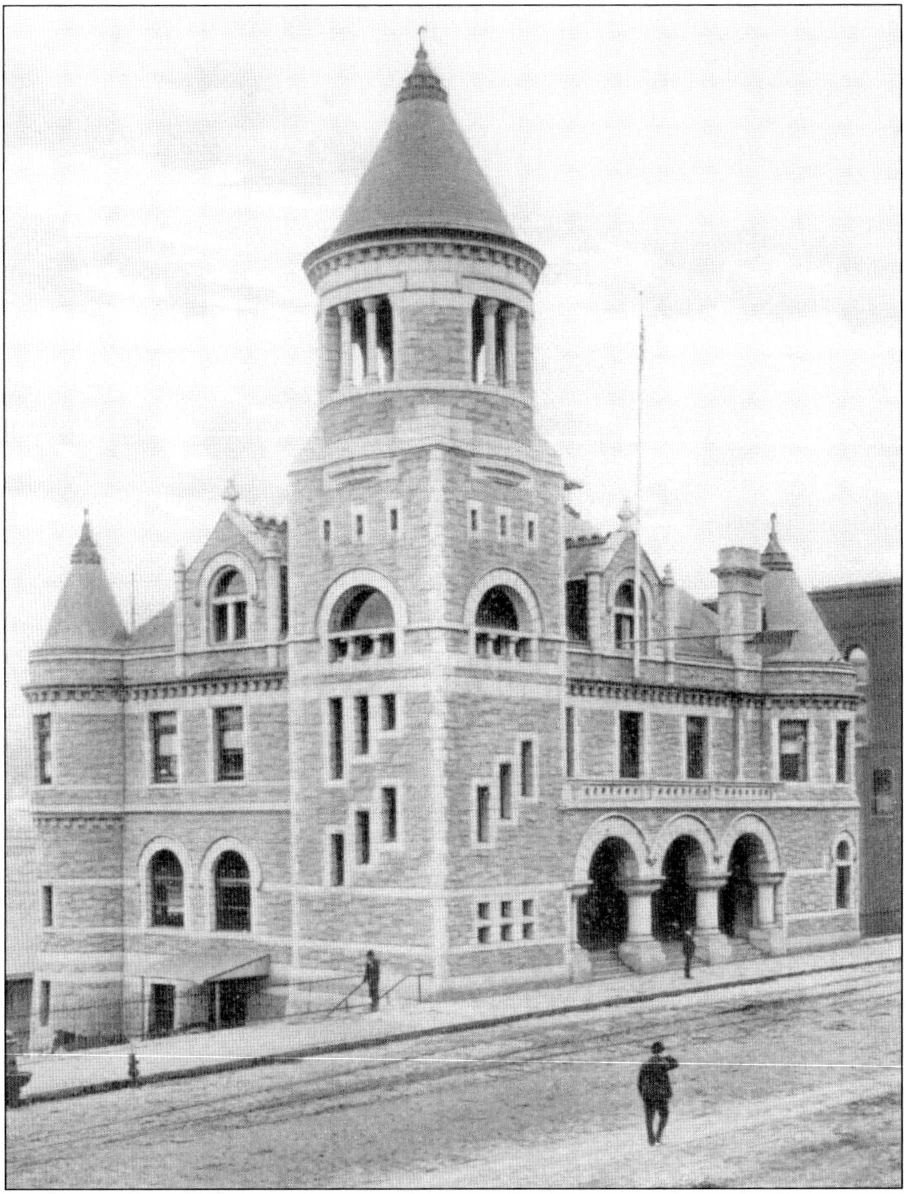

In August 1794, James Burton became the first postmaster in what would become Augusta and operated the post office within his home, where Meonian Hall now stands. Mail was only received once per week, with one sack sent out via horseback. Over time, Augusta's post office expanded to two locations to handle the ever-increasing amount of magazines and newspapers, but with upwards of 40 tons of second-class mail being produced daily by the local publishing houses, a new post office that could handle the volume was required. Built of Hallowell granite in the Richardsonian Romanesque style, the 32,000-square-foot structure was completed at a cost of $250,000 and opened on January 17, 1890. The post office used the first floor, while a US courtroom, judge's room, and clerk's and pension rooms occupied the second floor. The entire basement was devoted to the newspaper mailing department. Under the watchful eye of postmaster Joseph H. Manley, the post office generated $600,000 in receipts annually for all mail, with a staff of 30 personnel working day and night.

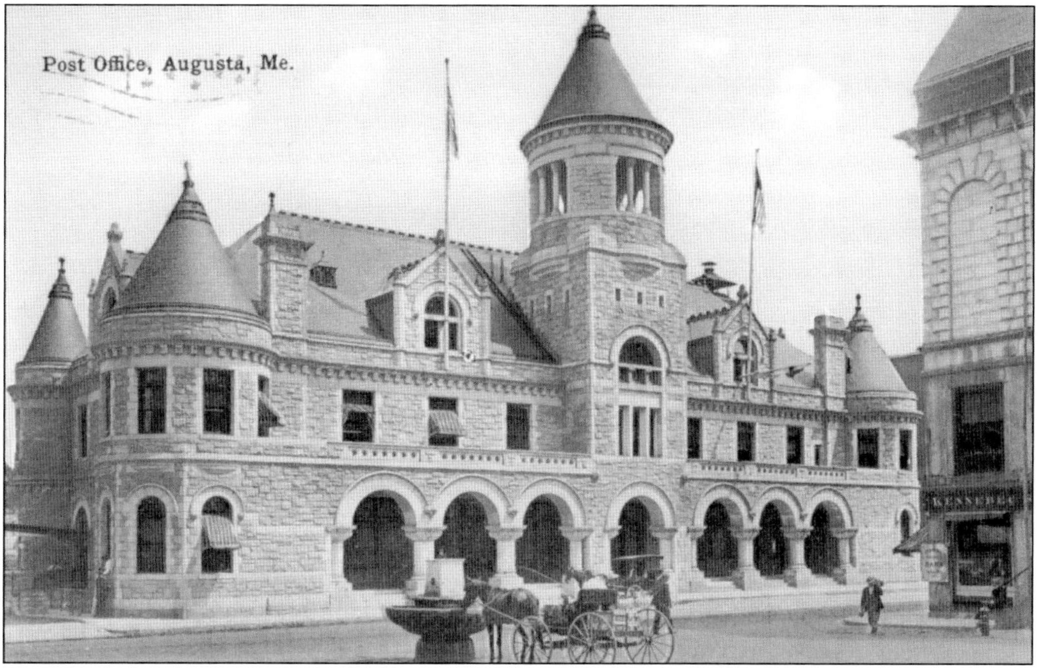

Within 20 years, it became obvious that the design by Mifflin Bell, supervising architect of the US Treasury Department, proved to be inadequate to handle the amount of mail required. The north wing was added in 1910, effectively doubling the floor space, and its 98-foot corner tower became the central focal point of the symmetrical structure.

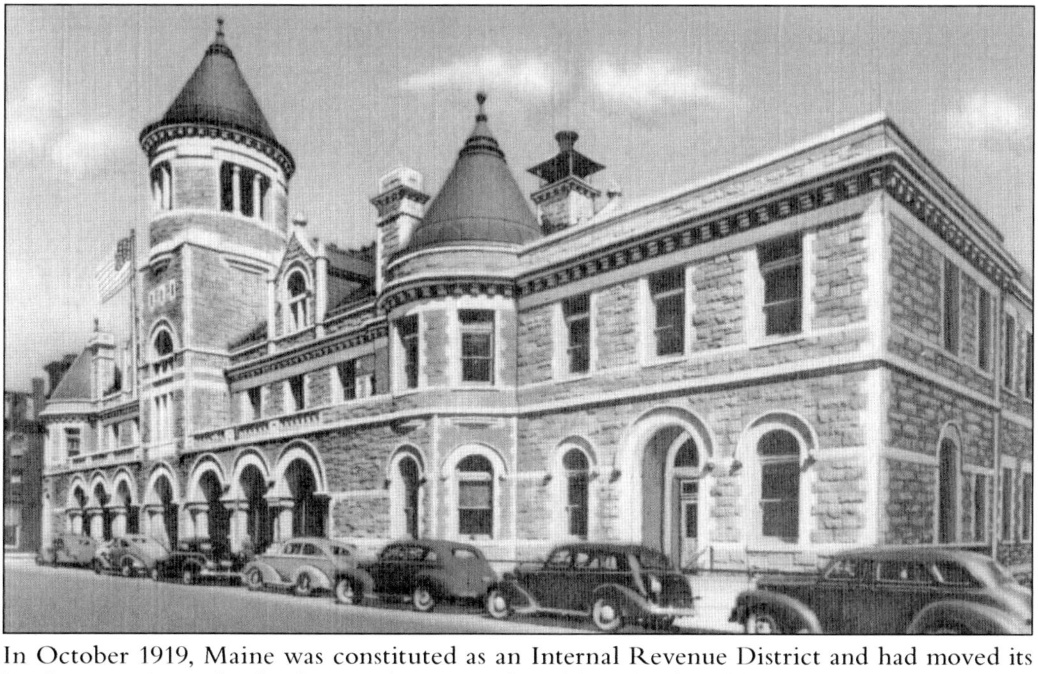

In October 1919, Maine was constituted as an Internal Revenue District and had moved its headquarters into what has become known as the Olde Federal Building. With the second floor being devoted almost exclusively to the tax department, it was not long before space was again at a premium, and by the mid-20th century, the south wing was added.

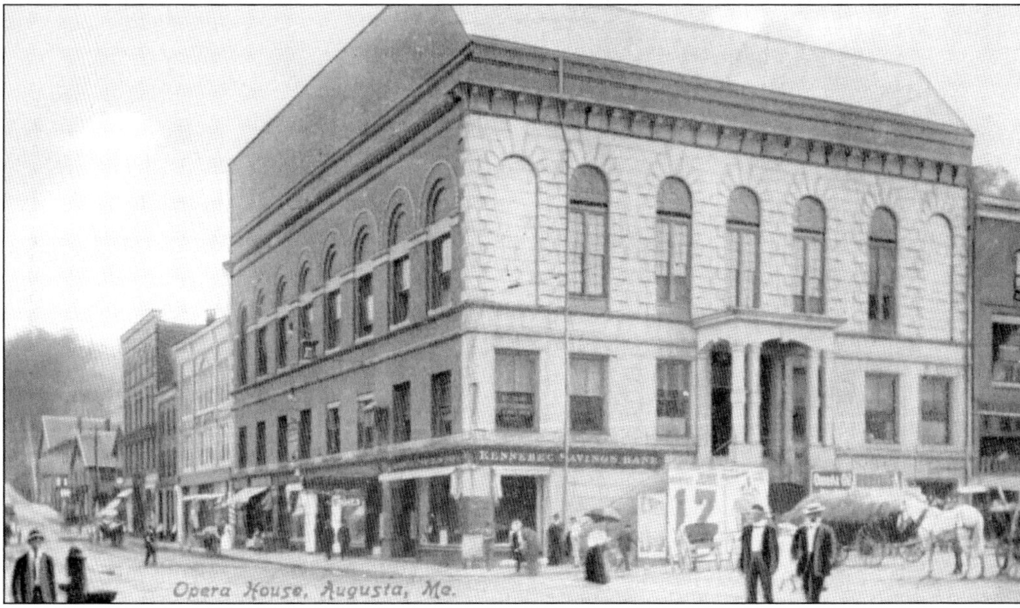

Granite Hall, later known as the Opera House, was built on the corner of Market Square and Water Street in 1866. The three-story edifice had businesses and offices on the first two floors and a 1,500-seat hall on the third. The structure survived fires in 1890 and 1896 and was rebuilt. After remodeling in the 1930s, it opened as the Capitol Movie Theater but, ultimately, was razed in 1983.

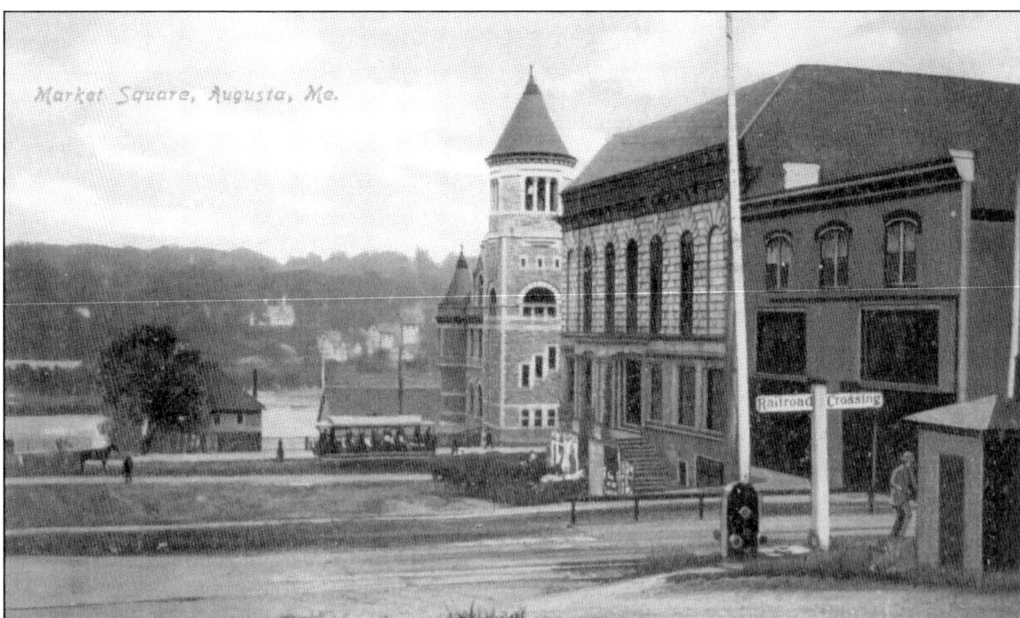

Granite Hall largely frames the southern side of Market Square. In front of it is the Cony Livery, which eventually became the location of R.W. Soule's furniture company. The post office can be seen on the other side of Water Street, along with the Augusta Yacht Club just behind the trees near the river. In the center of the street, a nine-bench open trolley car is heading toward Gardiner.

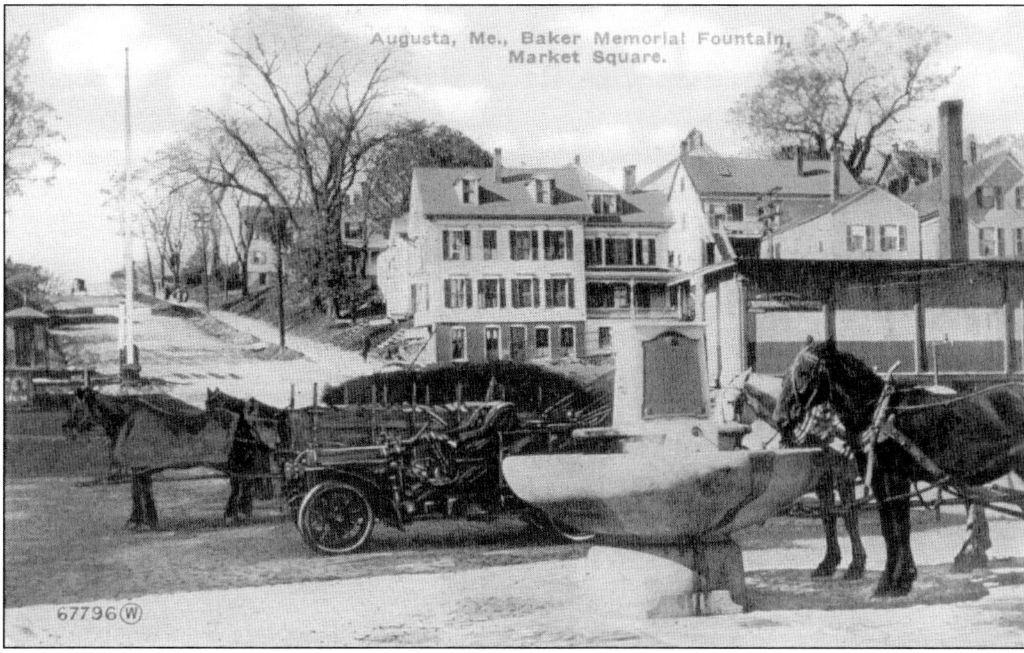

Looking toward lower Winthrop Street, a row of houses on Dickman Street can be seen peering from behind Maine Central Railroad's passenger station. The fire of 1865 had consumed the buildings up to this point. Peleg Morton built the house at center in 1875; it was a two-and-a-half-story Italianate home with a brick first floor. In 1974, the house was torn down for parking.

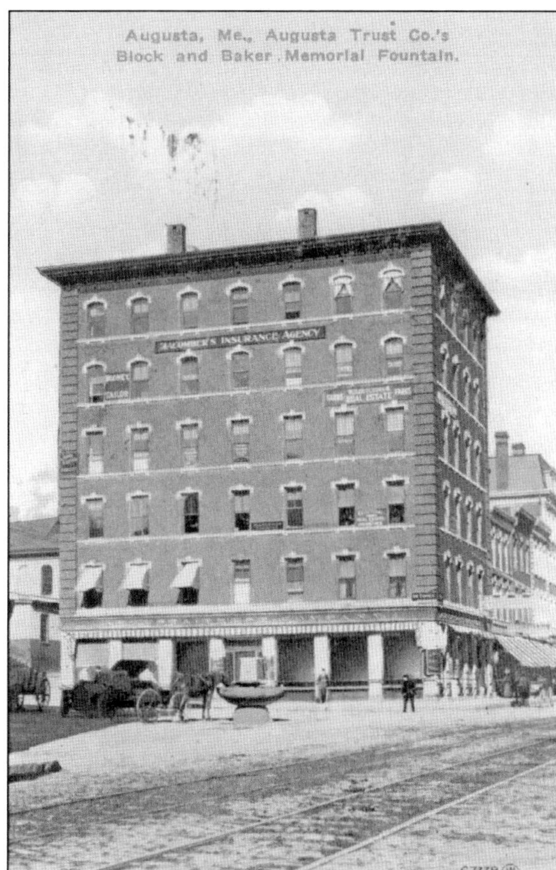

E.C. Allen had expanded yet again when he built this six-story structure at Market Square in 1880. Designed by George G. Stevens, it was erected opposite of Allen's original publishing house on Water Street and connected to it through an underground tunnel. After Allen's death in 1891, J. Manchester Haynes organized the Augusta Trust Company in 1894 and soon occupied the building.

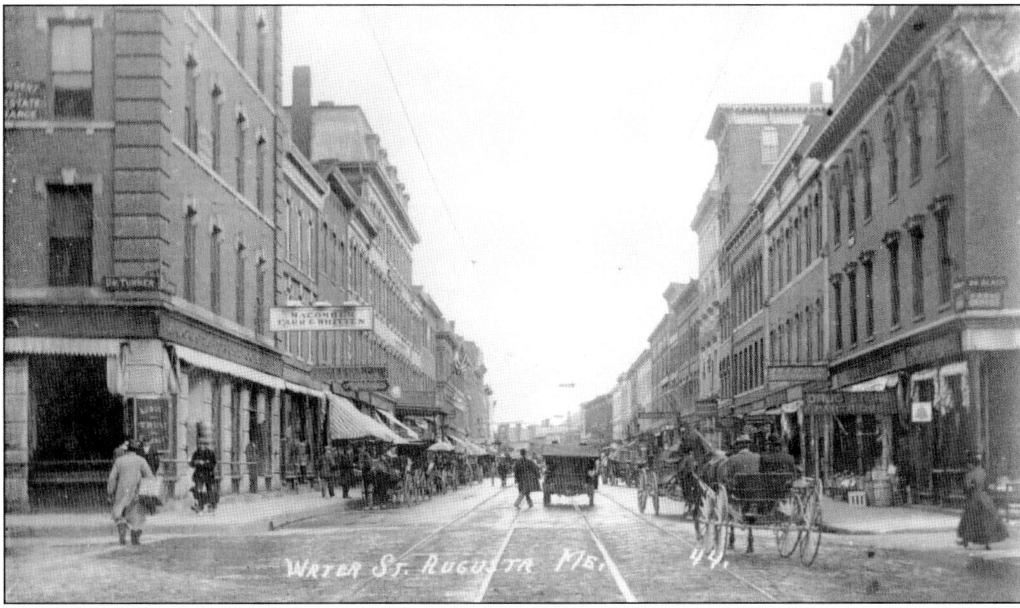

As one of Augusta's pioneering publishers, Edward Charles Allen was almost solely responsible for the need of the new post office. Outgrowing his rented accommodations, Allen built the mansard-roofed structure at right in 1872. Allen later expanded by erecting another building farther north in 1877. George G. Stevens designed both buildings. The first building's mansard roof has since been replaced with a fourth floor.

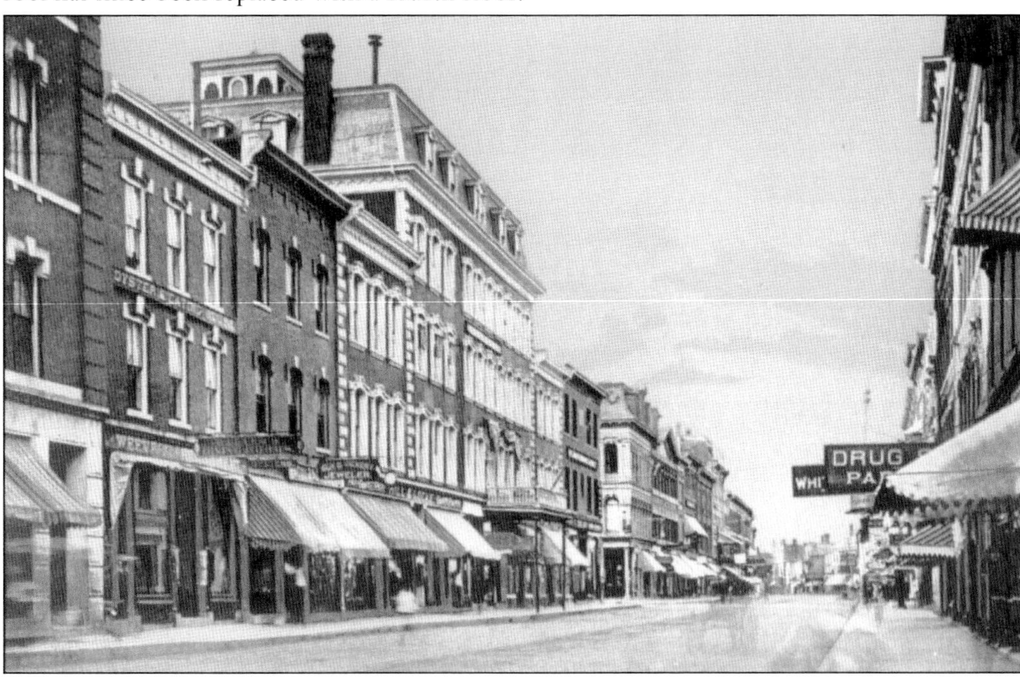

On the far left is the Potter Building, also called the Weaver Building. It was erected between 1872 and 1880 and served as a dining room for many years. Next to it is the Italianate-style Kinsman Block, built by Fred Kinsman around 1910. The Hotel North sits directly in the center, and the Day Building, or Alden Block, occupies the northernmost lot, constructed in 1902.

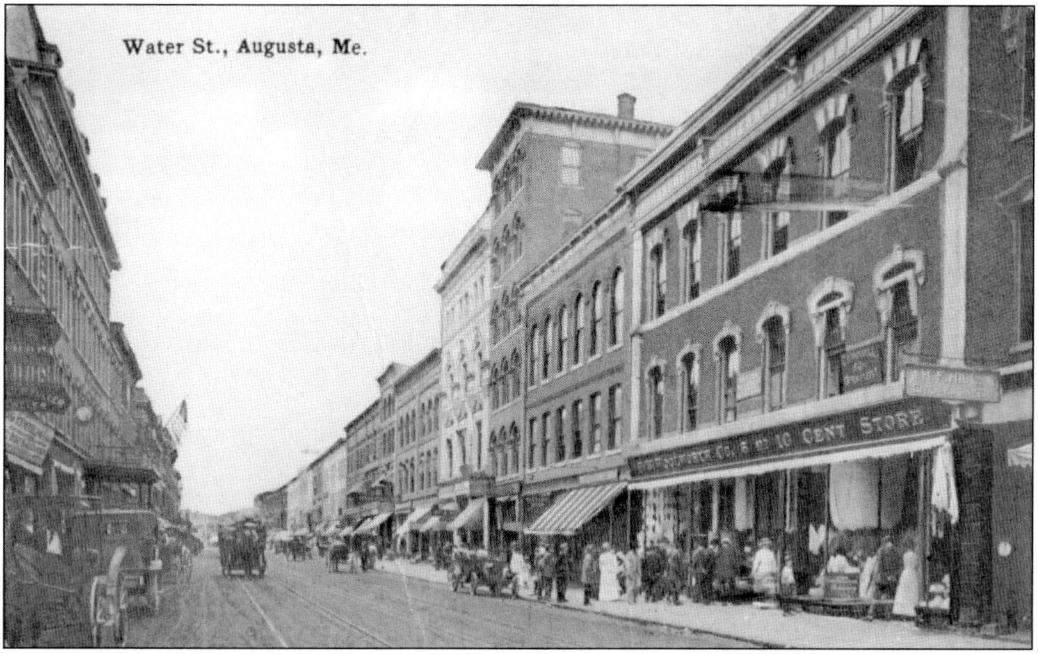

The F.W. Woolworth Company occupied the first floor of E.C. Allen's 1877 Italianate-style expansion to his publishing company. The building to its left originally was a two-story brick structure built by Parrott & Bradbury in 1866. In the 1880s, it was used as a sub–post office due to the large volume of magazines. The third floor had been added later.

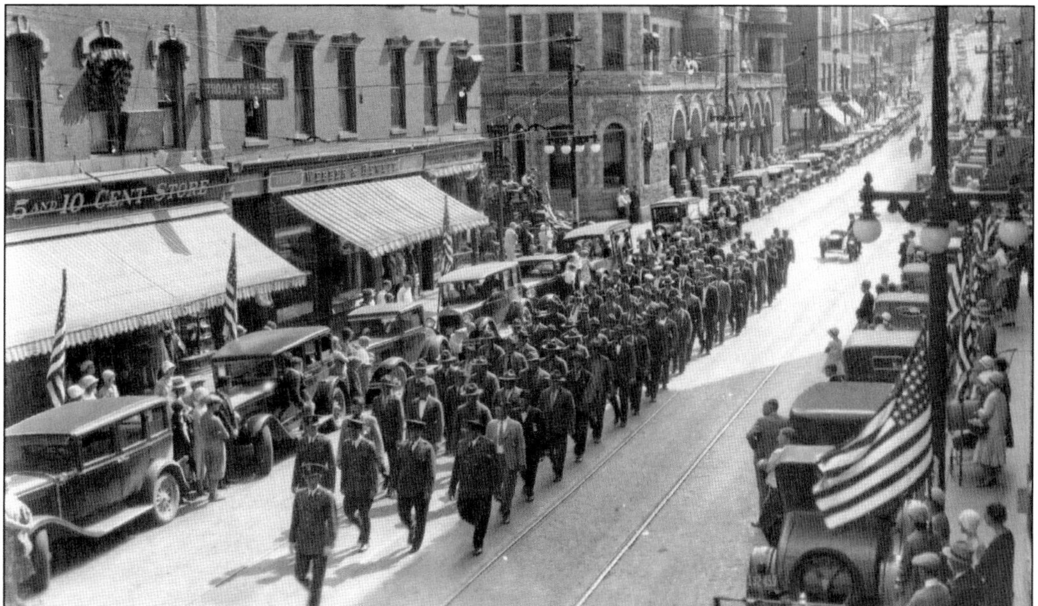

This real-photo postcard of an early 1930s parade was taken from the balcony of Hotel North. Woolworth's five-and-ten can be seen in the second of the Allen buildings, while Webber & Hewett's grocery store and George E. Frye's jewelry store is in the first. The balconies of the post office and the 1910 expansion also made wonderful vantage points from which to watch the parade.

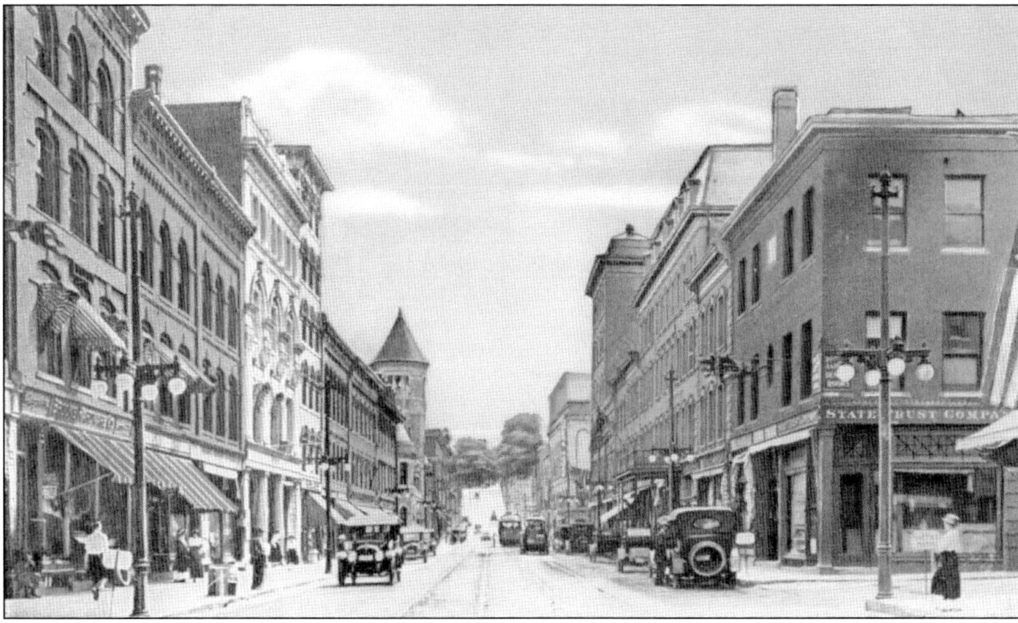

The Alden Block, located on the corner of Oak Street, was built in 1902. First occupied by the American Express Company, it was remodeled for the State Trust Company in 1913. Opposite are the Jones and Quimby buildings. John Spofford designed the Vickery Building, farther south, in an Italian Renaissance manner. Built for Peleg Vickery in 1893, it was used as the main office for his publishing firm.

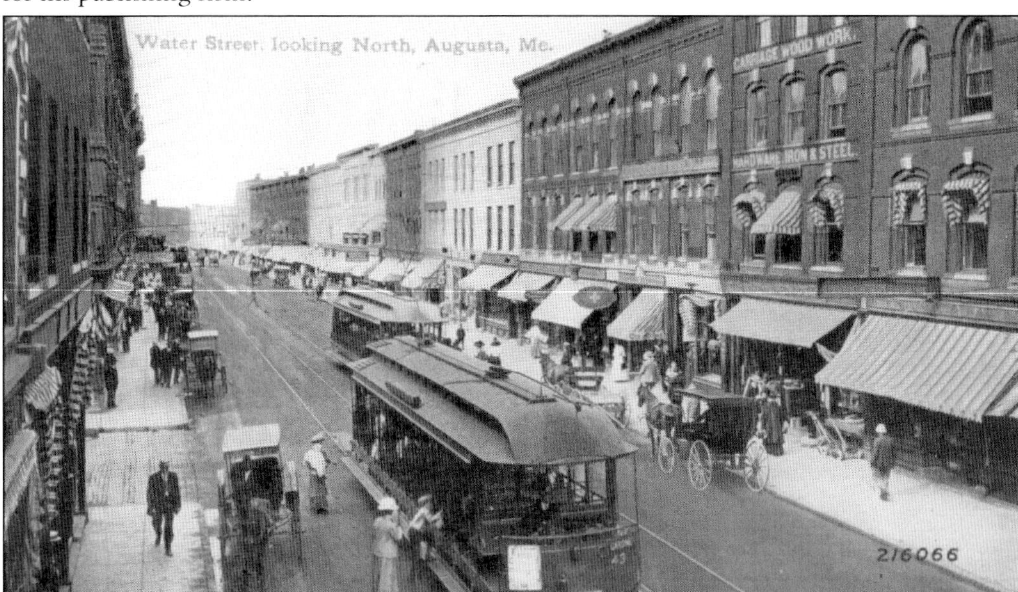

From the right, George Jones built the Italianate structure in 1877, the top floors of which were the original home to the YMCA. S.S. Brooks, hardware merchant, constructed the next block in 1876 and operated into the 20th century. The four buildings of the Parrott Block were erected in 1878 and once was the home of Dirigo Business College. Only the northernmost building remains today.

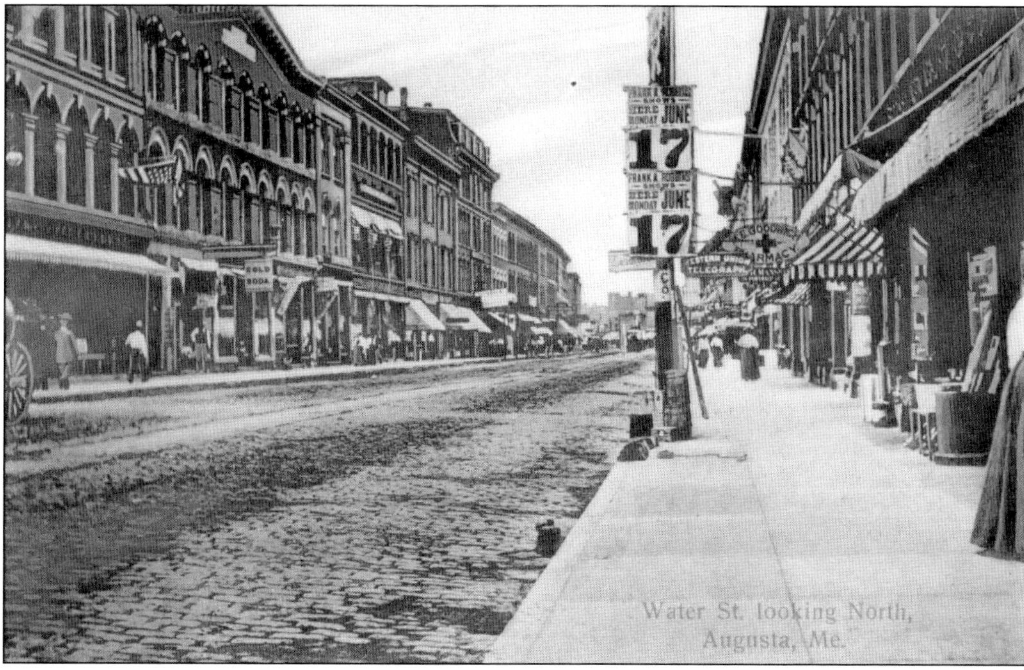

At a cost of $17,000, the Granite National Bank was built on the corner of Oak Street in 1866. The Hunts Block, adjacent to the bank, was designed with a peaked Italianate facade by Francis H. Fassett and built in the same year. Three buildings farther north is the Cony House. In 1894, a room at the hotel would cost around $2.

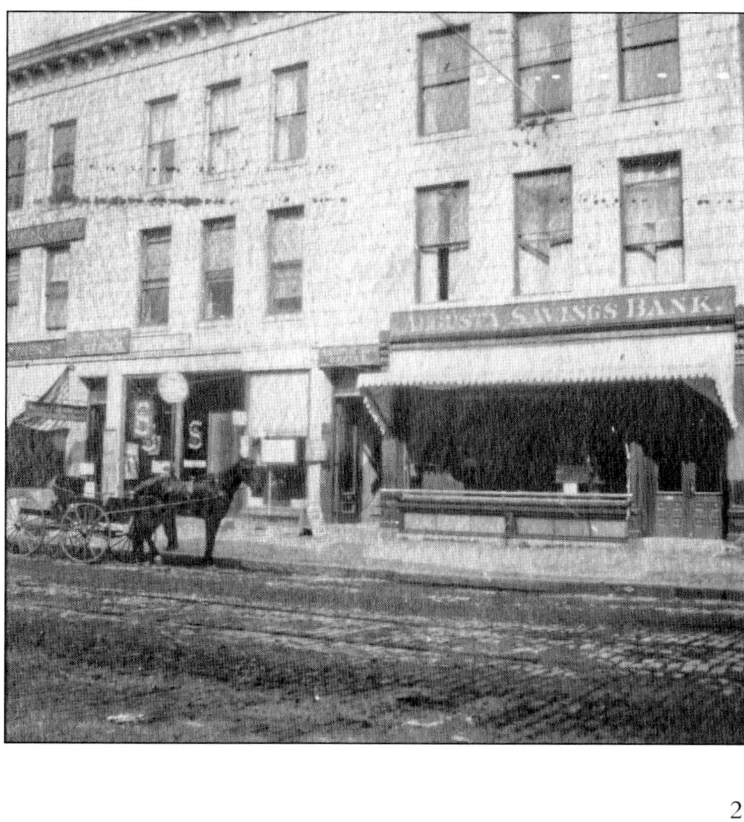

On September 17, 1865, the wooden structure previous to this granite edifice came to hold the distinction of being the ignition point of the great fire. Rebuilt the following year, this impressive Italianate block was built of rough-faced granite to house Libby's grocery, Cony and Farrar's meat market, and Dr. Hiram H. Hill's practice. In this image postmarked 1907, the Augusta Savings Bank, incorporated in 1848, occupies Hill's former location.

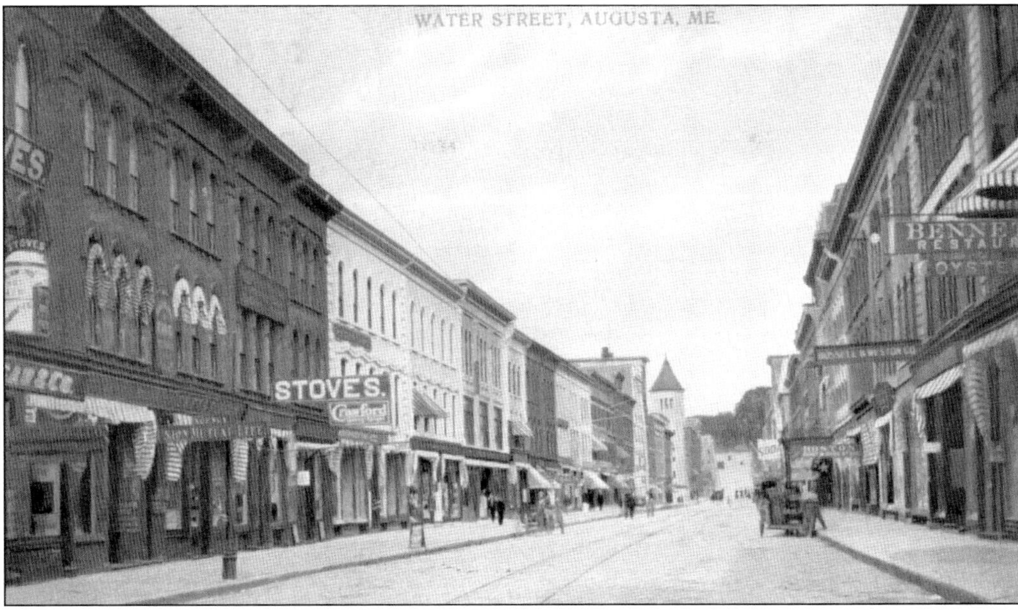

The four southernmost facades of the 1866 Italianate-style Williams Block can be seen on the left, followed by the light-colored edifice of North's Block. Although similar to Williams Block and built in the same year, North's was covered in mastic to give the appearance of brownstone. Beyond that is Meonian Hall. It was erected by James North in 1856, then rebuilt after the fire of 1865 and once again in 1904.

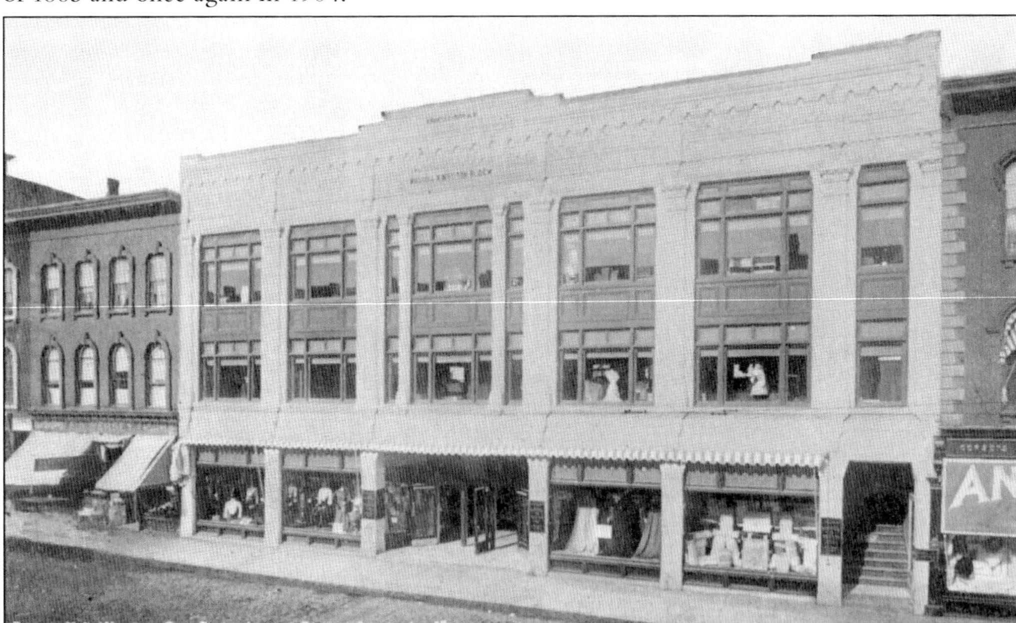

The Bussell & Weston Company, a dealer of dry goods established in 1881, originally was located under the Cony House. Just over two decades later, a few lots were purchased farther north on Water Street, the Classic Revival building was erected in 1909, and the new Bussell & Weston Department Store was opened. In the 1920s, Delbert W. Adams purchased the building, where he operated his own store until 1982.

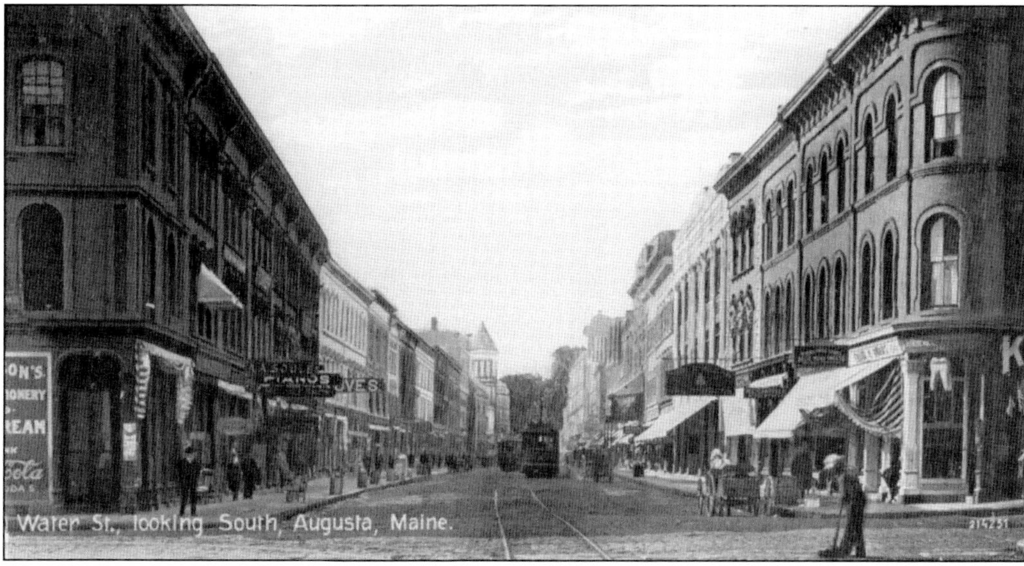

At left are the Stephen Deering building and the seven buildings of the Williams Block, designed by Francis H. Fassett. Only the first four structures, built in Italianate refinery in 1862, survived the fire of 1865. The corner building was removed in 1971 for the current downtown bridge. Of the same style, the Sturgis and Haskell building was designed by John C. Tibbetts and erected across the street in 1867; it still stands there today.

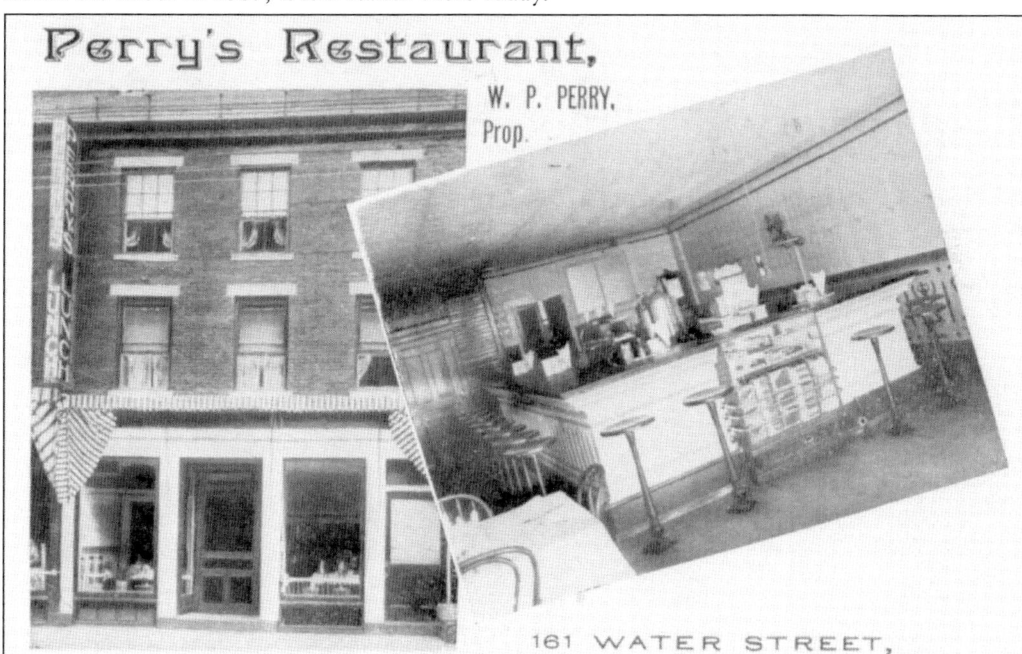

Wilfred P. Perry opened his first restaurant around 1905, in the Union Block north of the Kennebec Bridge, and his second in 1914, under the Opera House across from the post office. Though he sold his first eatery to Bernard Butterfield in 1920, he maintained his second location into the 1930s before selling. Perhaps his longevity could be attributed to his slogan: "Where Foods Taste Like You Get at Home."

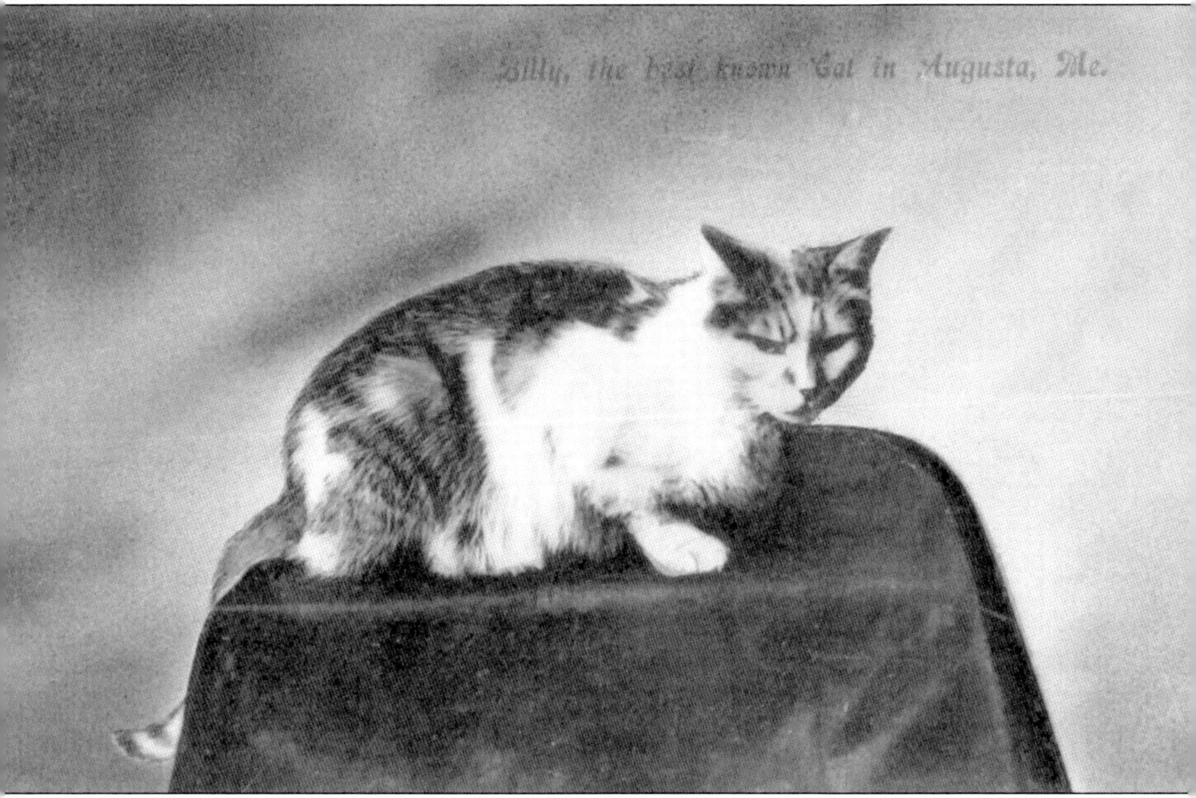

W.W. Morse ran a novelty and fruit store on Water Street with his onetime business associate William H. Gannett. Several years after Morse and Gannett parted company, Morse took on a partner of the feline persuasion named Billy. Although the extent of his renown is unclear, Billy was distinguished enough to have his obituary printed when he departed at the tender age of 13. In the *Daily Kennebec Journal* on March 1, 1911, a touching tribute states, "[Billy] enjoyed the distinction of being the best known cat in town, not only by personal contact, it might be said, but by reputation, for he had his photograph taken (under protest) and printed on some 5000 post cards, and these were sold at the store and sent all over the country, brute evidence that there was at least one cat in Augusta. And Billy was that cat."

Two

Public Buildings

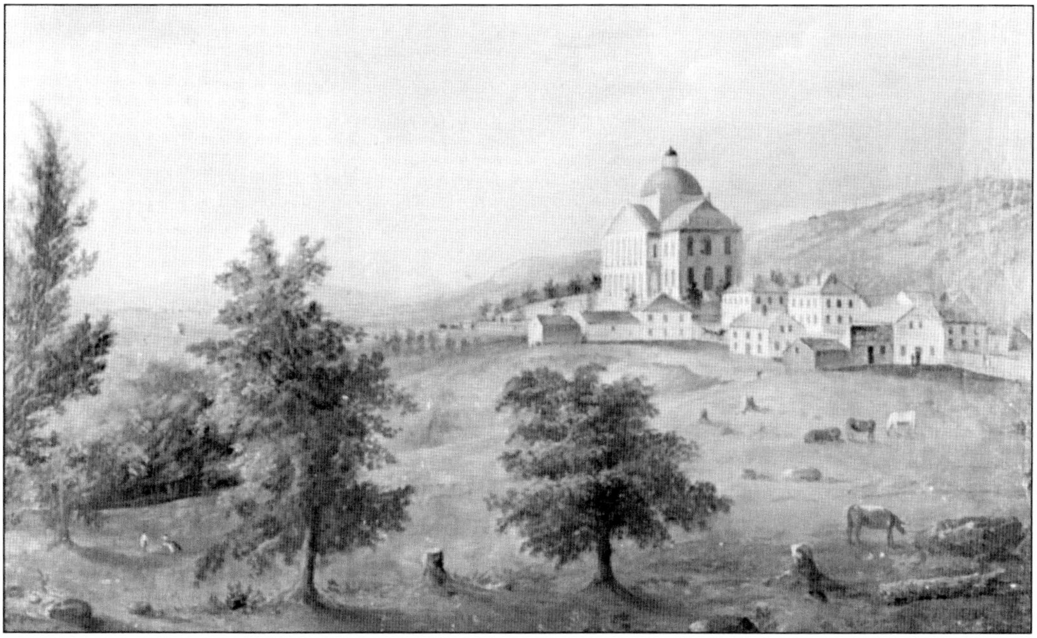

Native Maine artist Charles Codman's painting memorialized the newly constructed State House and its surroundings in 1836, four years after it had been built. Directly to the right of the capitol building is the Hall House, built in 1833, which would later come to be known as the Blaine House, though its distinctive cupola has not yet been added.

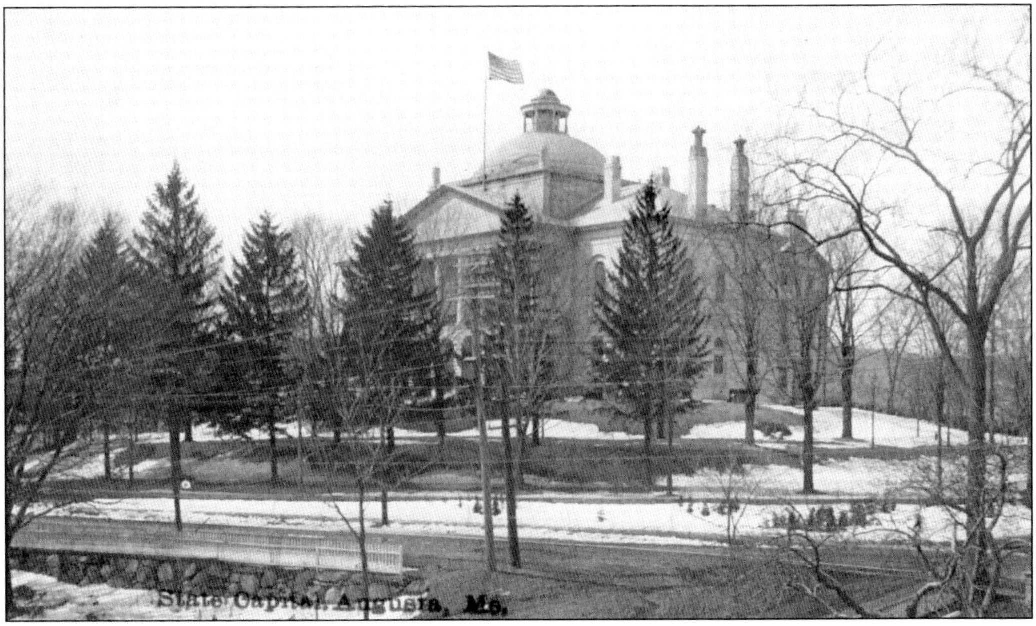

On July 4, 1829, two years after Augusta became the capital of Maine, the cornerstone of the State House was laid on Weston's Hill. Charles Bulfinch of Boston designed the Greek Revival capitol building, constructed of Hallowell granite for the princely sum of $145,000. The initial phase of construction took four years to complete; the legislature convened here for the first time on January 4, 1832.

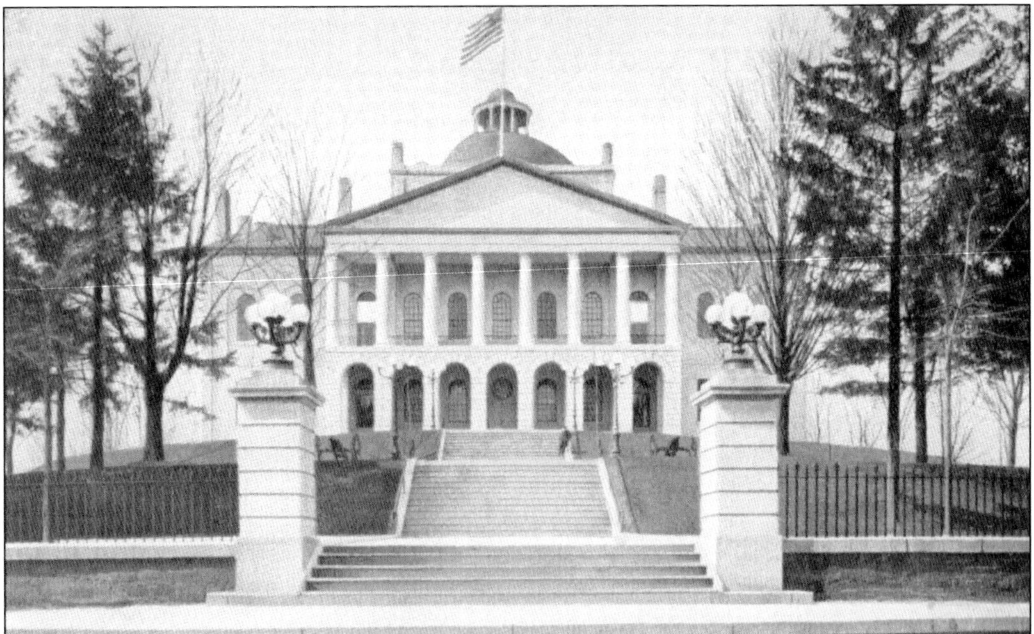

The central portion of the State House was 84 feet wide by 56 feet deep, with an additional 33-foot wing on either side. The arcaded colonnade has eight massive Doric pillars reaching 81 feet in height, and the cupola is 114 feet tall from base to top. Flanked by six-pound brass cannons, steep granite steps lead down the terraced front lawn from the State House to State Street.

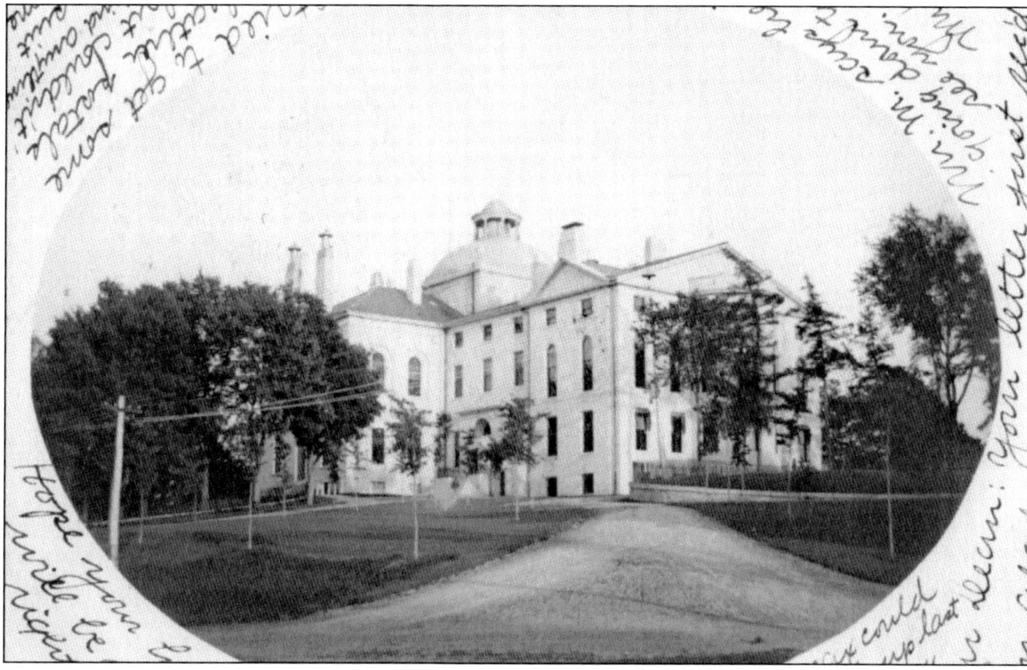

In 1891, the three-story west wing, designed by Brigham and Spofford of Boston, was added to the rear of the State House at a cost of $150,000, and with its Neo-Greek Revival edifice, it blended well with Bulfinch's original design. In addition to more office space, the state library relocated its collections to the new wing.

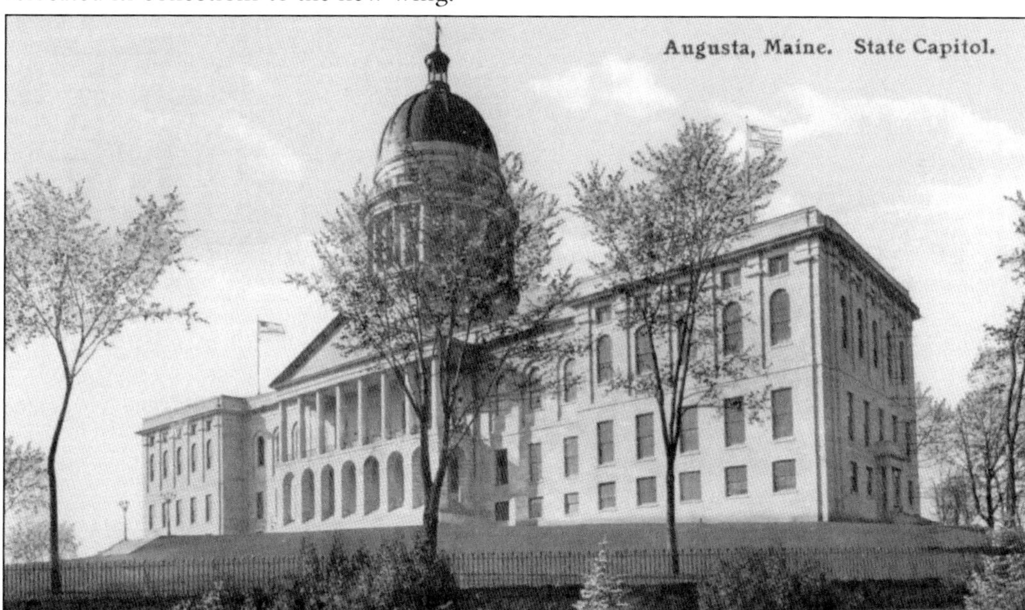

In 1910, the State House was expanded greatly into the grand edifice that is seen today. Based on designs by G. Henri Osmond of Boston, Charles S. Hichborn of Augusta supervised the construction of the new north and south wings, as well as the most prominent feature—the 185-foot dome. Care was given to preserve the front entrance designed by Bulfinch in 1832.

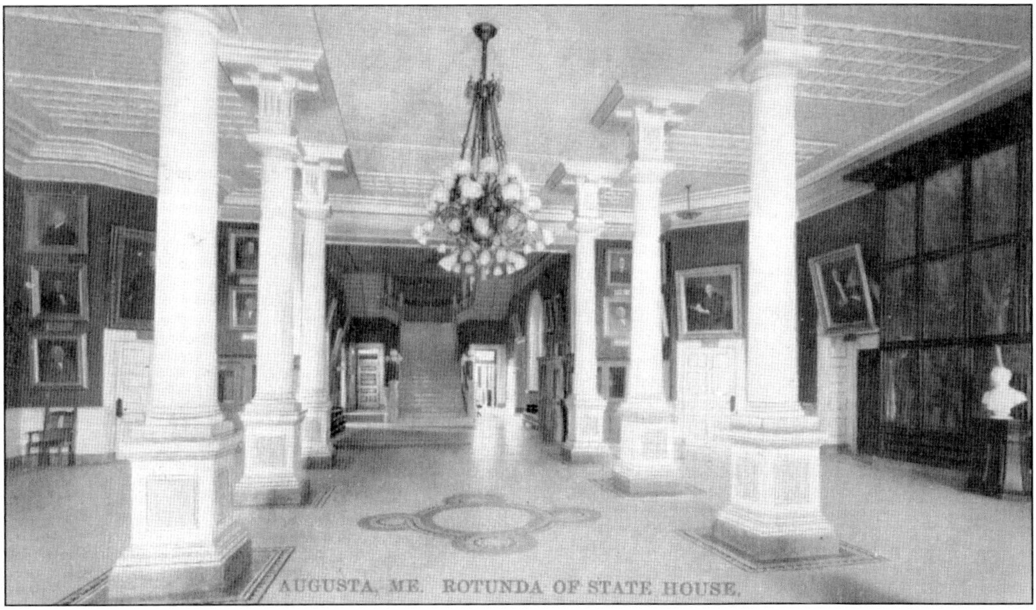

The Hall of Flags lies directly under the dome and, although not visible in this postcard, displays many of Maine's battle flags, beginning with the Civil War. Seen through the Doric pillars are portraits of many prominent political figures and statesmen that line the walls. In the background is the west wing's marble staircase, which leads to the senate and house chambers on the third floor.

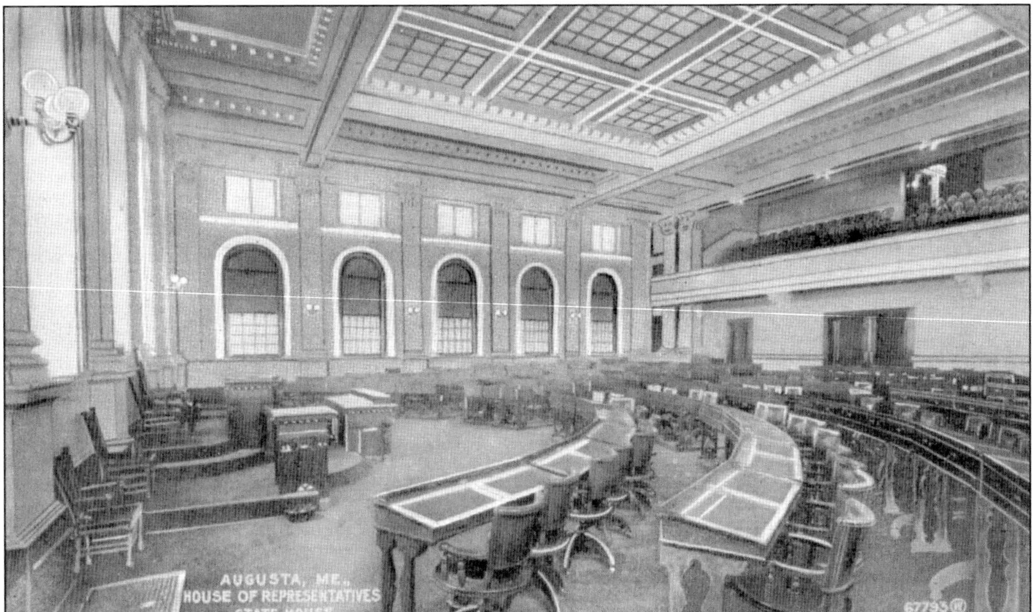

Occupying the third floor of the north wing, the chamber for the House of Representatives is two stories in height and is flooded with light from a double tier of windows on three sides and a frosted glass skylight. Slender Corinthian pilasters support the crossbeam ceiling high above the circular rows of desks for the representatives. The speaker's platform is directly across from the main entrance and the house gallery.

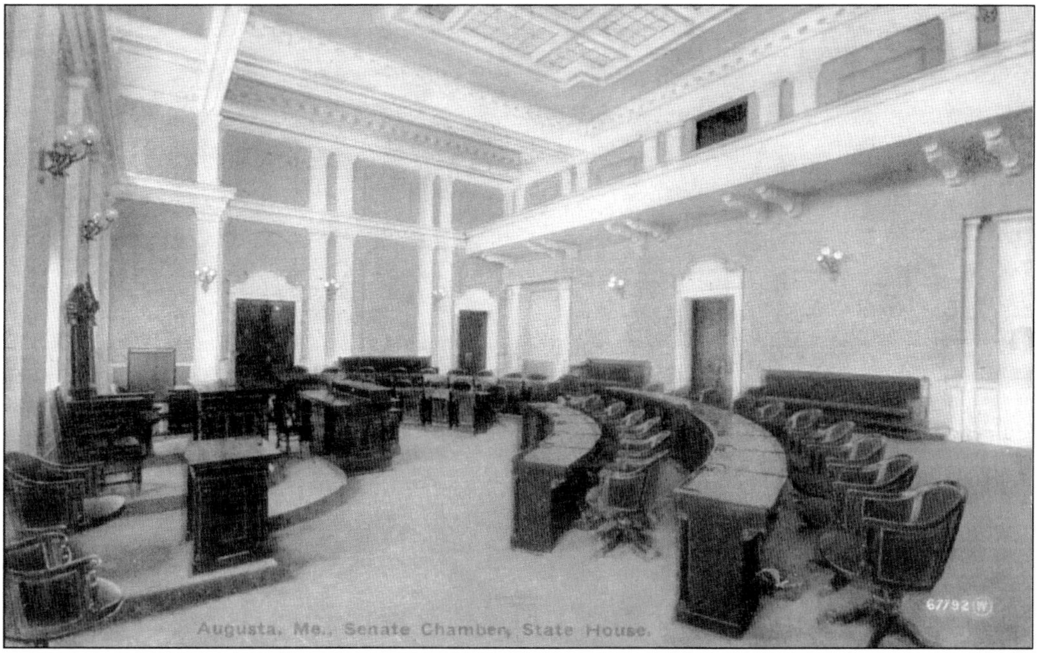

The senate chamber, located in the south wing, is similar to the house chamber, although smaller. The desks are arranged in two concentric semicircles facing the president's platform and sit upon mulberry-hued carpeting with a woven motif of the state seal. The walls are adorned with Doric pilasters that have gilt capitals, and the senate gallery overlooks the entire chamber.

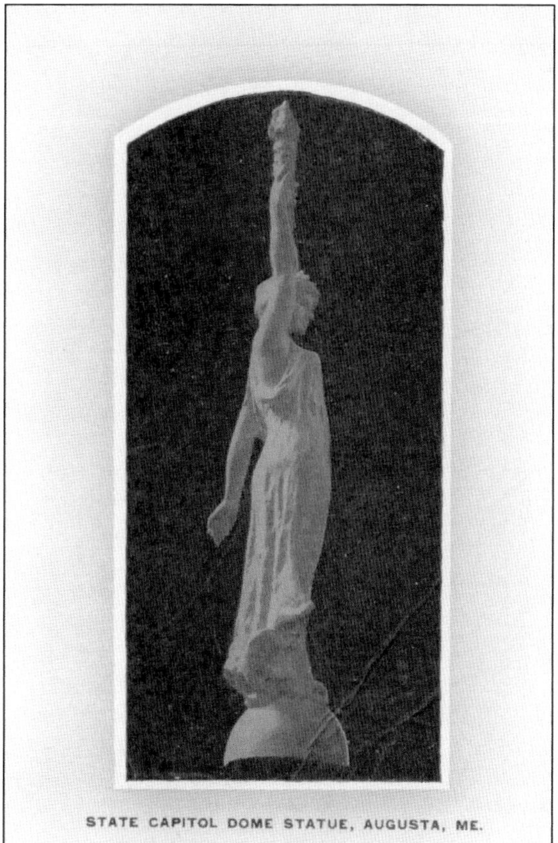

W. Clark Noble of Gardiner, Maine, sculpted *Lady of Wisdom*, the statue that graces the dome of the capitol building, around 1909. Standing 15 feet in height, she holds a pine bough torch high above her head in her right hand and a pinecone in her left. She is made from copper with a gold overlay.

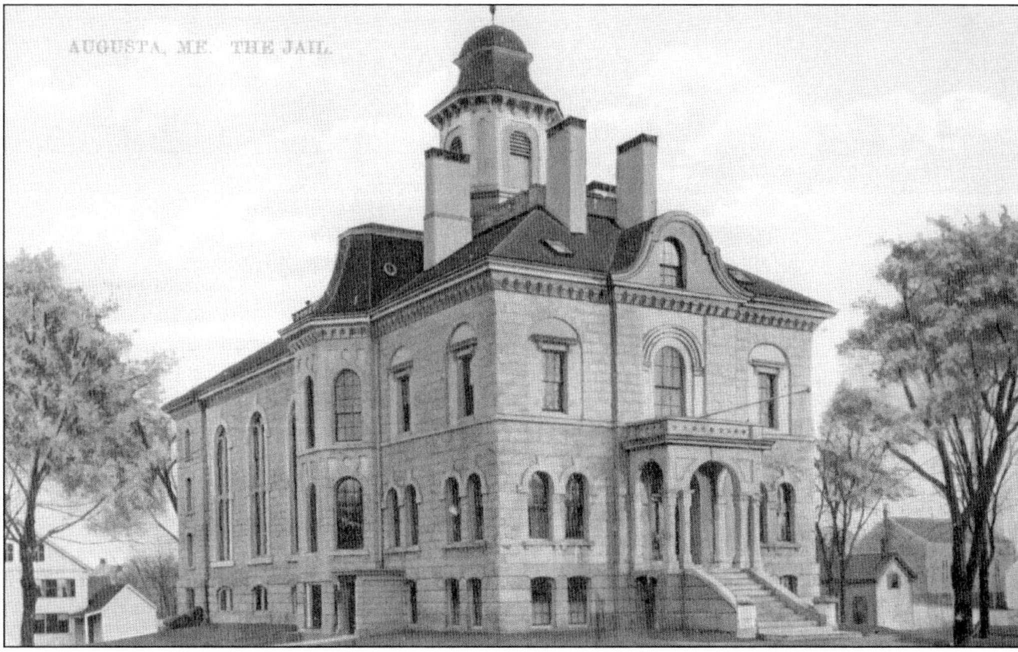

Although built in 1858, this jail was not Augusta's first—it was its fourth. The first jail was erected in 1793 on the corner of Winthrop and State Streets, the former site of the YMCA. The two-story hewn timber structure, not surprisingly, was not very secure. It burned in 1808, and a temporary facility was quickly built. In December 1808, construction of a stone jail began. By 1857, it had been deemed that the stone jail was unfit, and Gridley J.F. Bryant was hired to design the current jail. The jail was completed at its new location on State Street in January 1859. It was constructed of granite in a symmetrical Italianate style for a cost of about $60,000. On February 1, 1859, it was opened to public inspection—perhaps the only day people walked in voluntarily.

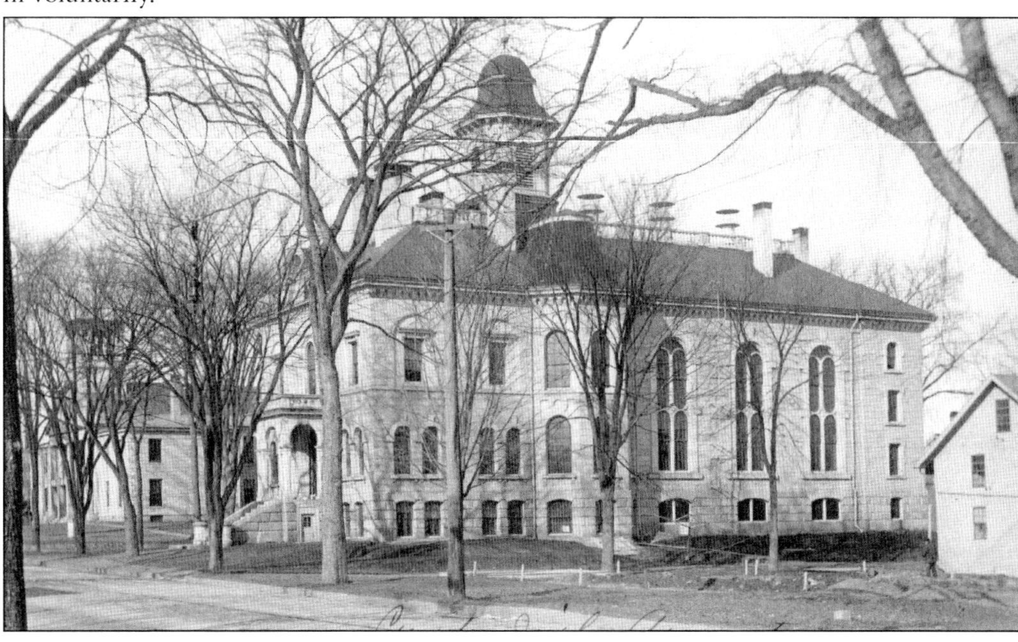

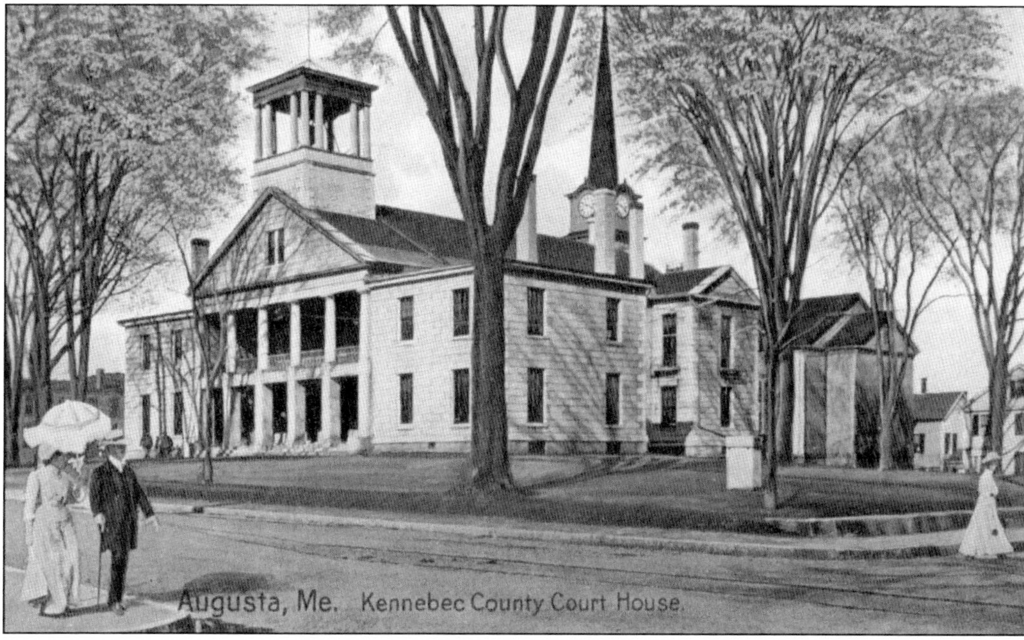

The original courthouse was a frame building erected at the foot of Winthrop Street, near the railroad crossing, in 1790. After Kennebec County was incorporated in 1799, a new courthouse was erected two years later on the site currently occupied by the jail. This structure served the county for almost three decades but was moved across the street and used as an amusement resort named the Concert Hall. In 1827, the county commissioners decided to replace the courthouse. John Cochran designed the Greek Revival structure, and Robert C. Vose constructed it from granite in 1829. The courthouse has been expanded three times: the north and south granite wings, a belfry, and the Greek Revival facade were added in 1851, followed by a second expansion in 1891, and in 1907, the probate building was constructed to the south.

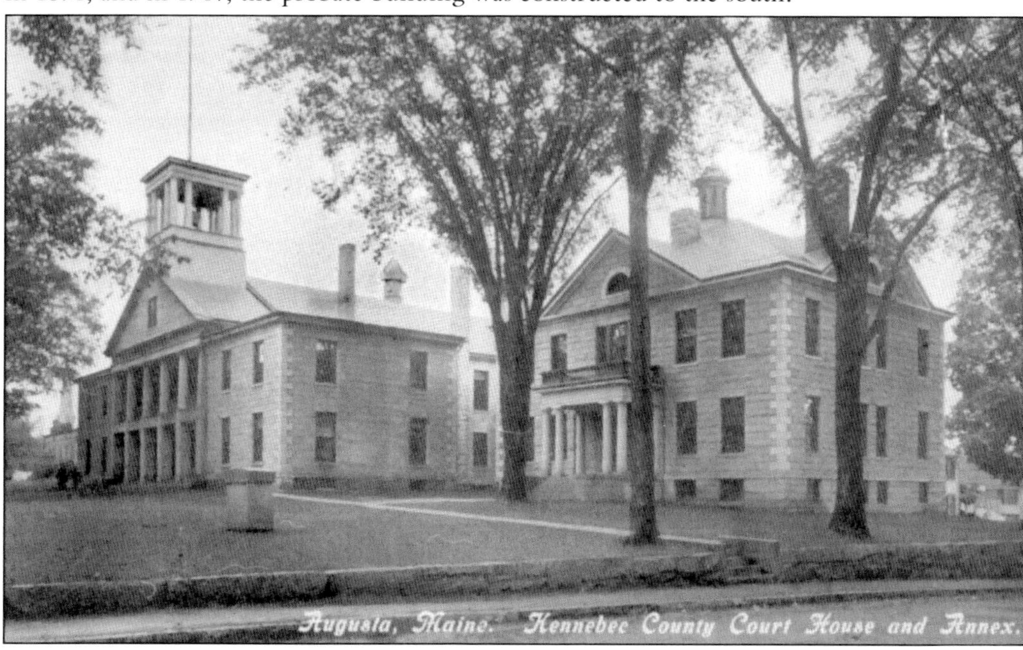

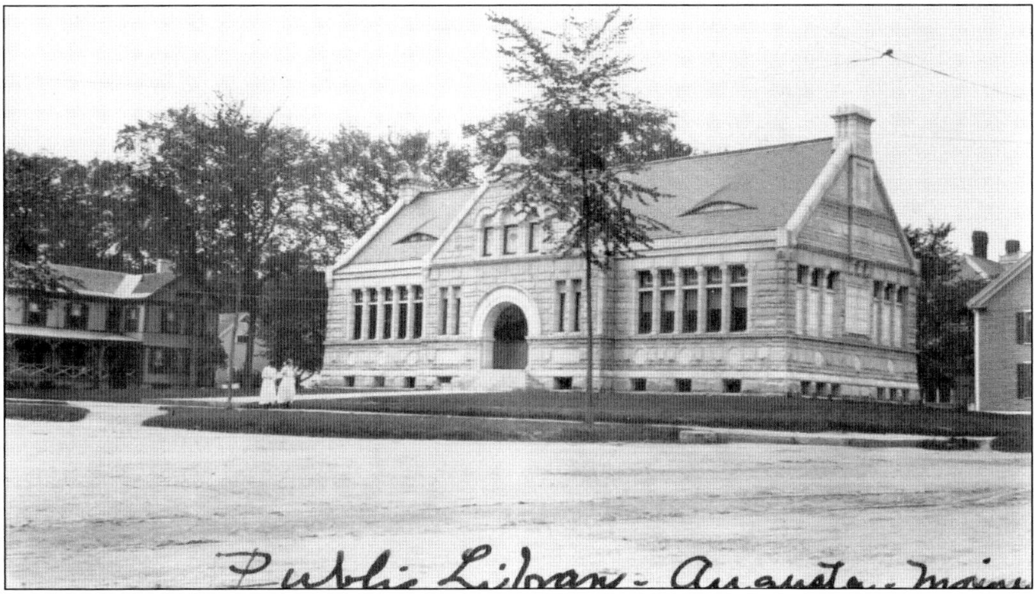

With the gift of a $20,000 endowment from Llewellyn W. Lithgow, the Lithgow Library and Reading Room opened its doors on Water Street in September 1882. It was not too long, however, before it outgrew that location, and in 1891, the Lithgow Library Trustees partnered with the city to raise contributions for this new structure. St. Mark's Home for Women can be seen on the left.

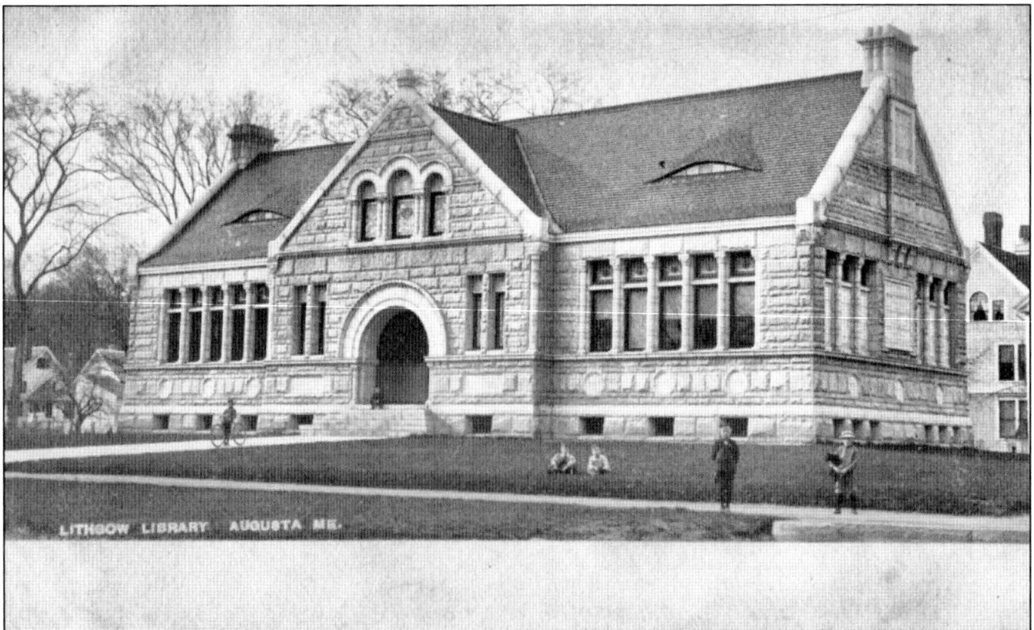

The cornerstone for the new Lithgow Library was laid on June 14, 1894. Designed by Joseph Ladd Neal, the Romanesque-Renaissance building was erected on the site of the former Cushnoc House, which had burned less than two years prior. Costing approximately $52,000 to complete, this impressive granite edifice was opened and dedicated on February 3, 1896. Within 30 years, the new library's shelves contained no less than 13,000 volumes.

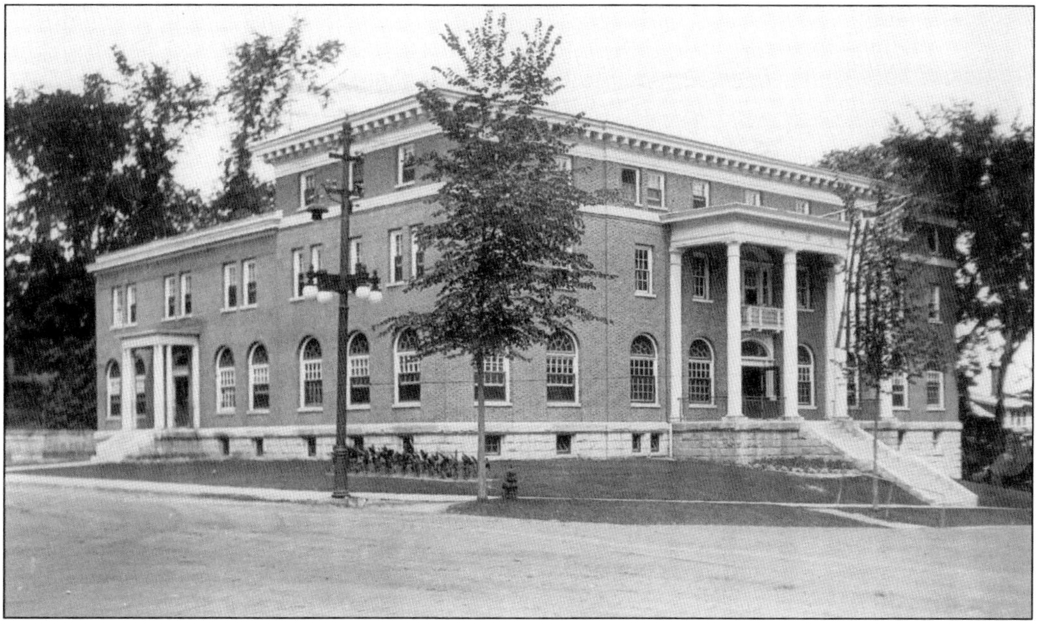

The YMCA was organized in 1881, but it was not until 1914 that they received their long-awaited building. Designed by Louis E. Jallade of New York City, this Neoclassical Revival structure was built by R.J. Noyes of Augusta on the corner of Winthrop and State Streets. It was replete with a gymnasium, dormitory rooms, a 45-foot pool, 600 lockers, pool and billiard tables, and even six bowling alleys.

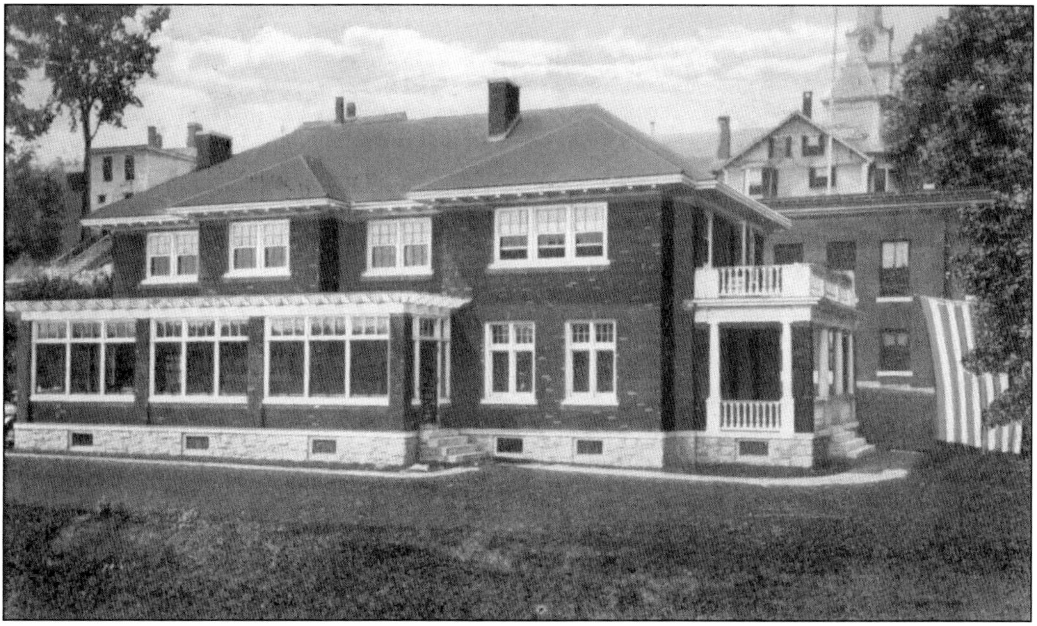

The Augusta Elks Lodge, instituted in May 1905 with about 50 members, required a permanent home. This brick Colonial Revival building was constructed on Winthrop Street and completed in 1917. As the membership grew, an addition that doubled the size of the structure was erected in 1972. Still being too small, the Elks moved to a new facility in 1989, and five years later, the lodge was torn down.

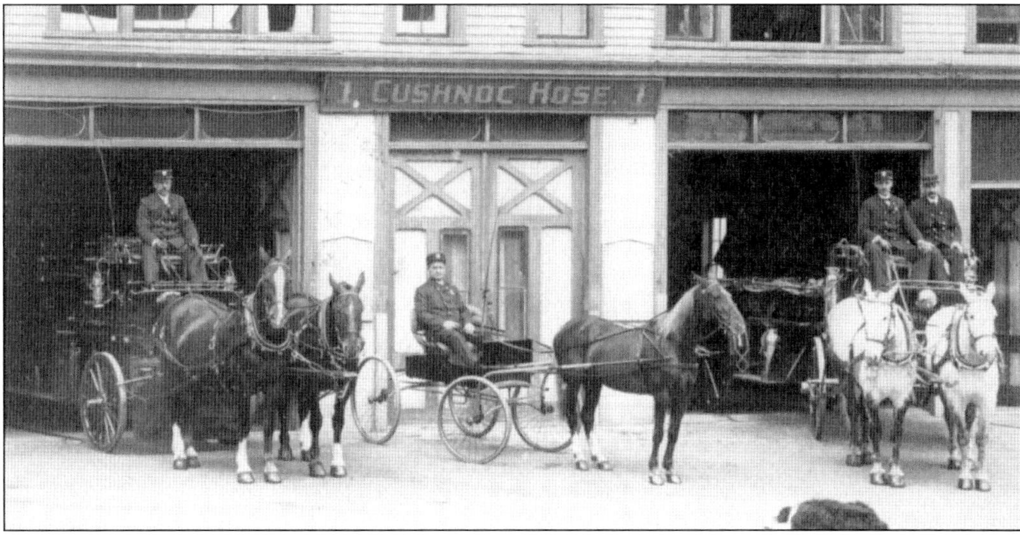

Built on Bridge Street in 1851, the Cushnoc Fire Station was one of Augusta's five hose companies. This c. 1897 image shows two key pieces of equipment: on the left is a horse-drawn hook-and-ladder truck, and to the right is the four-wheeled Cushnoc hose carriage. The hose carriage replaced the antiquated steamer Cushnoc once the water system was installed throughout the city in 1880.

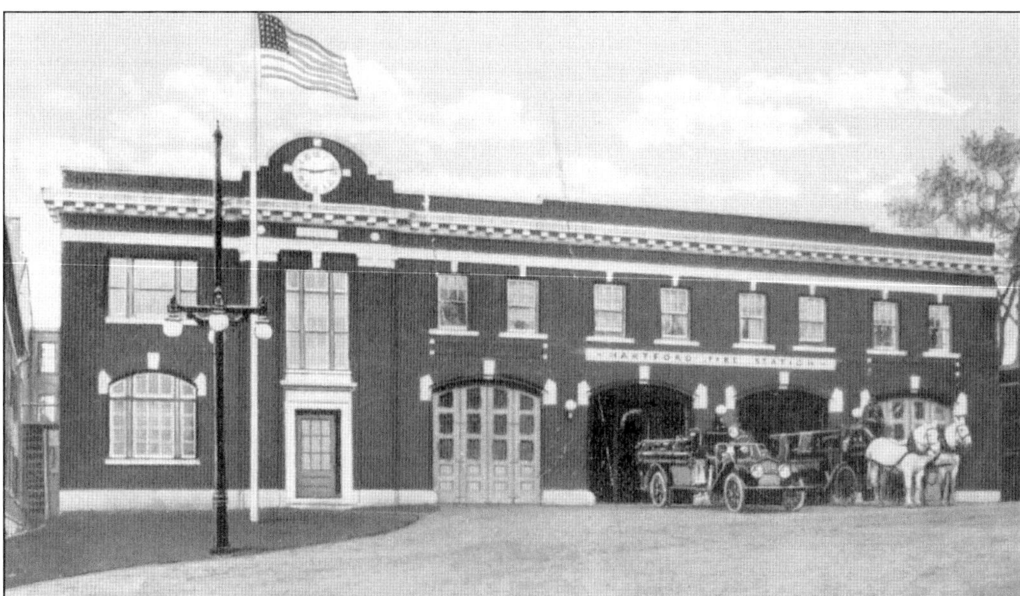

Generously donated by the heirs of George Huntington Hartford, founder of the Great Atlantic and Pacific Tea Company, the parcel of land atop Rines Hill was soon to become the site of Augusta's newest firehouse. Formally opened in 1921, the Hartford Fire Station had rooms for the chief engineer and five on-duty firefighters, along with a kitchenette and a modern fire alarm. But the showstopper was the new motorized electric-start fire truck.

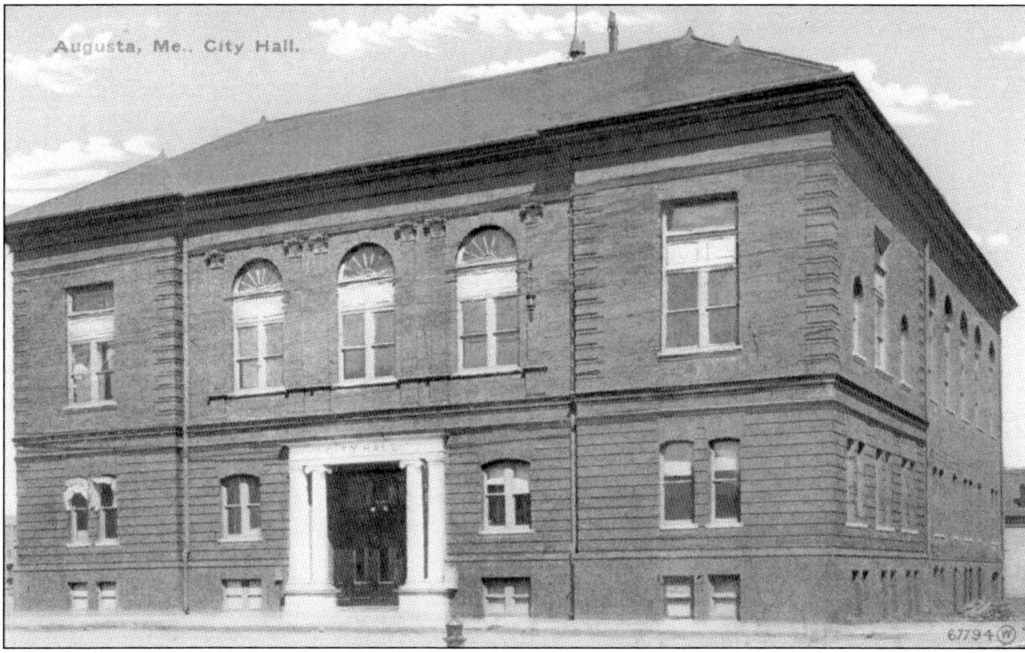

Designed by noted architect John Spofford, Augusta City Hall was dedicated on the Fourth of July 1896. The brick-and-granite structure housed various city offices, the Augusta-Hallowell Chamber of Commerce, the Augusta Police Department, and a large auditorium. But this grand building was not all work and no play, for here, John Philips Sousa debuted what would become his most famous march, "Stars and Stripes Forever," to an enraptured audience on May 1, 1897.

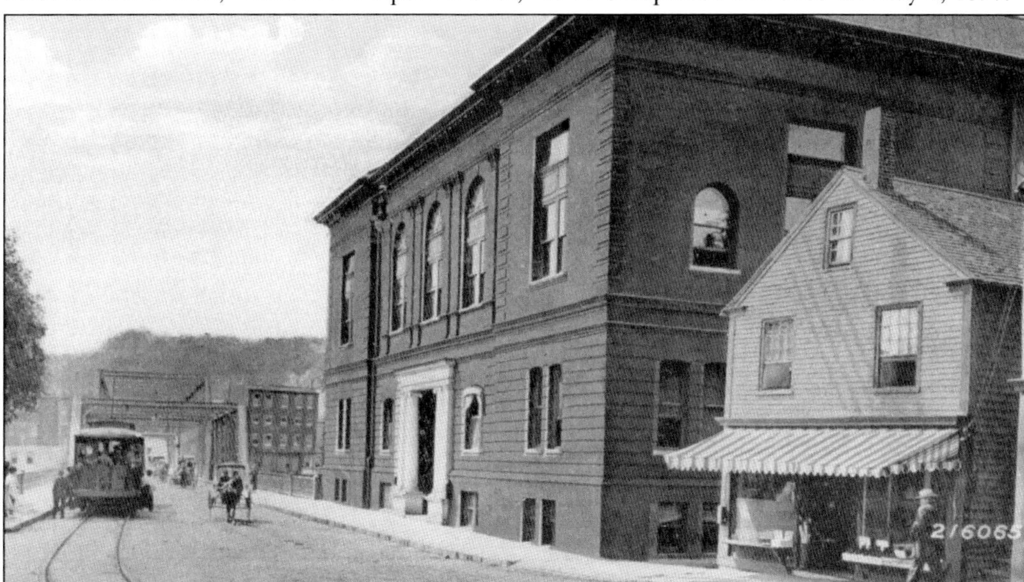

Situated at the east end of the Kennebec Bridge, city hall was easily accessible to all modes of conveyance. At right, Max Slosberg, a Russian Jew who immigrated in 1885, operated a clothing store, and located at far right was Tom's Variety Shop. In 1986, construction of the new Augusta City Center began. The stores are now gone and the former city hall has been converted into an assisted-living facility.

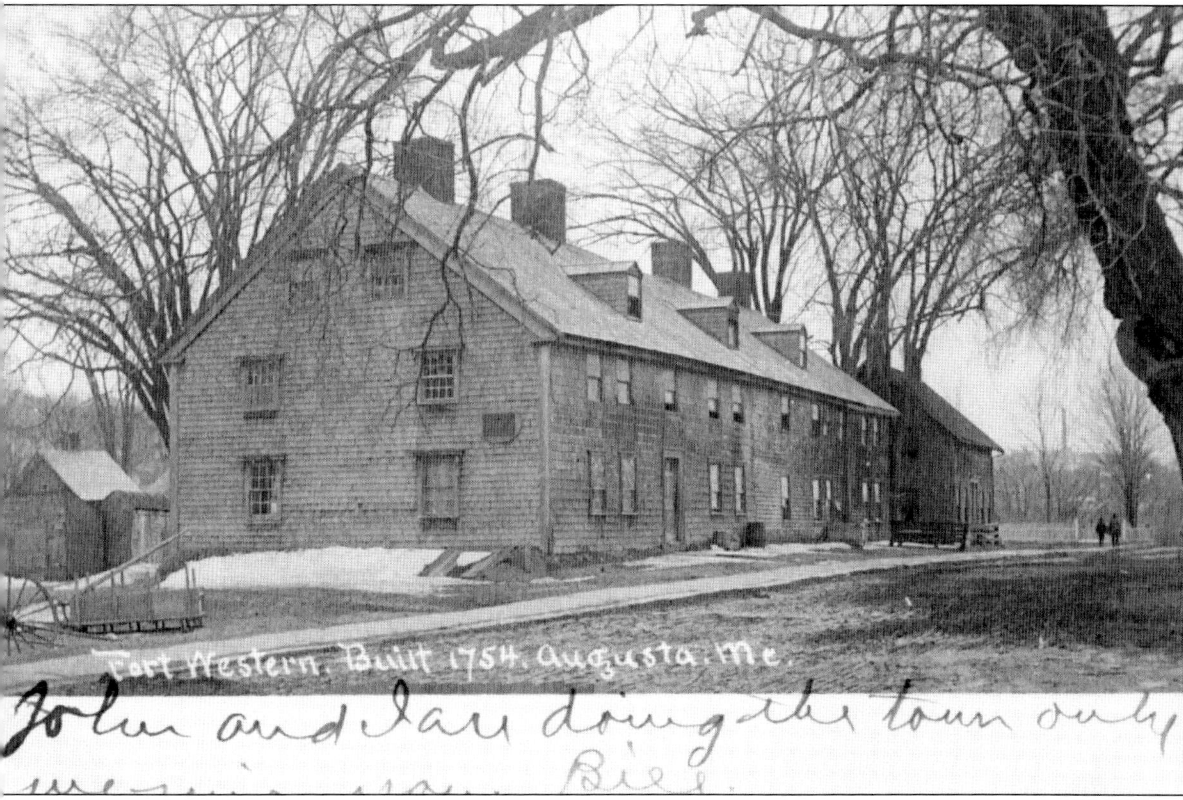

The Cushnoc Trading Post was established in 1628 to trade with the Abenaki people of the area. Though profitable for several decades, it was abandoned in 1675 due to waning revenue and increasing tension with the French and Abenaki. The site lay dormant for nearly 75 years, until Fort Western was erected nearby in 1754. With Capt. James Howard in command, the fort served as a trading post and provided protection from attacks. The large garrison house was built with 12-inch-thick timbers and housed officers' quarters and barracks. Although the fort never saw battle, it was well prepared, as it had two armed blockhouses surrounded by a heavy log stockade fence. The fort was decommissioned in 1769, and Captain Howard purchased it, along with 900 acres of forestland, for $500. The following year, he converted the main structure into both a store and his home. With ties to Boston, Newfoundland, and the West Indies, the store became a center of trade for the next 50 years.

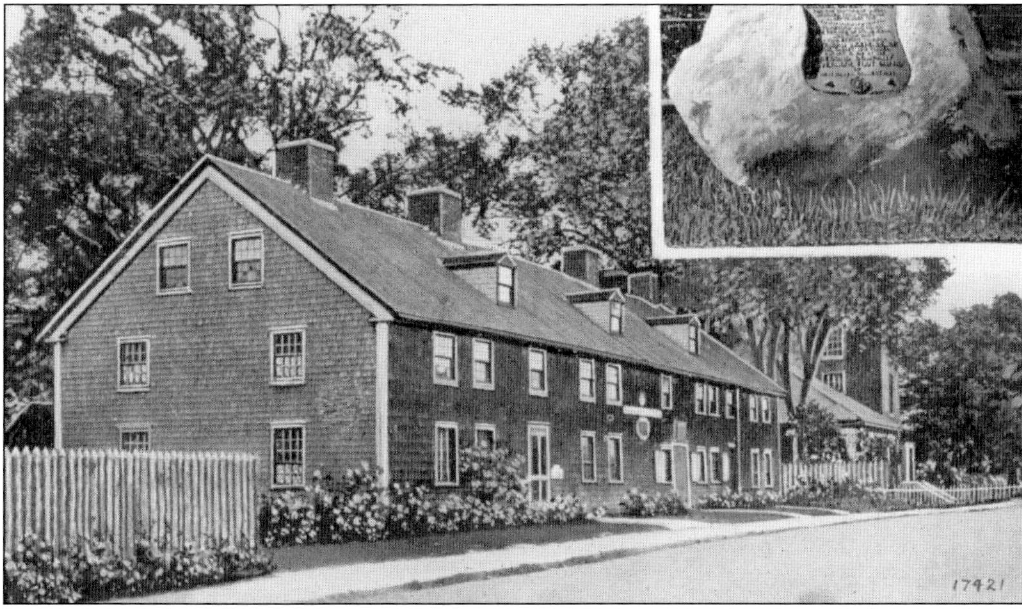

During his ill-fated 1775 march to Quebec, Benedict Arnold and his 1,100 men, including the 19-year-old Aaron Burr, camped for six days on the Fort Western grounds. In 1912, the 2nd Company of the Governor's Foot Guard of New Haven, Connecticut, attached a bronze plaque to a large boulder in commemoration of Arnold's exploits. Eventually, the fortification fell into disrepair, and the main house was refitted as tenements.

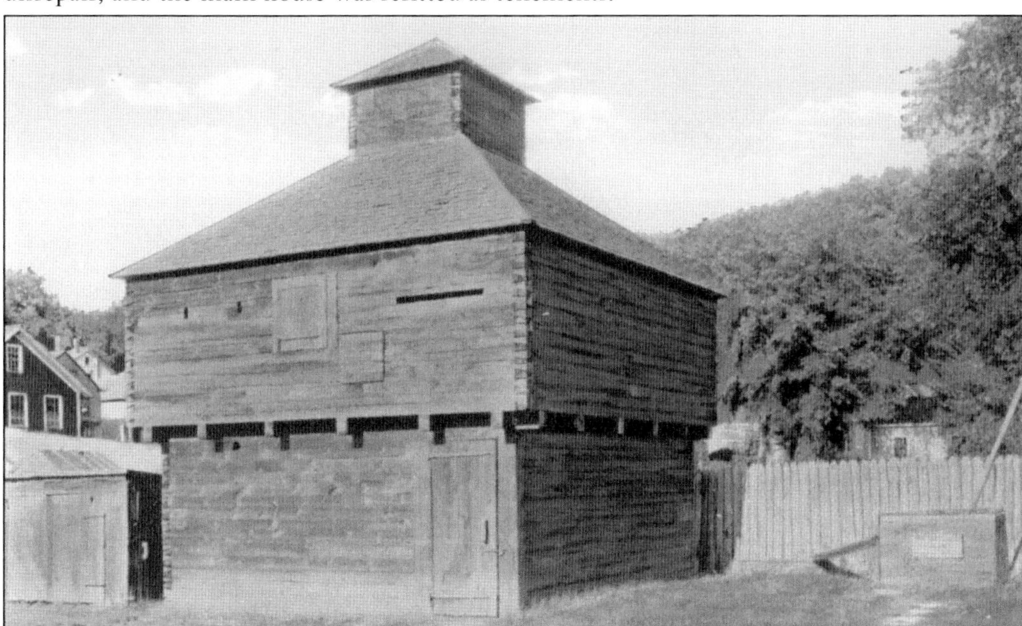

Since the historic fort had deteriorated so badly, the city took the property by eminent domain in 1919 for the purpose of demolition. Guy P. Gannett, a direct descendant of Captain Howard, acquired the property in 1921. He restored the complex the following year, complete with new blockhouses and a surrounding palisade, and decorated the garrison with period furniture and amenities. Fort Western is America's oldest surviving wooden fort.

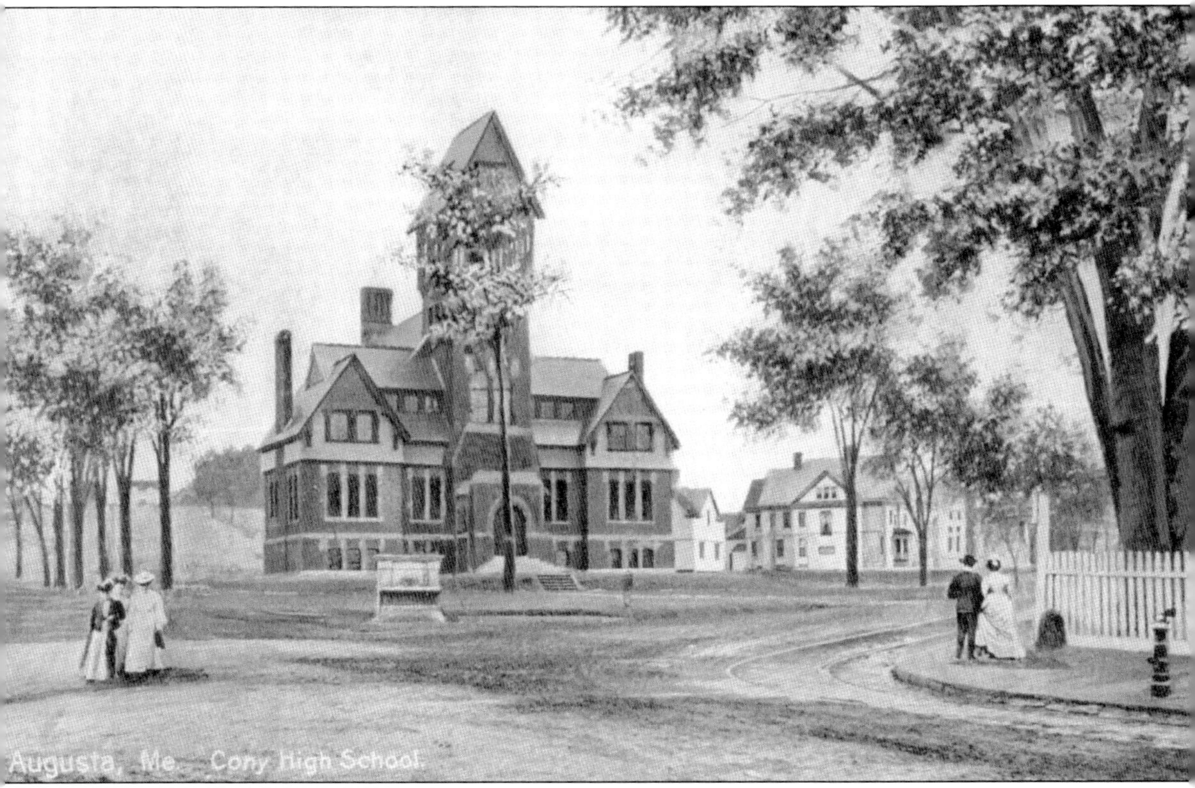

Judge Daniel Cony opened the academy in 1816 to provide free education to orphans and other girls under the age of 16. Built at the corner of Cony and Bangor Streets, the Cony Female Academy later moved to the old Bethlehem Church, located between Cony and Stone Streets, around 1844. Though Judge Cony passed away in 1842, the academy persevered until 1857, when it closed its doors. Cony's trustees built a new high school, seen here, for the city in 1881, with the stipulation that it remain free. Designed in the Queen Anne style by Gridley J.F. Bryant of Boston, the school's first and second floors were built of brick, as was the tower as far as the corbelled cornice, with wood for the upper open feature. The first year of school opened with 75 students and three teachers.

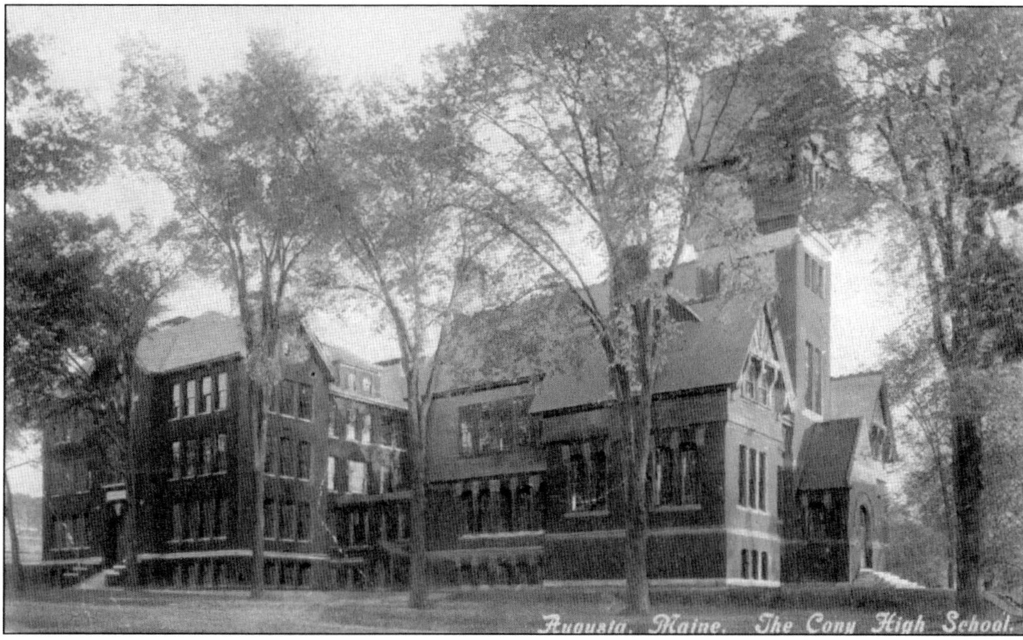

By 1908, the city had taken control of the property, and it was voted at a school meeting to build an addition to Cony High School. With $45,000 appropriated for the expansion, the new structure, designed by William R. Miller of Lewiston, was erected to the east of the existing school the following year.

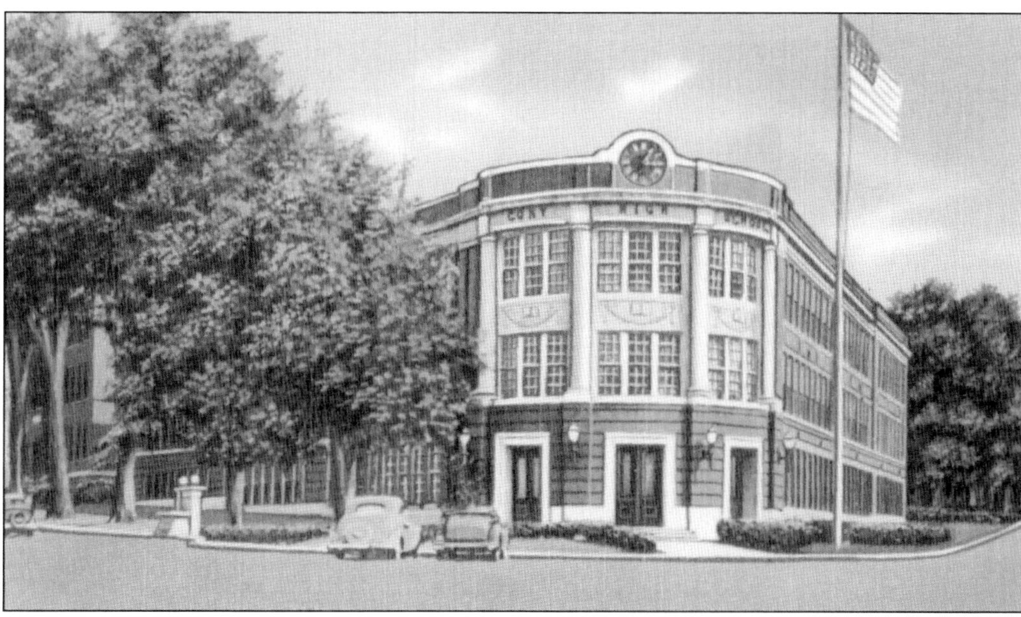

Construction of the Flatiron building to replace Cony's original school began in 1926 and was completed by 1930. The 1909 addition, seen through the trees, was demolished in the 1930s and replaced with a more modern structure in 1965. A new Cony High School opened on Pierce Drive in 2006. With a nod to its roots, it incorporated elements of the facade from the Flatiron.

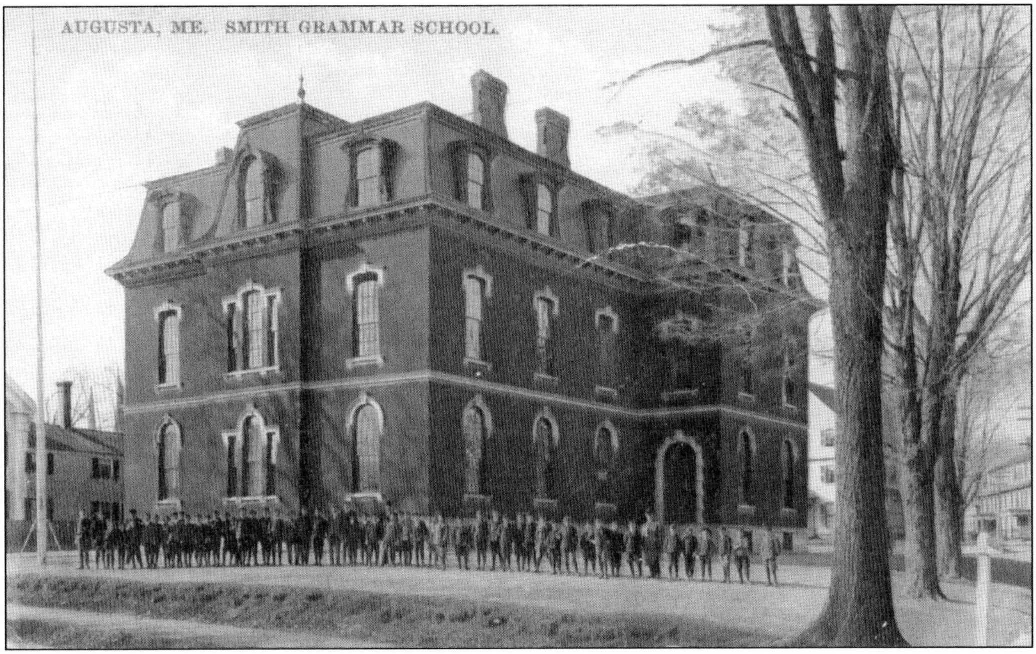

The Smith Grammar School opened on the corner of State and Bridge Streets in 1870. It had been designed to accommodate 400 students—200 grammar students on the first floor and the remaining high school students on the second. When Cony High School opened in 1881, the Smith School was used solely for grammar students. Part of Bridge Street can be seen on the right.

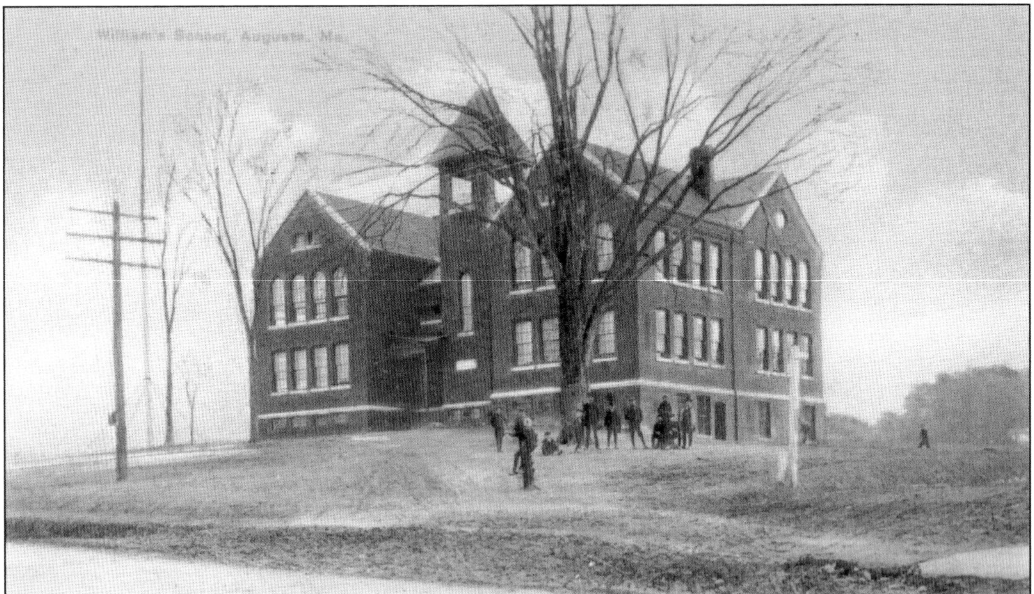

The brick-and-granite Williams Grammar School was built on top of Wedge Hill on Bangor Street in 1890. Consisting of four large rooms and two small, it became inadequate within 10 years. In the summer of 1902, an addition was built on the southern side to add four more large rooms, giving the school its symmetrical appearance seen here. The school closed in 1980 and was subsequently torn down.

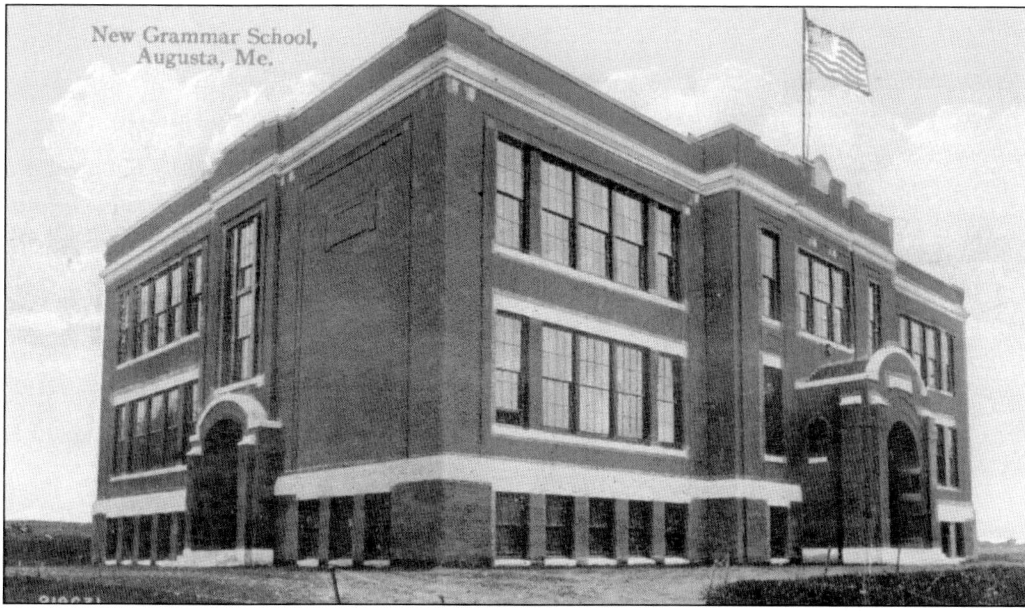

The Farrington Grammar School was to be built on the site of the old Middle Street School, but the area was deemed too small. Constructed with red brick and granite trimmings, the school was erected on a new site at the corner of Stone Street and Eastern Avenue. The school opened on September 15, 1913, and could accommodate 400 pupils. The building having been razed, the site is now occupied by a bank.

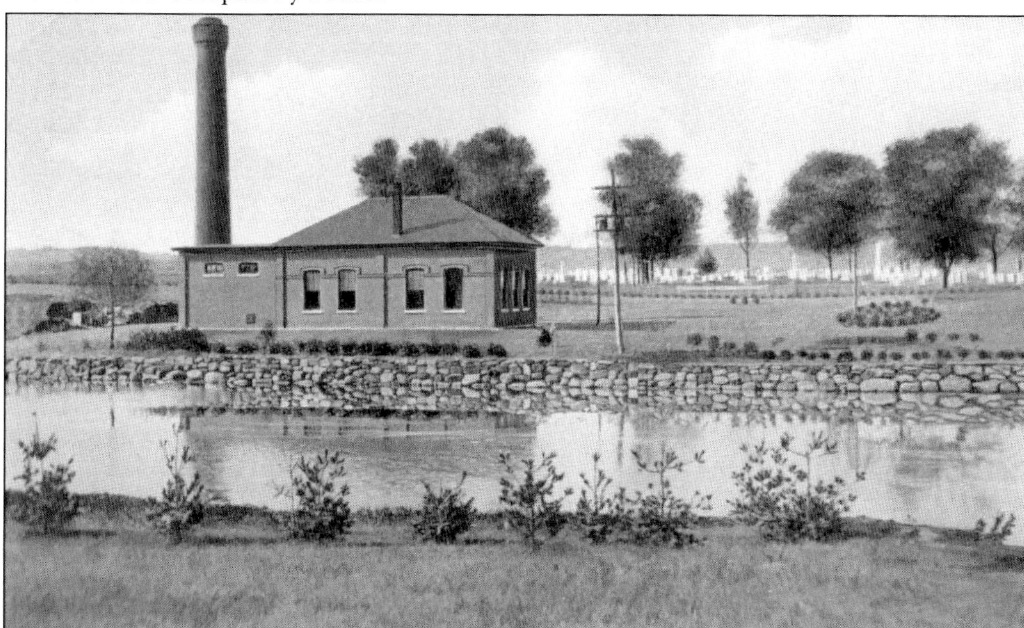

Augusta had filled its reservoir with water pumped from the Kennebec River starting in 1887, but with the increase in sewerage and manufacturing north of the city, another water source was needed. Carleton Pond and Cobbosseecontee Lake were selected, and a new pumping station was erected on the western bank of the lake in East Winthrop. With a 125-horsepower boiler and three pumps, this station went online in 1906.

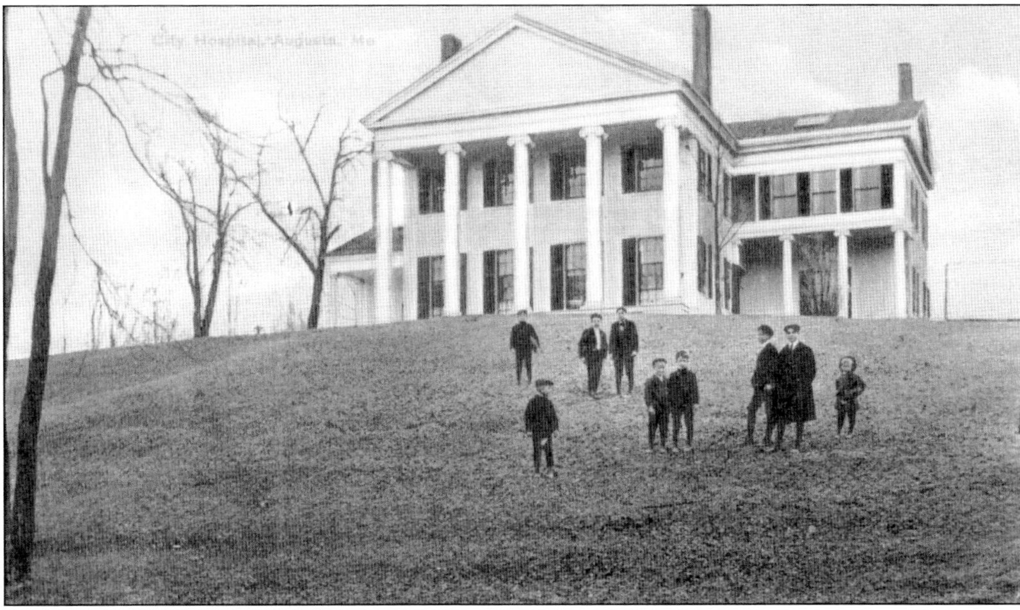

Originally built by Gen. Alfred Redington for his wife, Elizabeth, in 1837, this Greek Revival mansion was sold a mere two years later. In 1868, the structure was expanded and converted into St. Catherine's Hall, an Episcopal girls' school. The Augusta City Hospital purchased the hall in 1900. The hospital had its beginnings on Crosby Street in 1898, serving the soldiers of the Spanish-American War.

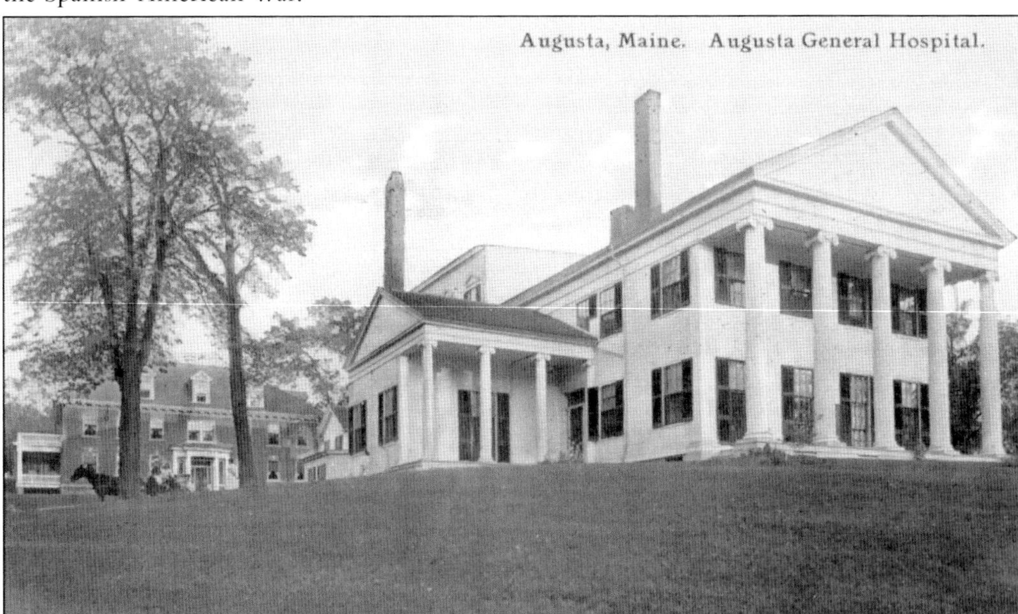

The new hospital had all the modern conveniences of the day, including two operating rooms, three wards, 15 private rooms, and a nursery. Student nurses also lived on the premises, but as the decade marched on, an increase in patients put space at a premium. The nurses needed their own quarters, thus the J. Manchester Haynes Home for Nurses was established to the east of the hospital.

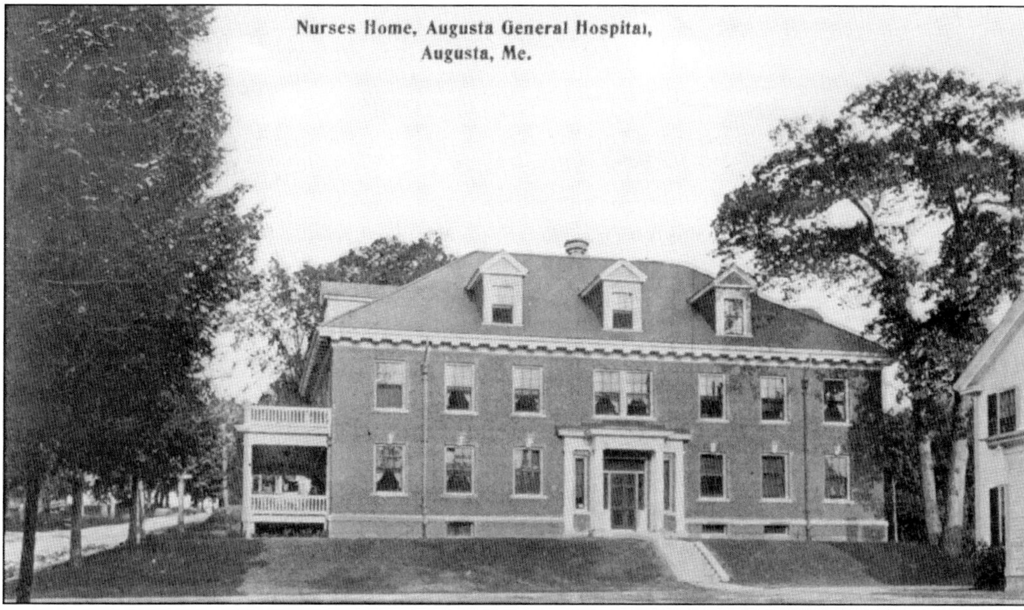

Josiah Manchester Haynes, philanthropist, took a deep interest in the hospital and its welfare. Though he died in 1906, his wife carried out the plans for the nurses' home, and Hanks & Wentworth of Augusta began construction in June 1907. With great ceremony, the keys and deed were presented to the hospital directors on September 28, 1908. The J. Manchester Haynes Home for Nurses was now open.

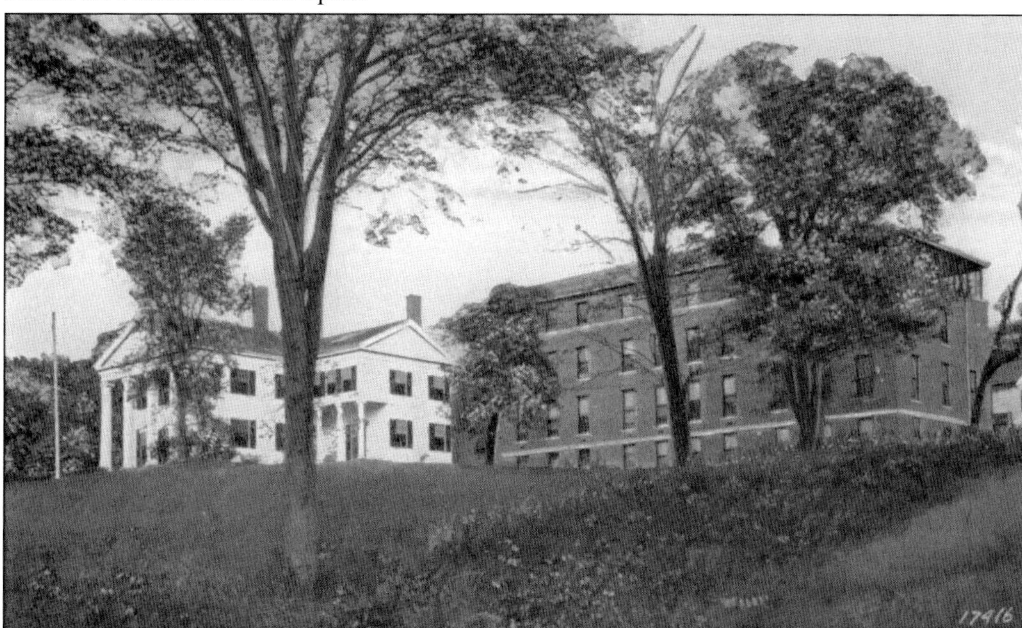

By 1917, the hospital had become overcrowded and fell into disrepair. Demands of the Great War were looming, and expansion became necessary. A hospital drive raised over $80,000 in one week, and although delayed, ground was finally broken on March 21, 1919, just south of the existing hospital. With three operating rooms, several wards, and private rooms, the state-of-the-art three-story brick wing opened in December 1920.

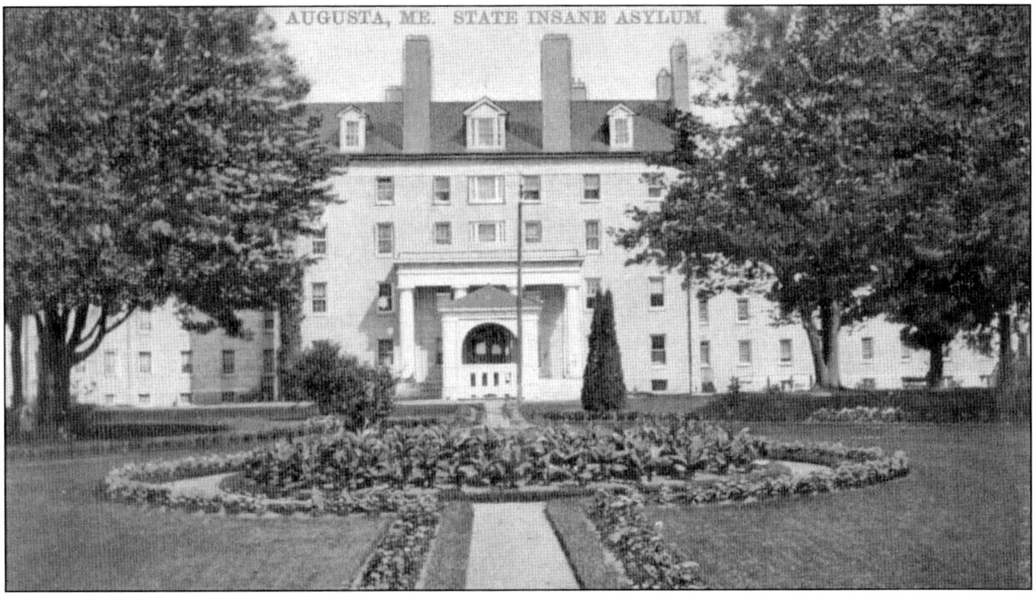

Established in 1834, the Maine Insane Asylum was built for the purpose of "the care and treatment of nervous and mental cases." In 1841, during its first full year of operation, the facility treated 133 patients, swelling to a number of 253 patients 10 years later. Tragedy struck on December 4, 1850, however, when a fire broke out, and 27 patients and one attendant lost their lives.

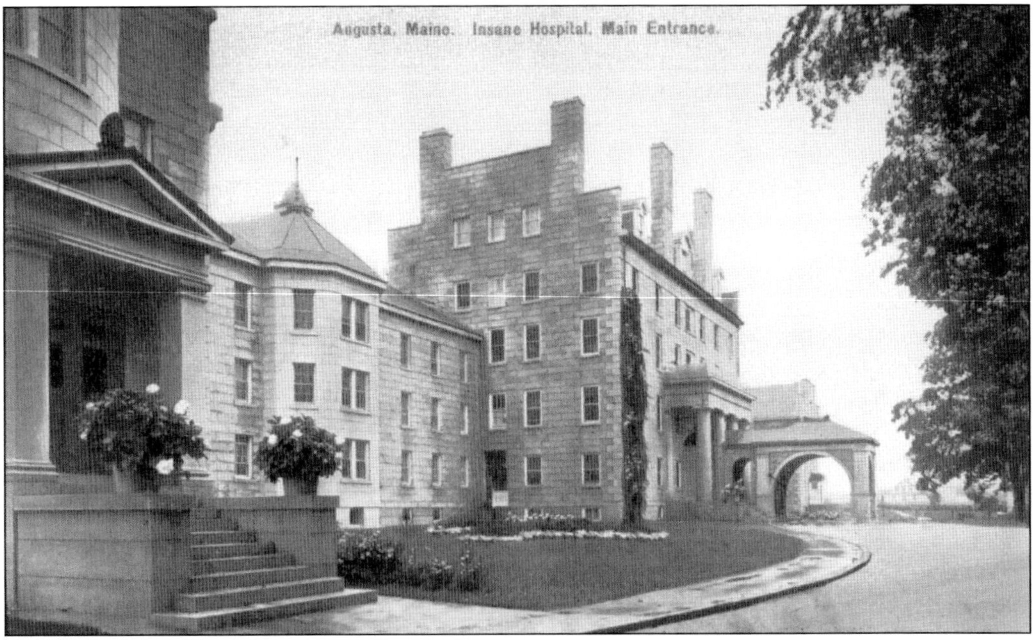

John D. Lord designed the asylum, widely known as the Augusta Mental Health Institute, in the Greek Revival style, and construction began in 1836, taking six years to complete. The central building and mirrored wings were built of Hallowell granite. Just to the right of the arched entryway are the faintly visible dairy cattle barns. At one time, there were stables, shops, and a straw barn located here.

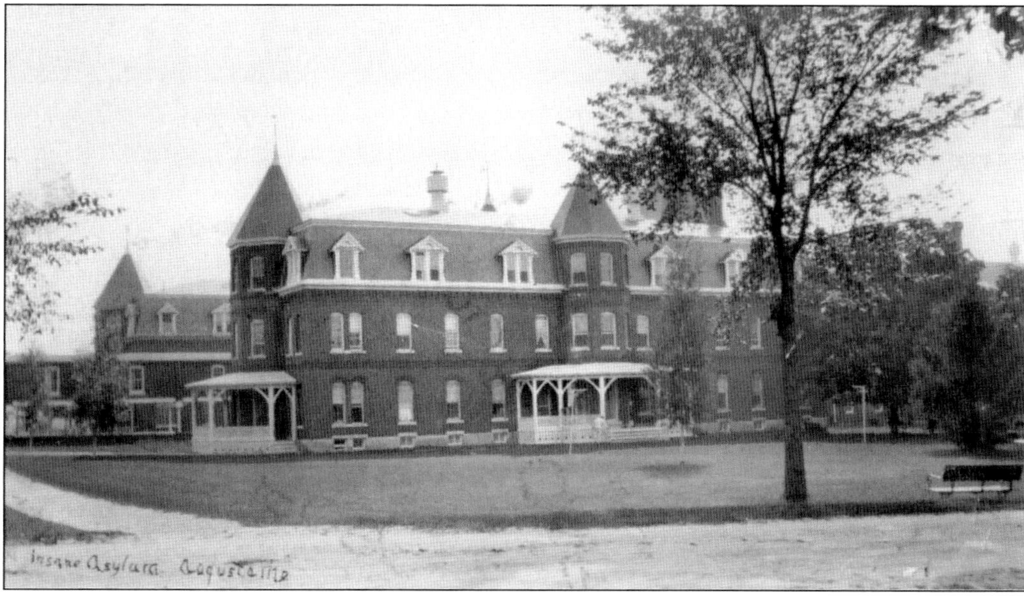

By the 1880s, the asylum was treating over 600 patients, which required more space. Dr. Bigelow T. Sanborn, physician and superintendent, was appropriated $40,000 in the spring of 1883, and later that year, two new wards were constructed. Essentially mirror images of each other, the southern ward was for men, and the northern ward, shown here, was for the women, who would move in the day after Thanksgiving.

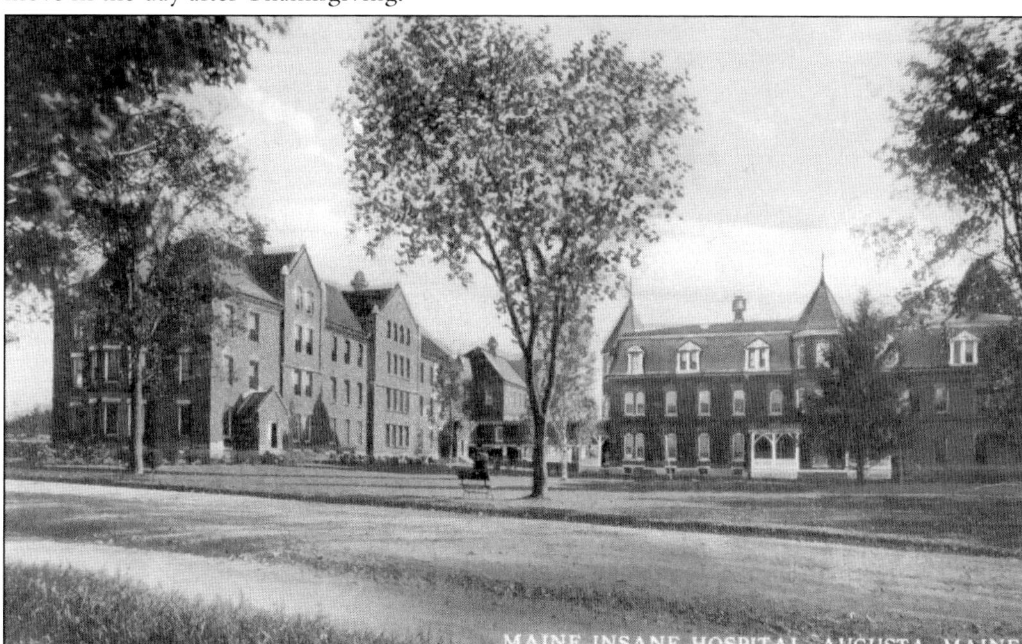

Contracts for two pavilions were awarded in April 1889 for $80,000, and construction began the following month. Patients were occupying the brick-and-granite buildings by August 1890. On the left is the northern pavilion for women; the men's pavilion can be seen at center, farther back. The women's ward is on the right. An elevated brick corridor connects all the pavilions, wards, and the asylum proper.

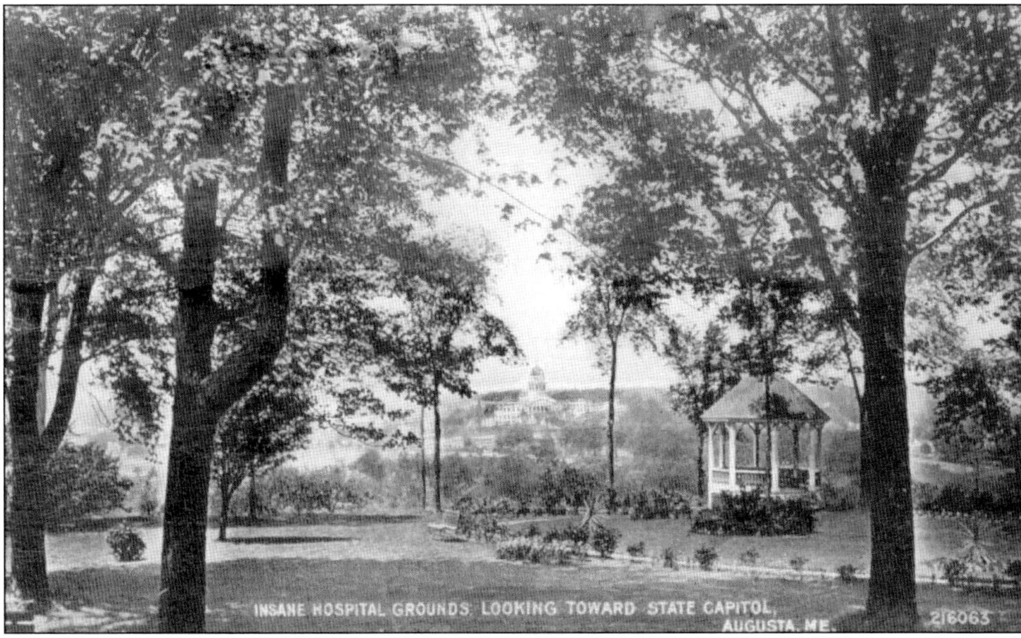

Although this picturesque view of the state capitol from the Maine Insane Asylum, beautifully framed by shade trees, gardens, and a quaint gazebo, would be soothing to any temperament, the location of the asylum was actually chosen for the opposite perspective. The site was selected so that each successive governor and members of the legislature would never forget the hospital or those cared for there.

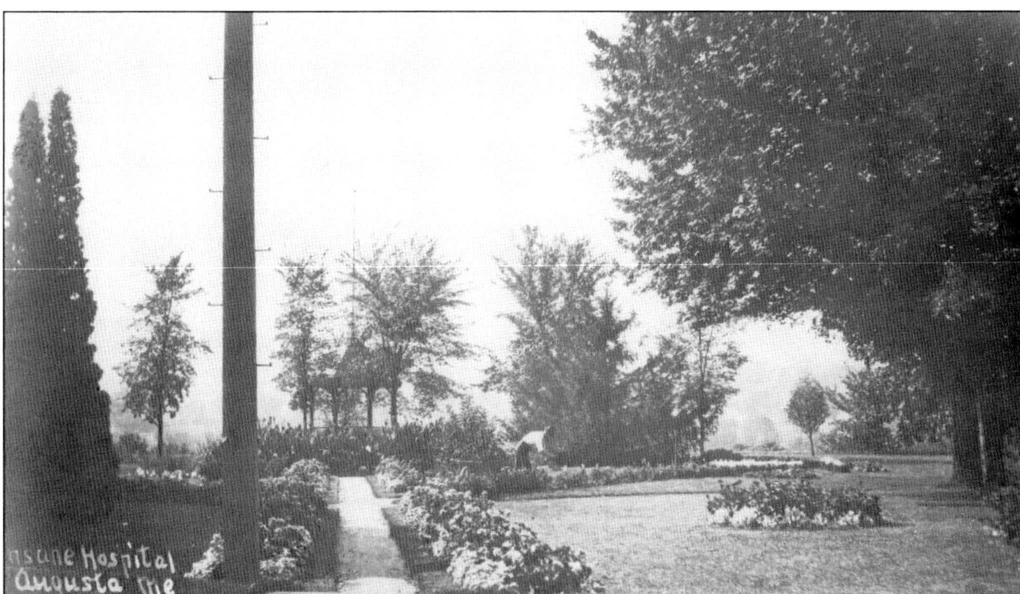

For therapeutic and practical reasons, the patients performed much of the work. Many of them were employed in various departments, such as the laundry, kitchen, mechanical room, barn, garages, and wards. In addition, a large number were engaged in exterior maintenance, including lawn care as well as farming and gardening. Such may be the case for this fellow tending the flower beds shown here.

Three

Churches

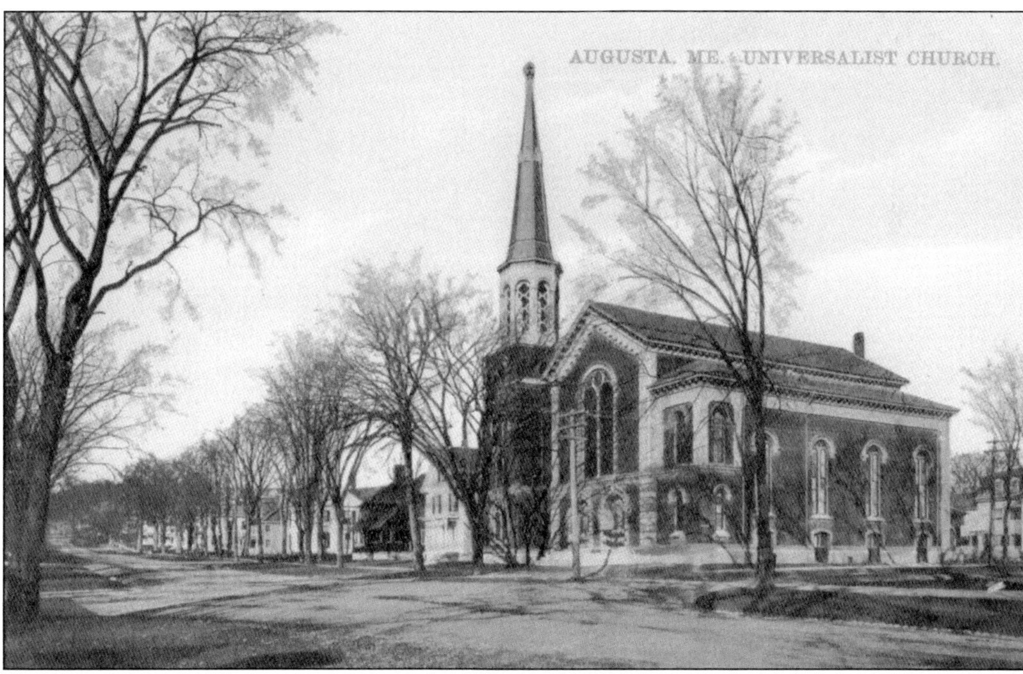

Financed with the sale of pews, the Universalist Society built their first church on Chapel Street in 1835 and dedicated it on Thanksgiving later that year. The prosperous and growing congregation later erected this Romanesque edifice on Winthrop Street in 1868. Large and proportionate, the brick-and-mortar church could hold 500 parishioners, while the belfry stood at 135 feet and housed a 1,500-pound bell.

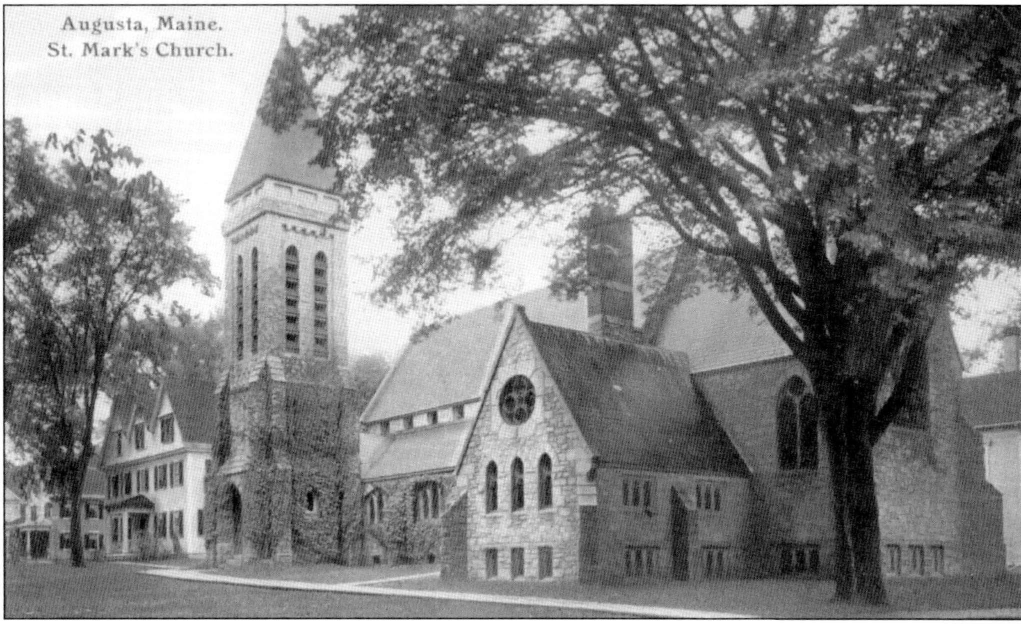

From the first Episcopal services held at Old Fort Western in 1763, St. Mark's Episcopal Church grew into a substantial congregation requiring a proper place of worship. Richard M. Upjohn of New York, brother of the then rector, Rev. Samuel Upjohn, designed the Gothic-style structure. At a cost of $40,000, the church was built of Maine granite in 1886, then consecrated the following year. Weighing over 12,000 pounds, 11 bells were installed in the 92-foot spire.

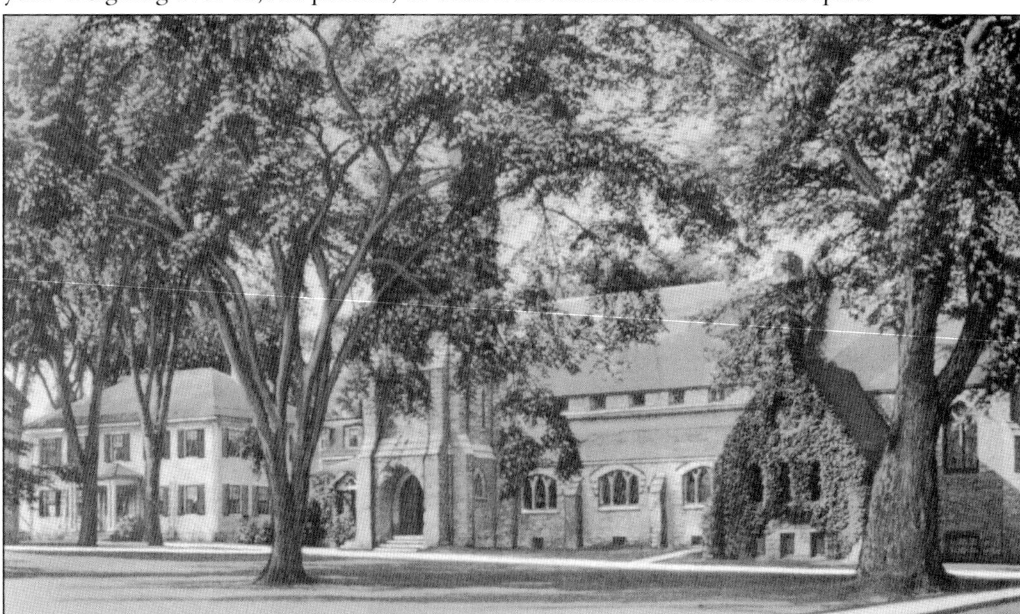

The Fuller-Weston House, seen on the left, is used as the rectory for St. Mark's Church. Built in 1818, this Federal-style house was the residence of Judge Henry Weld Fuller, a probate judge of Kennebec County. By 1832, Judge Nathan Weston, a chief justice of the Maine Supreme Judicial Court, and his family had moved into the dwelling. The house exchanged hands several more times before being deeded to the church in 1888.

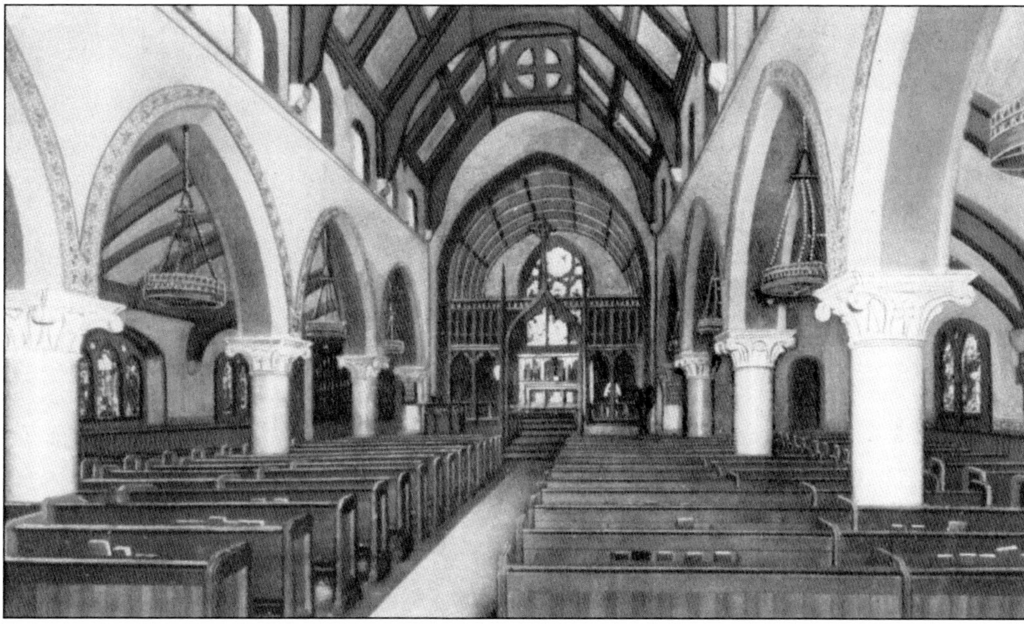

St. Mark's interior is proportioned well in that the polished granite pillars beautifully frame its reredos, with ample natural light from the open clerestory. The altar, made mostly of French cream-colored sandstone, is a memorial to Sibyl Angier Farnham Lambard, the first communicant of this parish. The stained-glass window behind the altar faces east, providing an impressive backdrop during the morning hours.

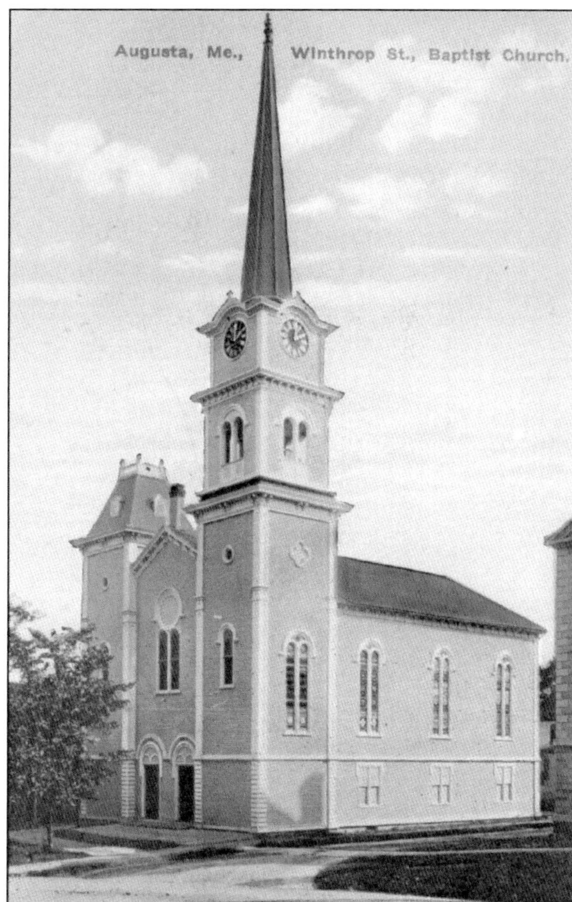

Organized in 1831, the First Baptist Church met at the old courthouse until the congregation built a Federal-style church on Winthrop Street in 1835. Having been extensively remodeled with an Italianate facade in 1868, the church had two towers, the tallest being 150 feet high. The First Baptist Church and the Freewill Baptist Church merged to become the Penney Memorial Baptist Church, and a new church was erected on Grove Street in 1906.

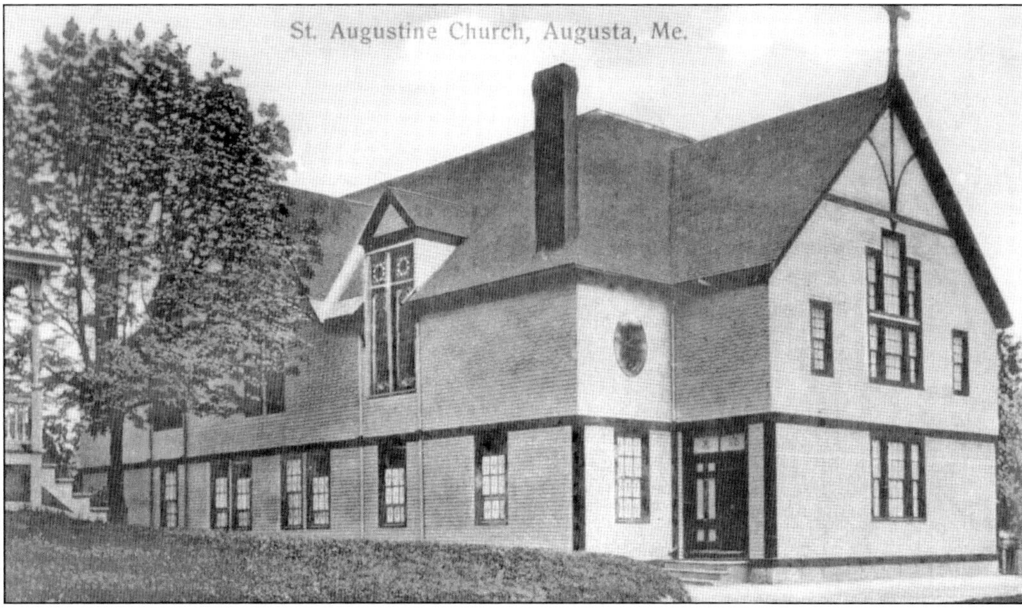

Although founded in 1887, it was another two years before St. Augustine's parish had erected this wood-frame structure on Washington Street. Initially, it housed a school and the church, but it became apparent that one building was too small for both, so a new church was built to the south in 1916. The original structure was devoted to use as a school, with the major renovations performed in the 1930s.

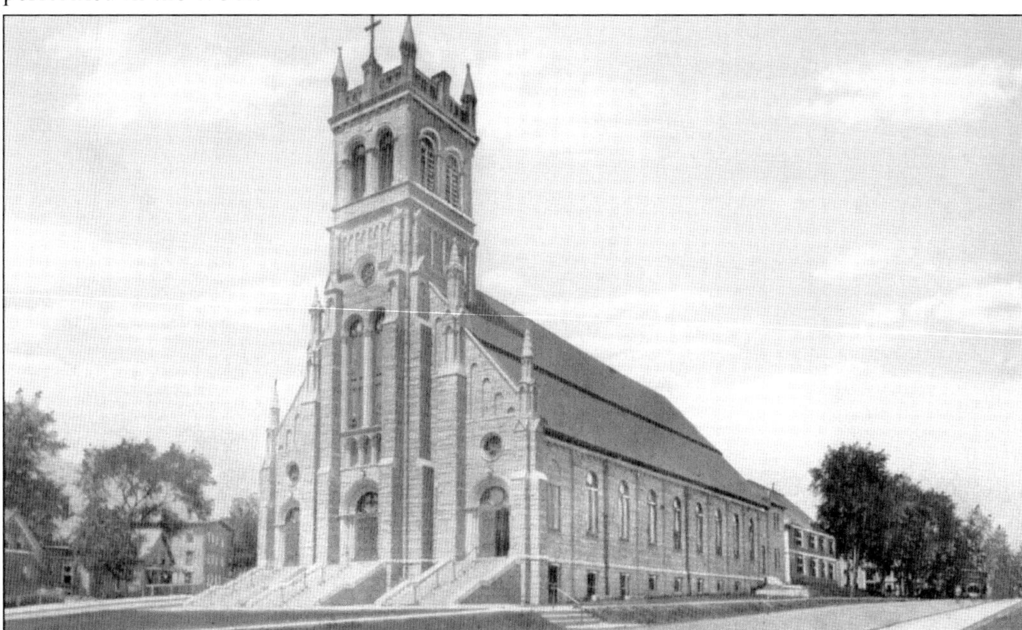

Designed by Thomas G. O'Connell of Boston, construction began on this Romanesque granite church in 1916 to replace the smaller wooden structure of St. Augustine's parish. The plans had originally included a spire, but only a parapet was actually built. Even though construction had not been finished, more than 1,500 people attended the church's dedication on Christmas Day 1916.

St. Augustine's Church finally received its spire in 1932, bringing its height to a towering 150 feet, although it lacked the ornamentation of its original design. Two years prior, the church had installed new bells and stained-glass windows. It has remained relatively unchanged since, standing as a testament to the French Canadian immigrants of Sand Hill who built it.

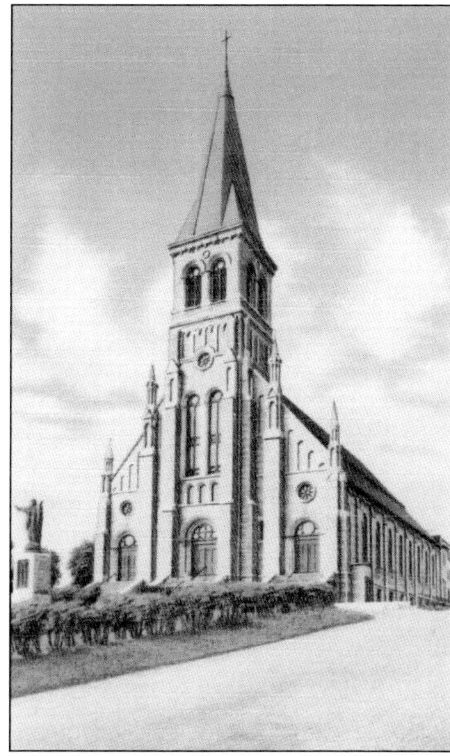

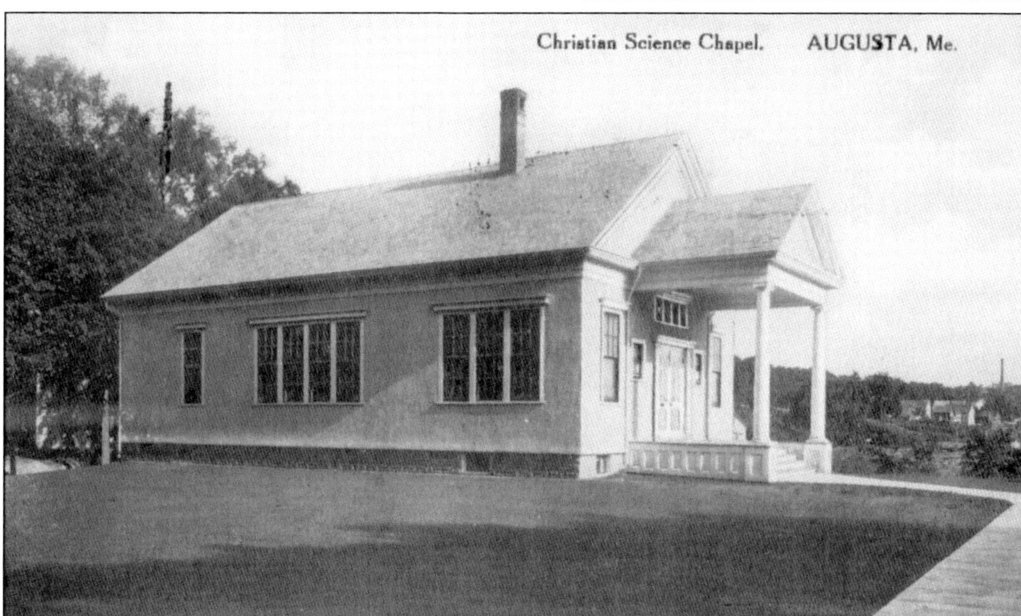

The Christian Science Chapel stands on the corner of Williams and Howard Streets, roughly where the Cushnoc Trading Post was once located. The church edifice, with simple Colonial lines and a stucco exterior, was completed in 1914. The chapel's main auditorium seats 175, along with a reading room on the south side. In 1934, the name was changed to First Church of Christ Scientist.

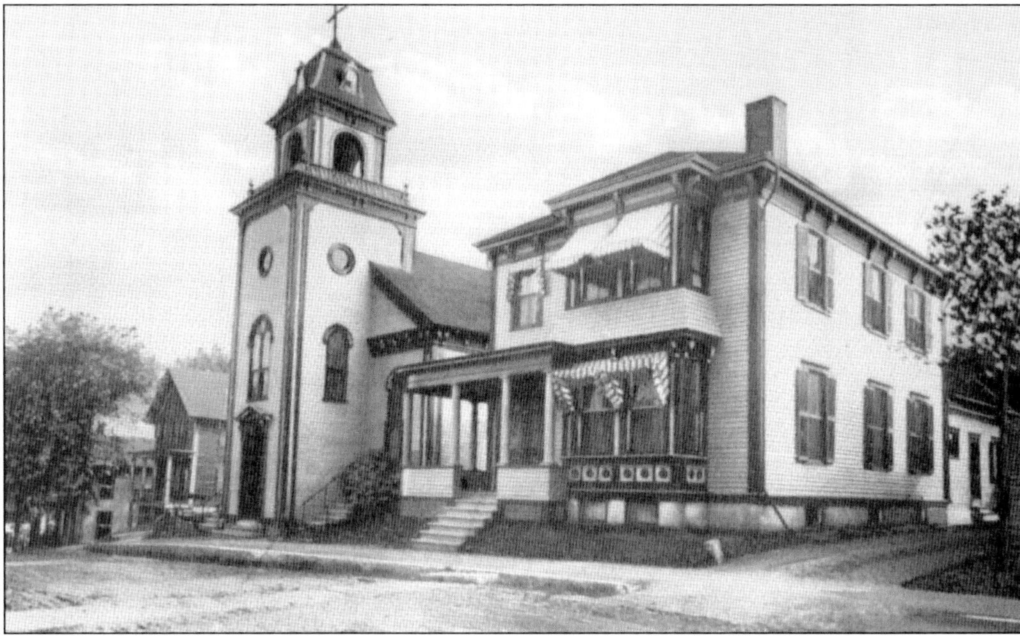

Due to the influx of Irish laborers, the Victorian-style St. Mary's Church was built on State Street in 1845 when the Catholics had outgrown the Bethlehem chapel, which was then sold to the Cony Female Academy. George G. Stevens of Augusta designed the church with Italianate trim and stained-glass windows. In 1868, the square tower was added to the church, seen here with the presbytery on the right.

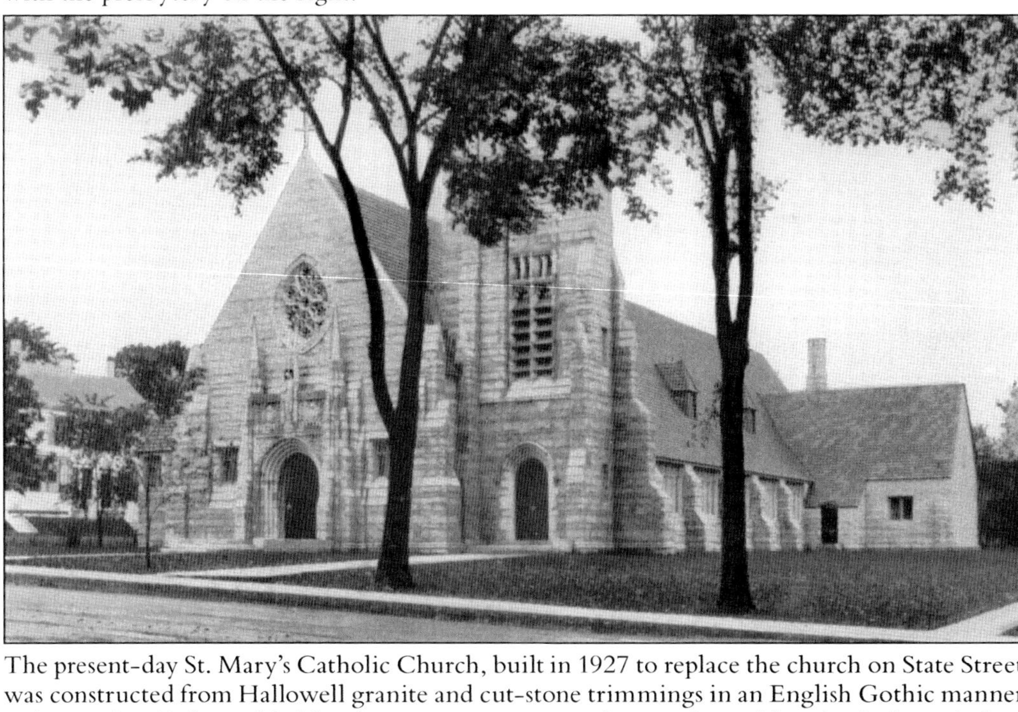

The present-day St. Mary's Catholic Church, built in 1927 to replace the church on State Street, was constructed from Hallowell granite and cut-stone trimmings in an English Gothic manner. Its impressive 60-foot gabled facade opens to a stone arcade, complete with stained-glass windows from Munich, Germany.

Few churches have been modified as often as the Methodist church on Green Street. Built in 1828, the church's first remodel occurred in 1848, when the north end was extended by 14 feet to make room for more pews. The second remodel, which included raising the structure by 2 feet and digging a 10-foot basement, was done in 1856. Lastly, in 1868, the church was cut at pew height and raised 5 feet 7 inches.

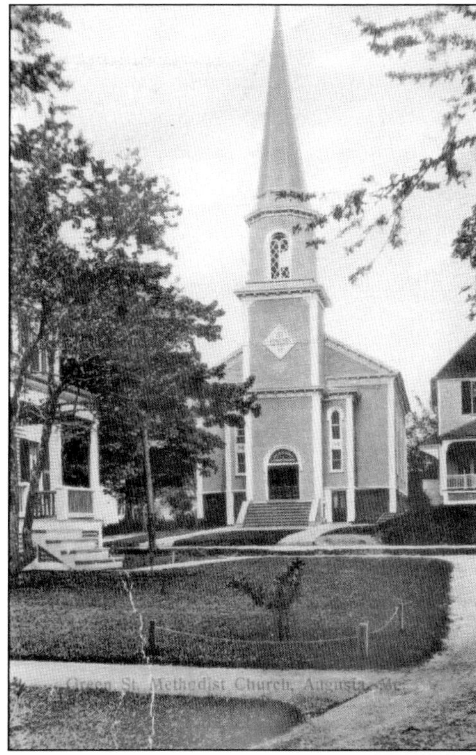

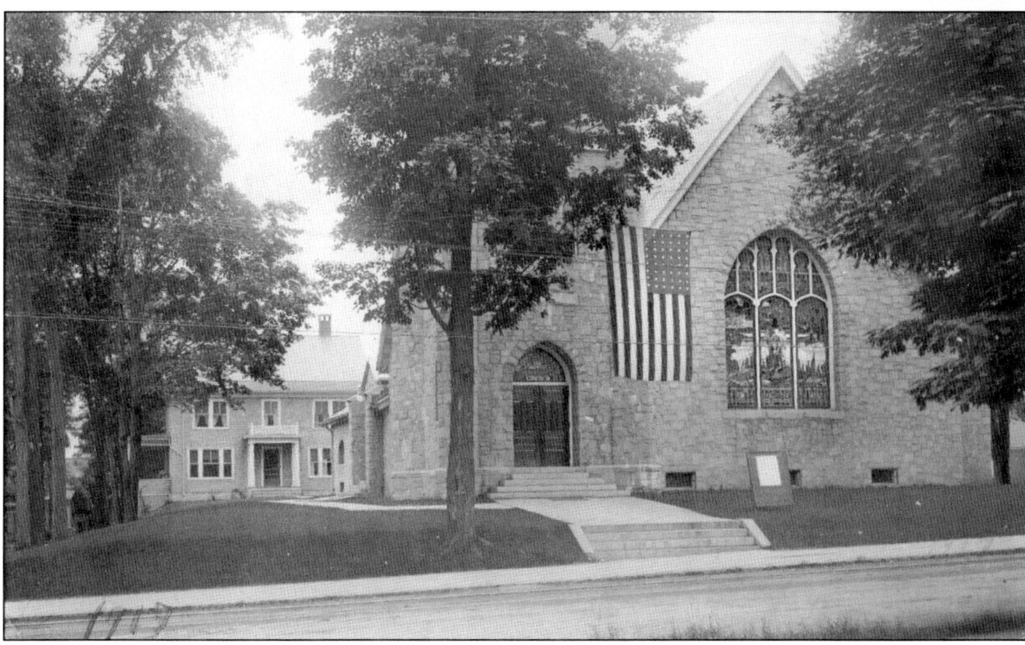

Penney Memorial Church was named in memoriam of Rev. Charles Fox Penney, pastor of the First Baptist Church from 1862 to 1886. Construction of the Gothic edifice, built of Hallowell granite, began in April or May 1906. Interestingly, the cornerstone was not laid until July 31 because the tower was slated for the final stage of construction. Completed at a cost of about $40,000, the church was dedicated on September 17, 1907.

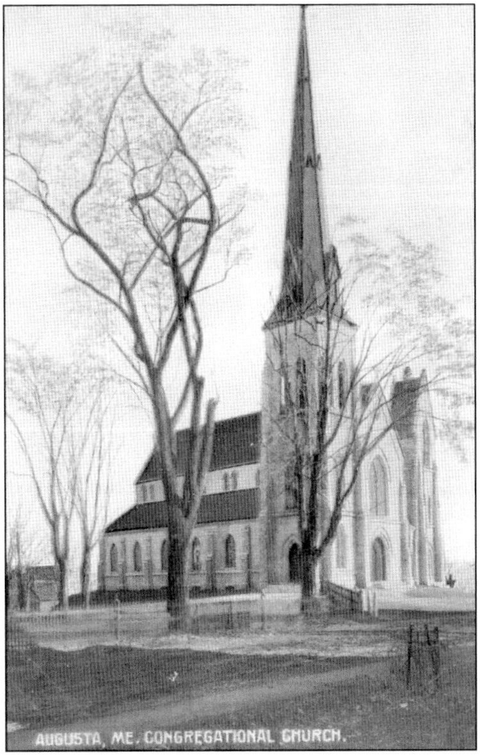

The current granite edifice of the South Parish Congregational Church was built in the Gothic Revival style to replace the 1809 structure that was struck by lightning and burned to the ground on July 11, 1864. Able to accommodate 750 parishioners, this grand church has a towering 178-foot spire and a 57-foot ceiling. It was dedicated on July 5, 1866, making it the oldest church in Augusta.

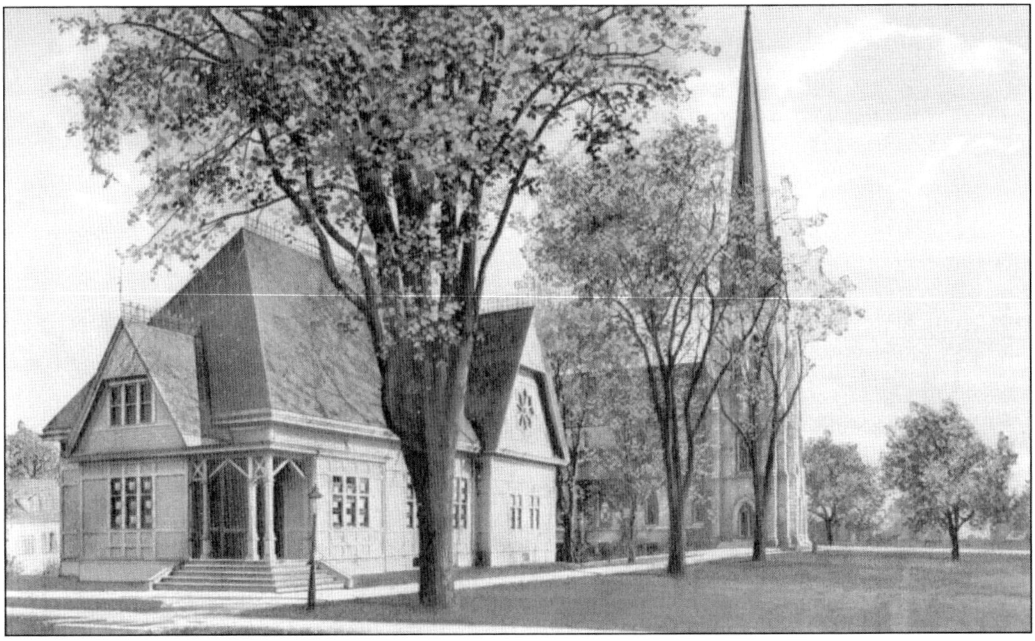

With the previous chapel deemed unsafe, the South Parish congregation had it removed and built this new structure in its stead. James H. Cochrane of Augusta was the designer, and John P. Wyman completed construction in the spring of 1889, with a final cost of about $6,300. By May, it was being used regularly for meetings. At one time, the chapel had a tower located on the near corner.

Four

Homes

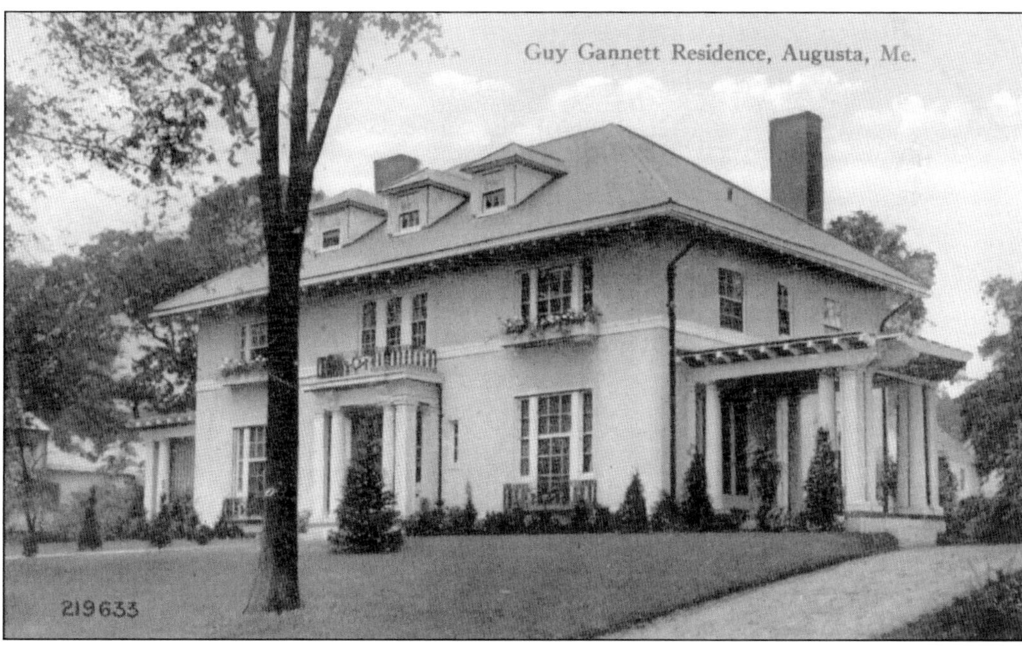

In 1911, Guy P. Gannett completed his luxurious mansion on State Street for a cost of about $20,000, including furnishings. Designed by Thomas M. James of Boston, it was the first stucco house in central Maine. The home had many modern conveniences, including a gas water heater, an elevator for firewood, and a central vacuum system.

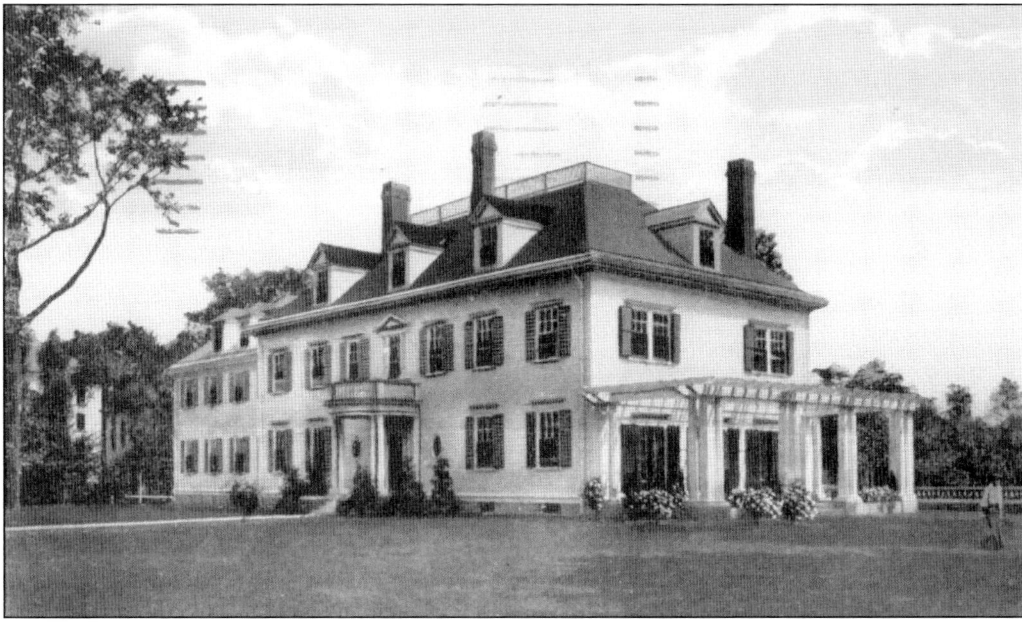

Percy Vickery Hill, the son of ex-governor John F. Hill, built his palatial mansion on State Street, not far from his father's house, in 1915. Designed by Charles N. Cogswell of Boston, this Colonial-style manor had 23 rooms and six bathrooms, all of which cost nearly $100,000 to build, including furnishings and landscaping. The estate grounds required the removal of five houses to cover its approximately four acres.

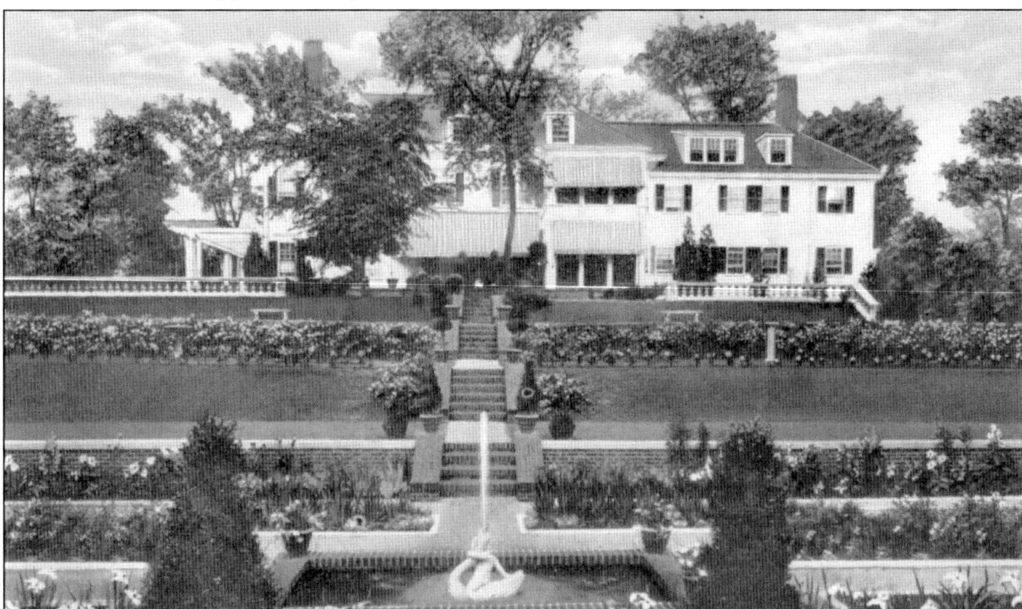

On the first floor, to the left, the large living room has a southerly view under the pergola. Behind the awnings is the dining room with French windows looking out over a brick-paved terrace. Four large bedrooms, each with separate bath, occupy the second floor. The third floor houses a cavernous ballroom. The servants' ell, on the right, contains six bedrooms and baths, as well as a kitchen, butler's pantry, and dining room.

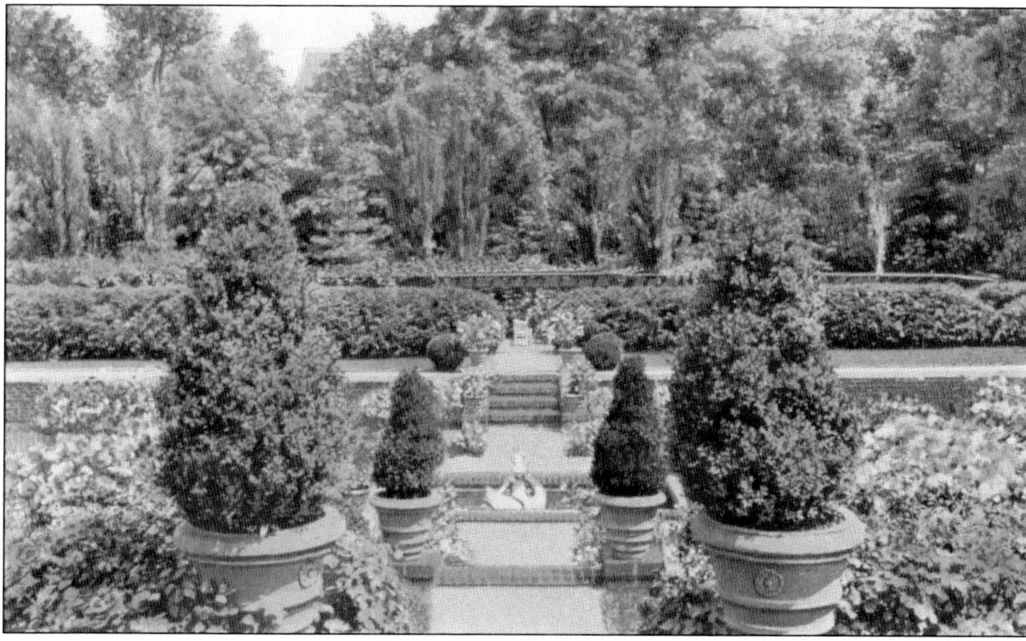

Landscape architect Carl Rust Parker of Portland designed the grounds for the estate. Three 20-foot-wide terraces led from the garden to the house, the second of which was brimming with roses. The terraced area was enclosed by a brick retaining wall with a concrete balustrade. The garden itself was 40 feet by 80 feet, containing a center pool built of tapestry brick and red tile and filled with lilies and fish. A garden house, built of brick with a mottled green tile roof, was erected at the south end; a greenhouse was proposed for the north end. Another flight of steps led from the garden to the tennis courts, not pictured. The courts were surrounded by an attractive fence of brick posts with ornamental wire panels, covered with an ivy-veiled pergola, the top of which is barely visible.

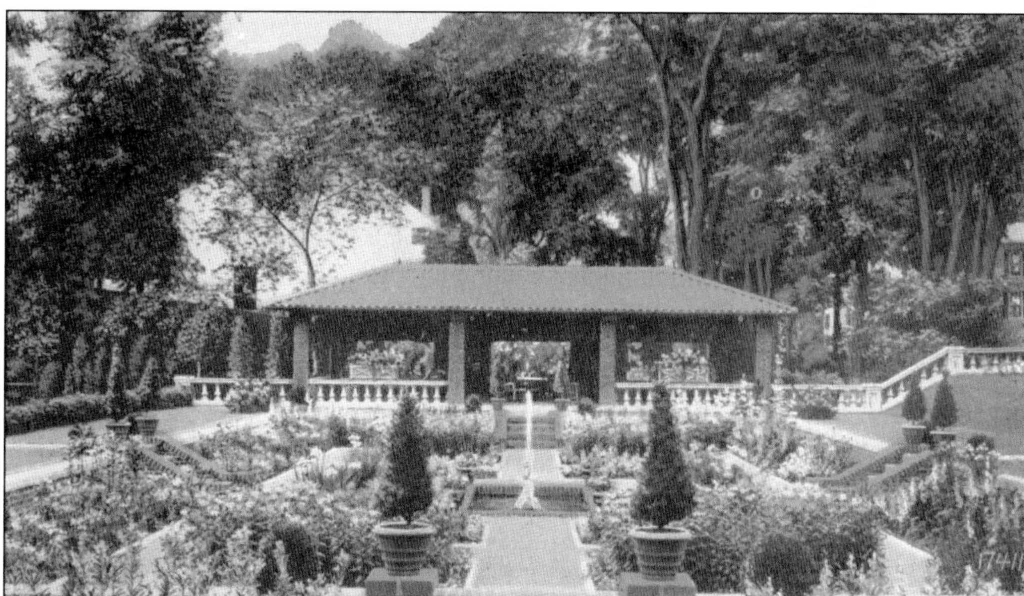

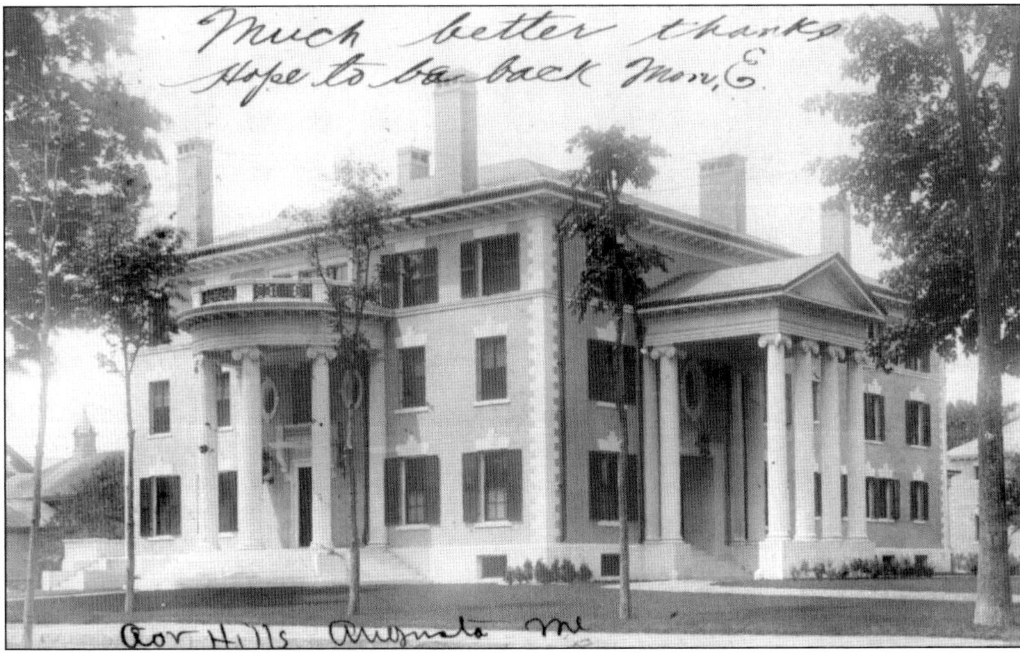

The 45th governor of Maine, John Freemont Hill, built his ornate Colonial Revival home at the junction of State and Green Streets in 1902. Designed by John Calvin Stevens, this three-story mansion was constructed with bricks from St. Louis, trimmed with Hallowell granite, and dressed with Ionic columns along its two porticos. The formal entrances open to a hallway that connects the dining room, living room, parlor, and library.

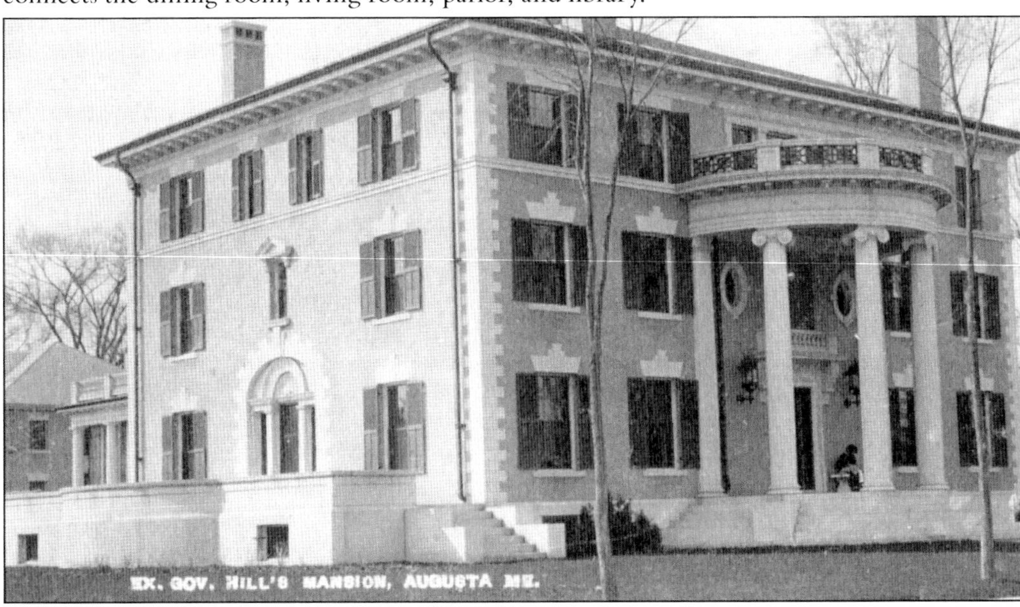

The first floor of the Hills' mansion was used mostly for receiving and entertaining guests, while the second floor contained the family's bedrooms. The servants' quarters were located on the third floor. The stable is seen on the left. Although John F. Hill passed away in 1912, the residence stayed in the care of his daughter Katherine Merrill until 1948, when it was given to the Oblate order of priests and used as a retreat home.

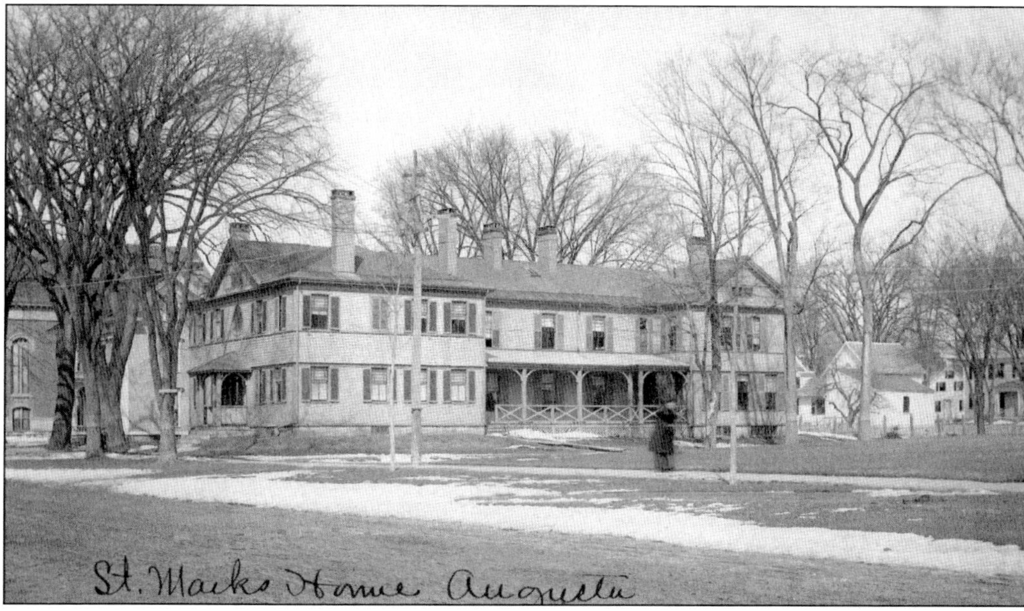

Dr. Issachar Snell built this beautiful mansion on lower Winthrop Street in 1805. Allen Lambard purchased it in 1870, then donated it to St. Mark's Parish to provide residential living for homeless women. Originally accommodating 17 women of all faiths and backgrounds, the home has 25 rooms, two parlors, and a dining room that can seat all residents at once. Sadly, it closed its doors at the end of 2014.

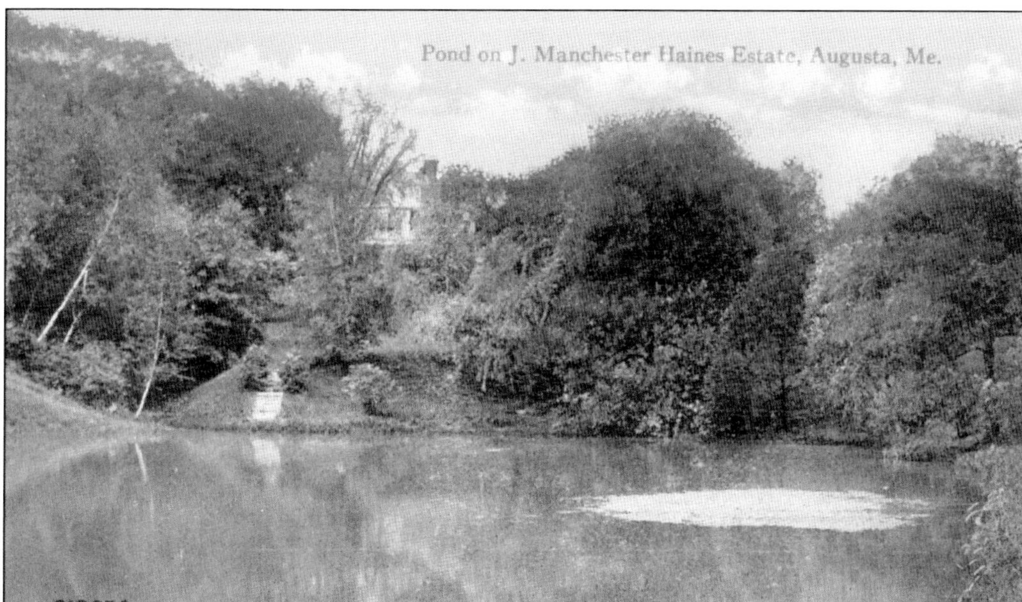

Surrounded by the Haynes Woods, the J. Manchester Haynes estate, known as Glenmere, was located on lower Western Avenue. The pond, where children once ice-skated in winter, occupied the corner of the estate, now the site of the post office. The rose-and-ivy-covered home can be seen beyond the steps leading from the pond. The house has since been replaced by a shopping mall.

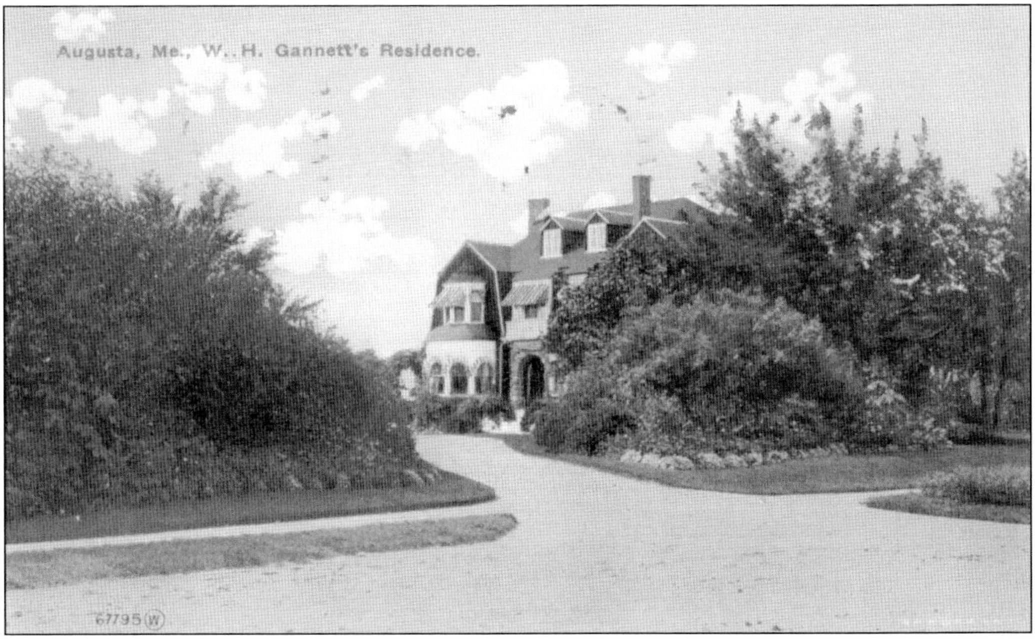

In the 1890s, William H. Gannett purchased over 450 acres of land south of Western Avenue, where he built his home, along with Ganneston Park, which the public was welcome to enjoy. He built his palatial two-and-a-half-story home atop Howard Hill around 1898, and in 1949, the mansion was deeded to the city, then later moved south of Capitol Street due to urban development.

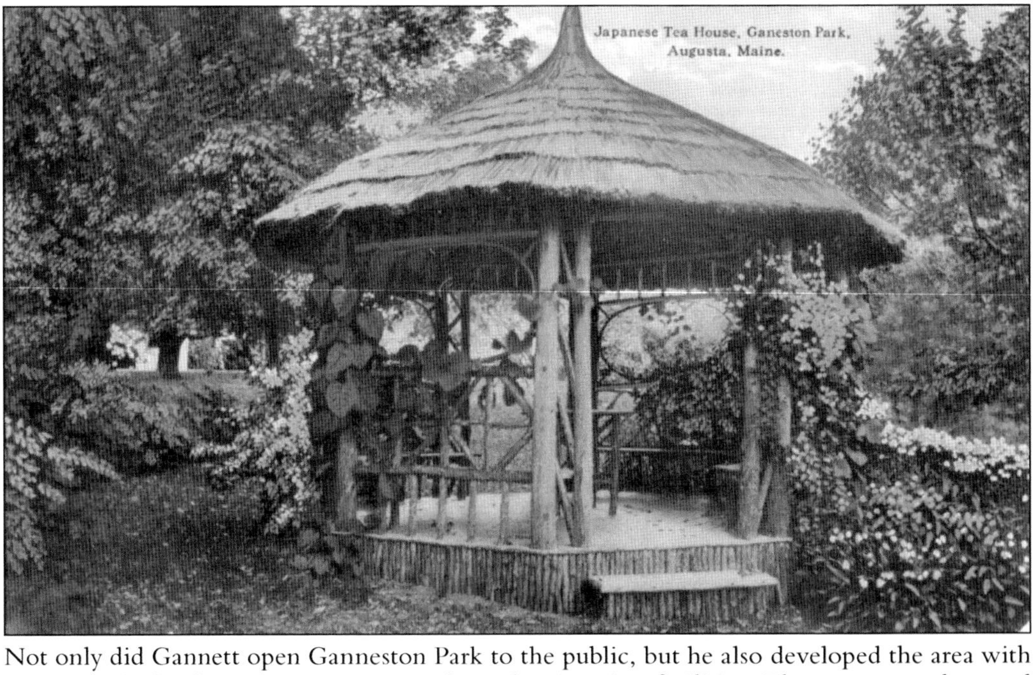

Not only did Gannett open Ganneston Park to the public, but he also developed the area with hiking trails, bridle paths, picnic grounds, and swimming facilities. There were gardens and artificial lakes, with Kennedy Brook winding its way throughout the foliage. He further enhanced the charm by adding unique structures, such as the House in the Trees, a Philippine bungalow, and even this quaint Japanese teahouse.

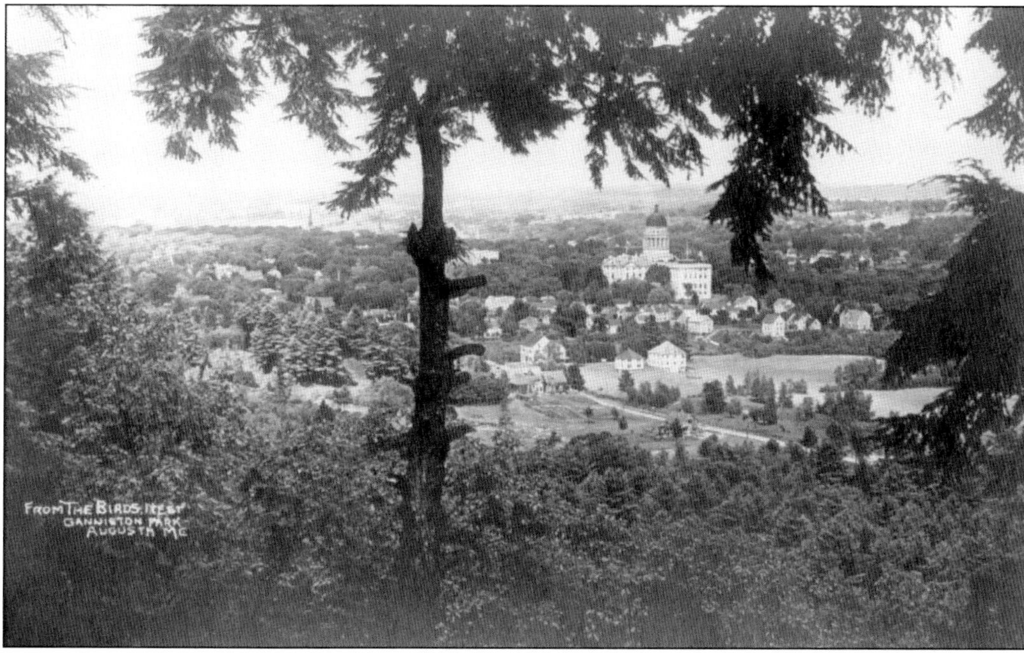

Gannett built the House in the Trees, a large cliffside tree house, for the use and enjoyment of the public. In 1915, it was erected on the cliff above Sewall Street, offering an unparalleled view of the river, the State House, and the city of Augusta. Unfortunately, the tree house was vandalized to such an extent that Gannett ordered it removed so no one would get hurt.

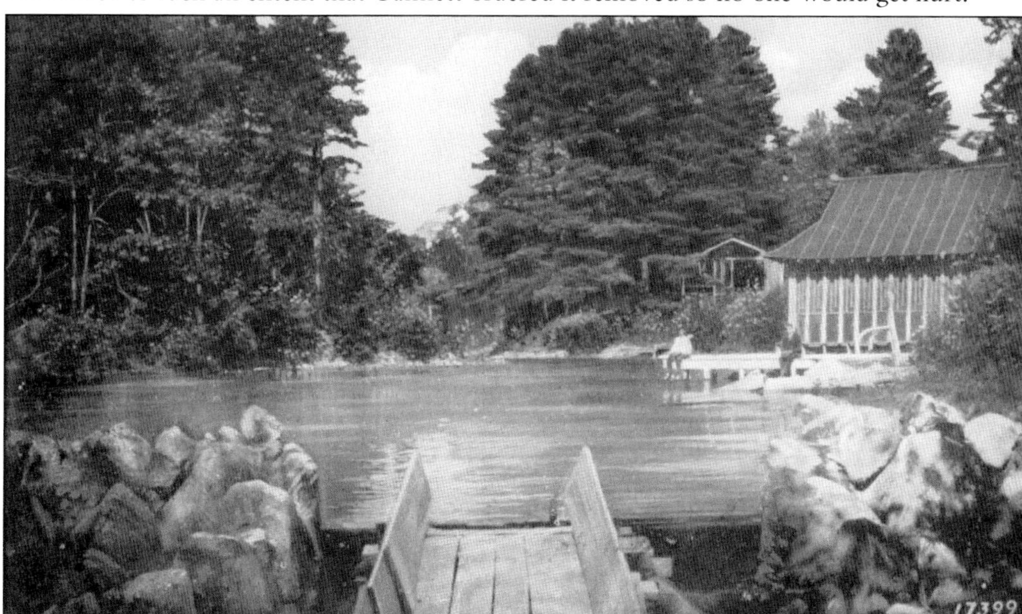

Around 1915, Gannett built a small dam on Kennedy Brook just above Johnson's Pond and below Gannett's Pond, forming a third lake in Ganneston Park. A small boathouse was added later on the edge of the swimming hole. Children would ice skate on these ponds during the winter, often seeing muskrats swimming under the ice. Two dams were breached in 1955 when Capitol Street was extended and these ponds were drained.

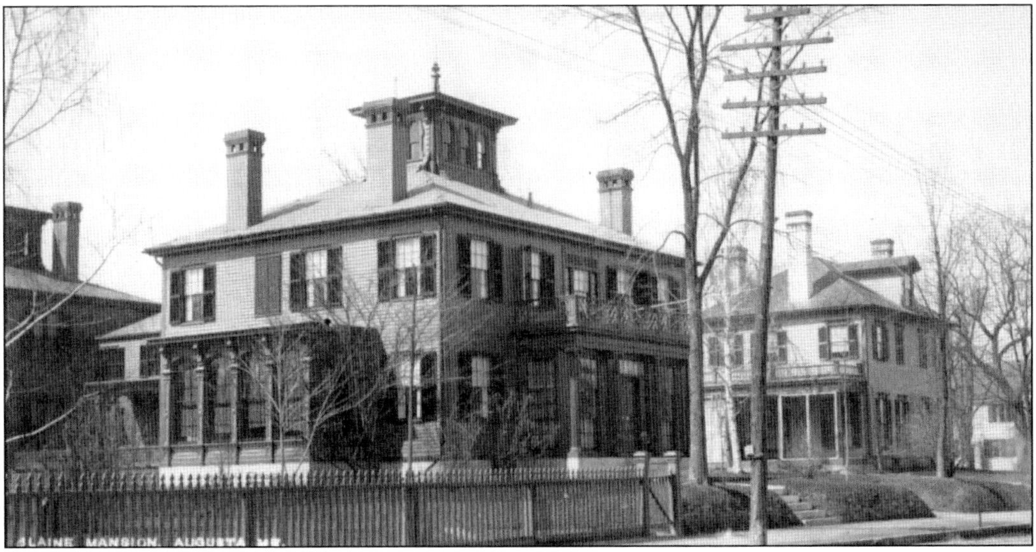

Capt. James Hall built his Classic Revival home on State Street in 1833, but the mansion acquired its signature features after 1862, when James G. Blaine purchased it as a birthday present for his wife. Blaine remodeled in 1869, adding the ell porch and hip roof on the carriage house, and again in 1872, incorporating the bay window and cupola and building a new wing.

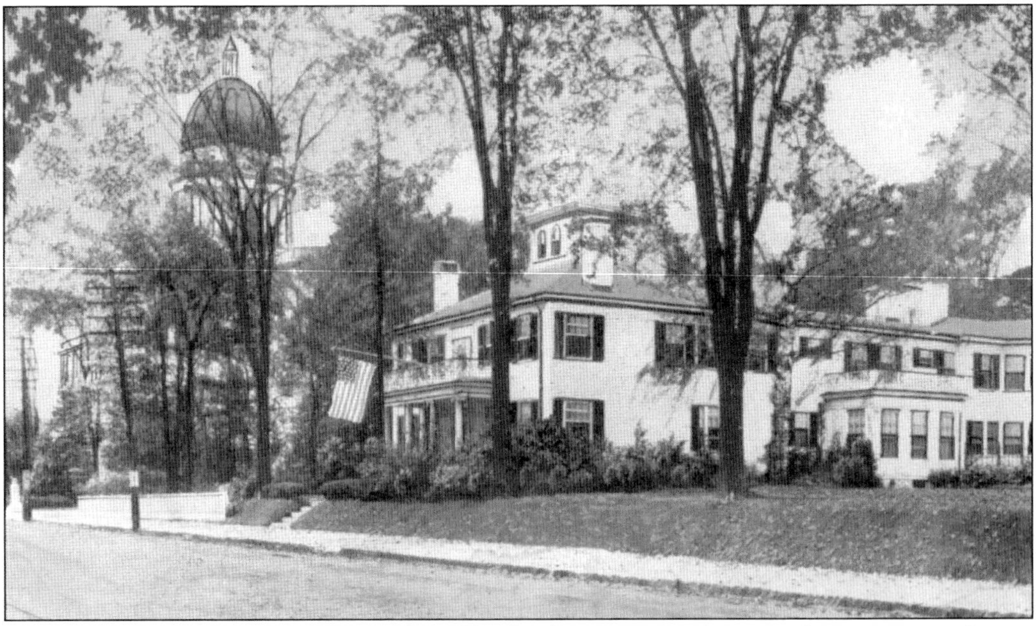

James G. Blaine was an important political leader from Maine who served as secretary of state, as well as in the US House of Representatives and Senate; he also lost a close presidential race to Grover Cleveland in 1884. Though Blaine died on January 15, 1893, his wife, Harriet Stanwood Blaine, lived in the mansion for another decade. The 1869 ell can be seen on the right, as viewed from the north.

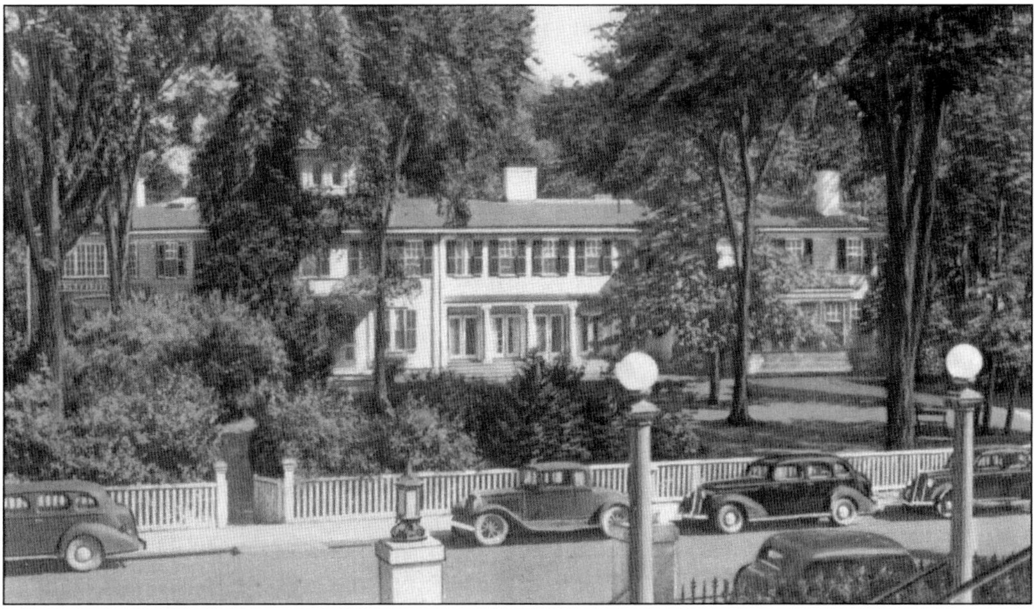

Harriet Stanwood Blaine died in 1903 and left the mansion to her children. By 1919, daughter Harriet Blaine Beale would own the estate outright. Beale donated the home to the state in memory of her son Walker, who had perished in France during World War I, and the Blaine House has remained the official residence of the governor since 1920. This beautiful view across Capitol Street shows the estate during the 1930s.

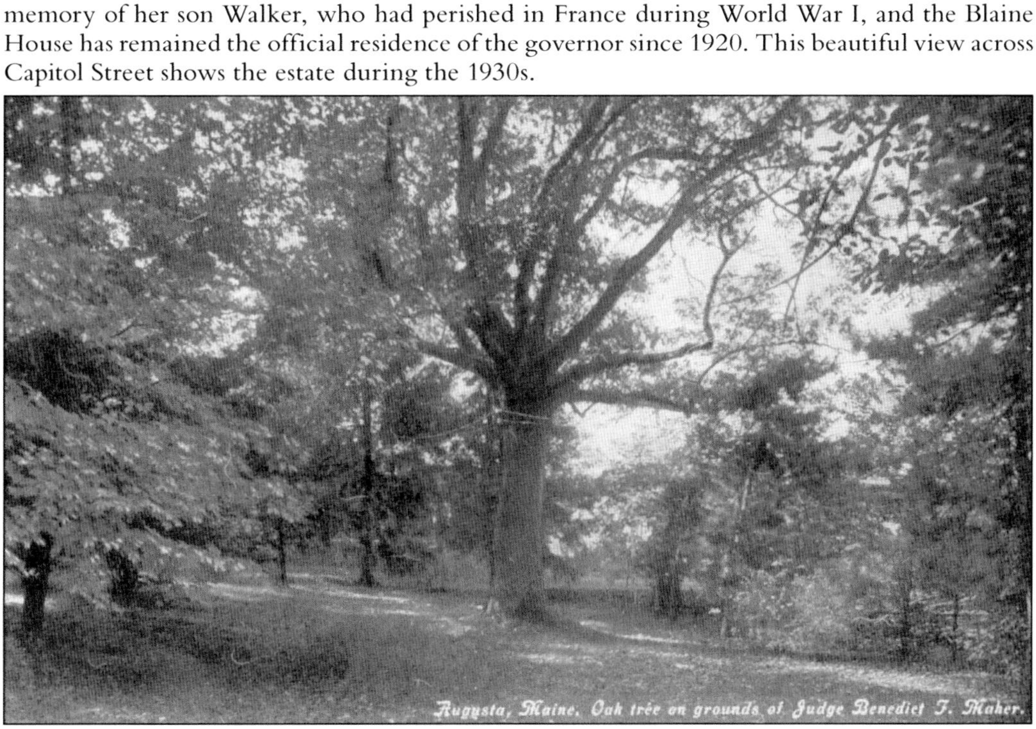

According to local legend, 19-year-old Aaron Burr wooed Indian princess Jacataqua underneath this old oak tree—on what became Judge Maher's property on lower Green Street—while on Benedict Arnold's 1775 expedition to Quebec. Supposedly, the pair was investigating why the cornfield was being eaten when they came upon a bear and her cubs, which they promptly dispatched and later served for dinner.

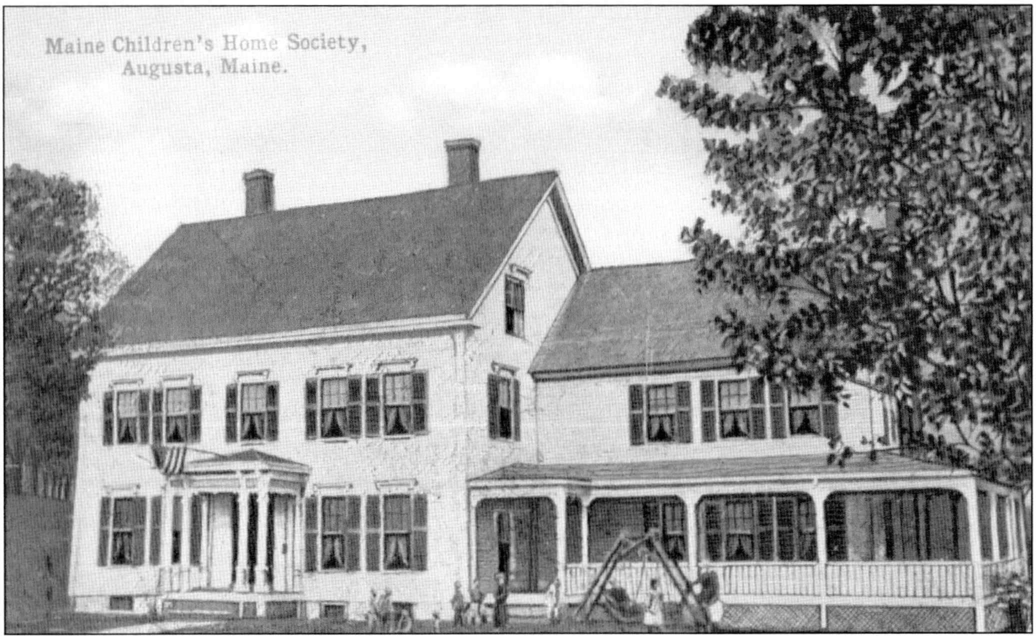

Established in 1899, the Maine Children's Home Society ultimately opened its doors at 129 Sewall Street in 1902. The home cared for many hundreds of orphaned and abandoned children before closing in 1915 due to the ever-increasing acceptance of foster care programs. Although the building is now gone, it once housed Edgar Jones Productions, Inc., and eventually would become Holman Day Productions, Augusta's only motion picture studio, from 1918 to 1922.

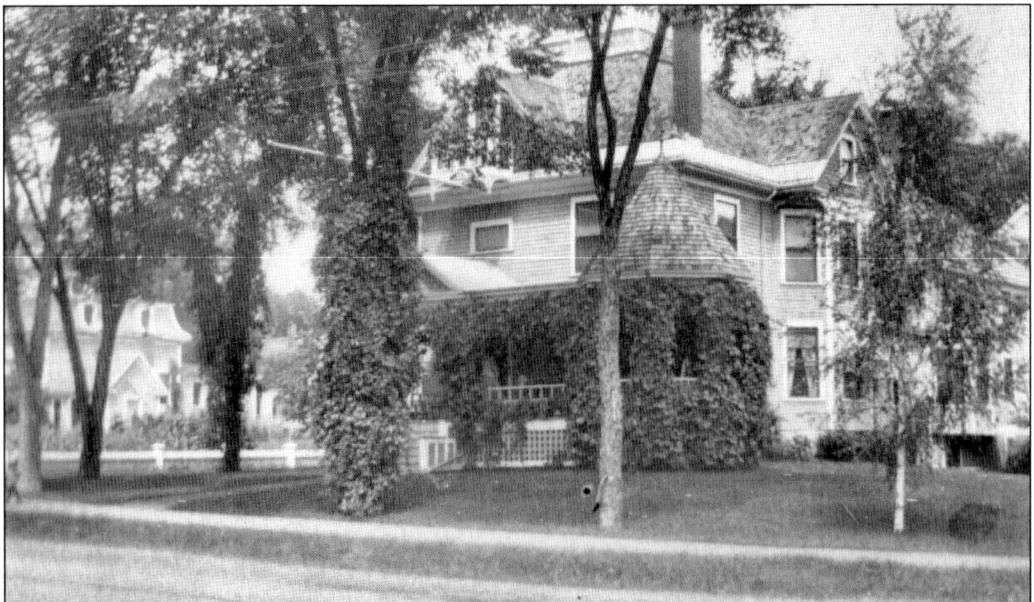

This beautiful home was typical of those built on Western Avenue in the late 19th century. Located at the corner of Melville Street, this structure still exists, although it has had many alterations over the years. At one time, the building at left with the mansard roof was the Bowdoin Inn, from the late 1910s into the 1920s.

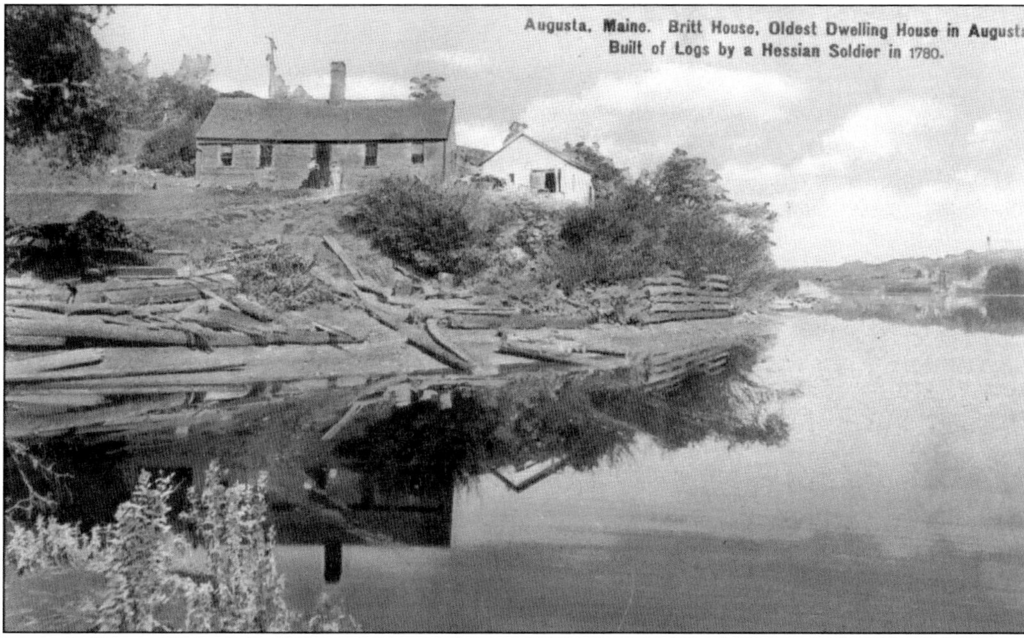

The Britt House was the oldest dwelling to have survived up to that time. It was built in 1780 by John Britt, a Hessian soldier (for whom it was named), who had settled on the west bank of the Kennebec River at the close of the Revolutionary War. Presumably, Britt came to this country with Baron von Steuben to assist George Washington in battle.

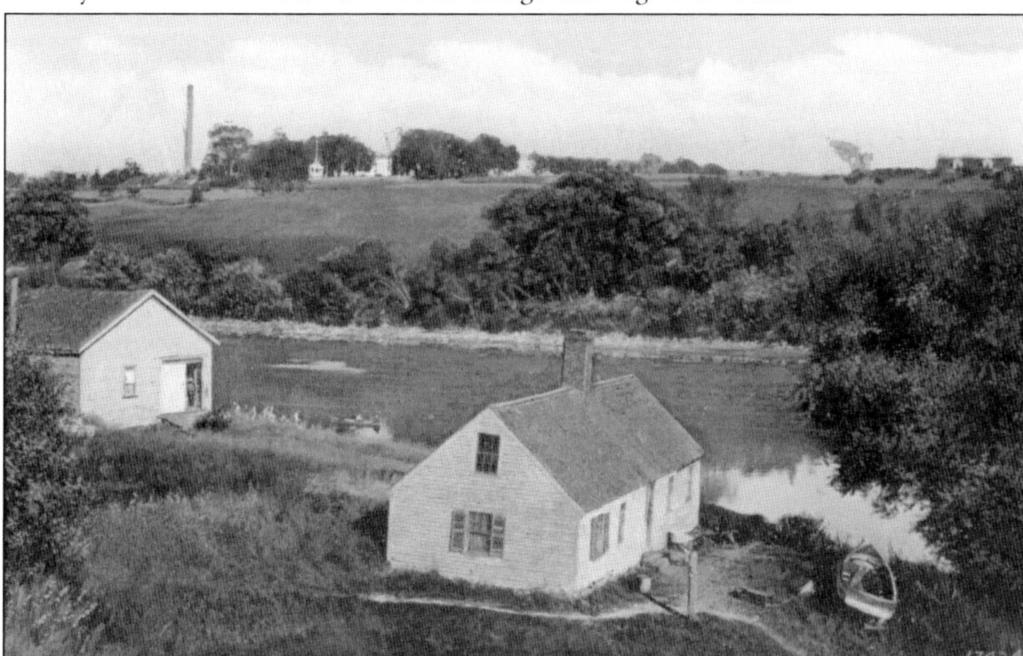

Located at the end of Britt Gully Road (now Jackson Avenue), the Britt House was constructed of logs, though it was covered in clapboard sometime in the early 1900s, as it had fallen into disrepair. At least seven generations of the original settler resided here before the house was lost to fire around 1930.

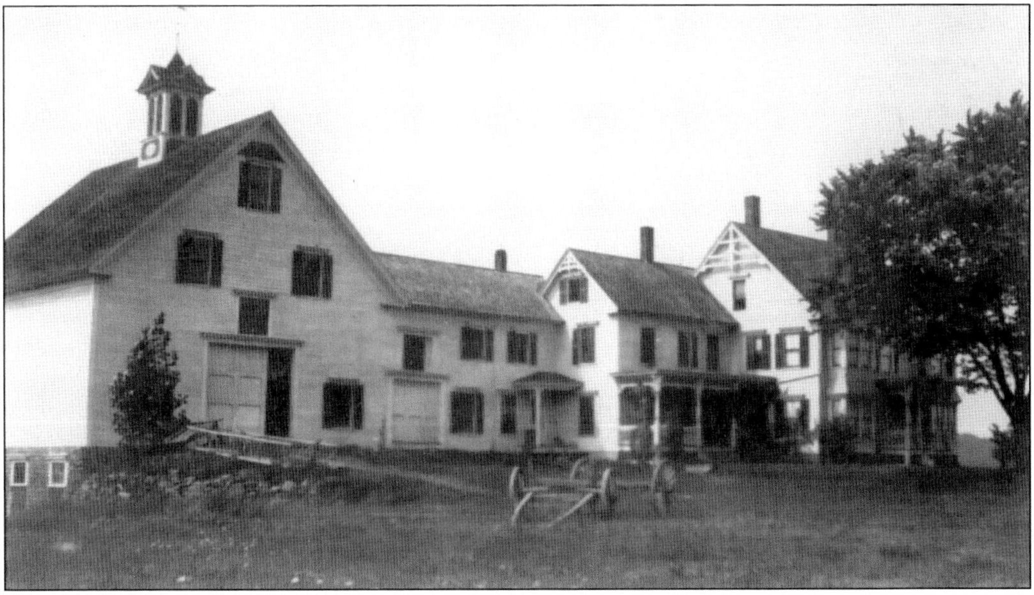

Built in 1850, this homestead on Riverside Drive, formerly known as East River Road, was typical of rural living in Augusta during the early 20th century. As was common in that day, neighbors helped neighbors; in this case, a gasoline engine was being used to pump springwater into a tank for a stable and two neighboring houses. The house and barn have since been remodeled and converted into apartments.

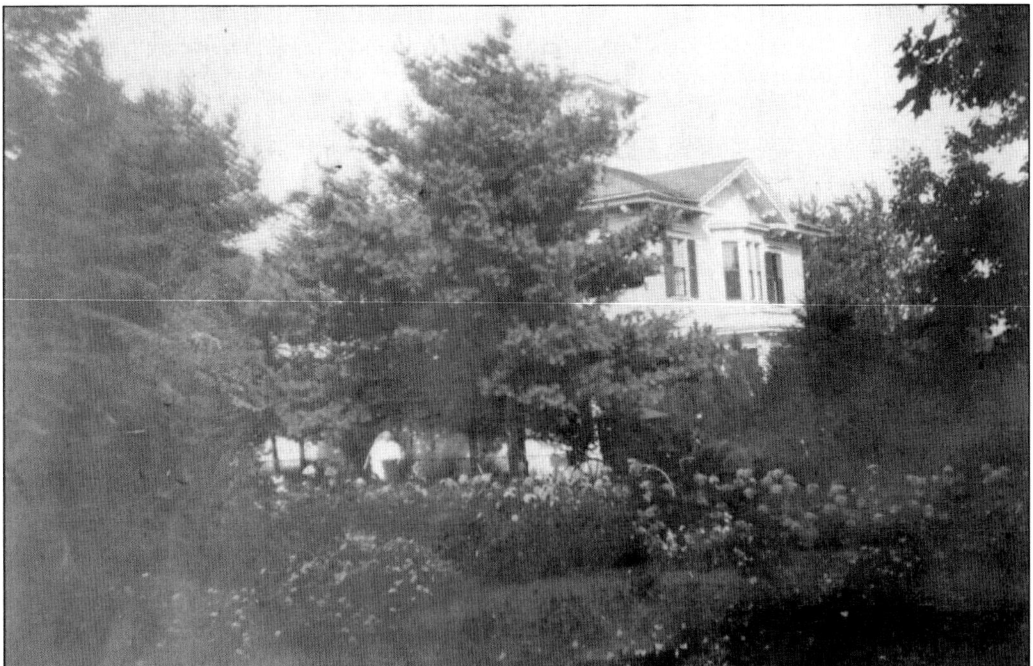

Barely visible through the trees is the home of the Honorable Charles A. Milliken as it appeared at 57 Western Avenue in 1905. First elected in 1894, Milliken served as a two-time mayor of Augusta. It is unclear as to the identity of the fellow in the white shirt; however, the postcard does include a message: "Greetings, congratulations and good wishes from the Milliken family."

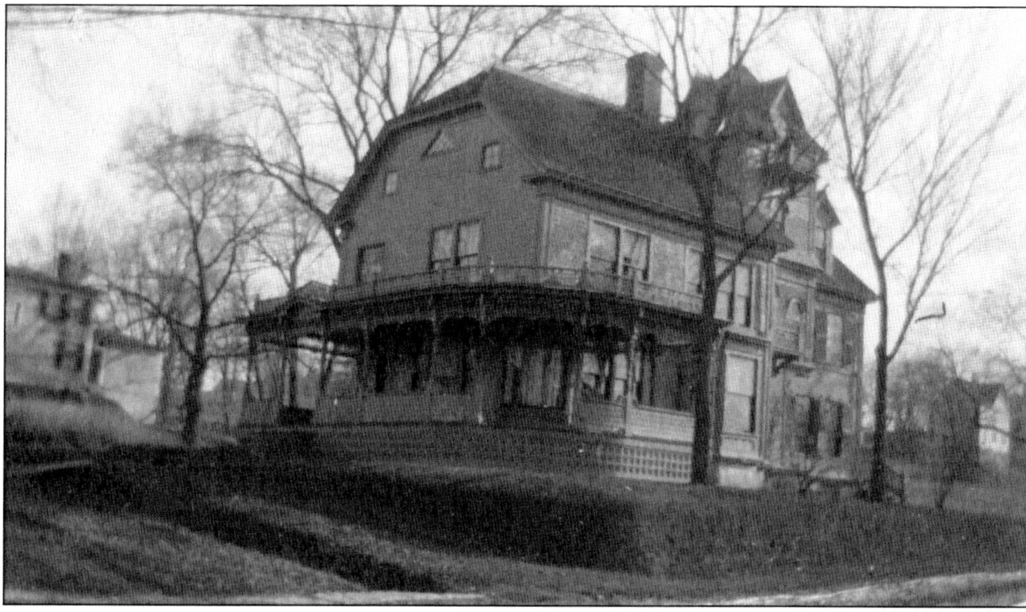

Eugene C. Carll and his wife, Lucie, purchased this ornate turn-of-the-century Victorian home in 1907. It was built on the corner of Chestnut and St. Catherine Streets, directly behind the J. Manchester Haynes Home for Nurses. They owned the estate until 1922, when they sold the property to the Augusta General Hospital. The facade has changed very little over the last 100 years.

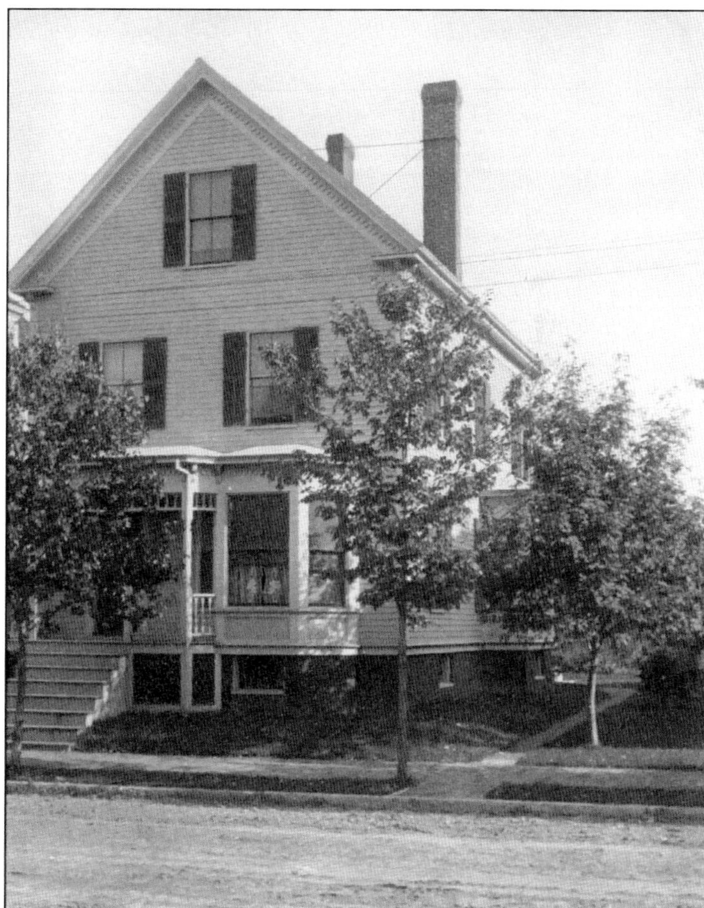

This Colonial-style home was one of the few residences located on Williams Street in the early 1900s. The house, along with more than half the block, was leveled when the Crossett Shoe Factory was constructed in 1915. With the factory now gone, the site is occupied by the Augusta City Center building and parking lot.

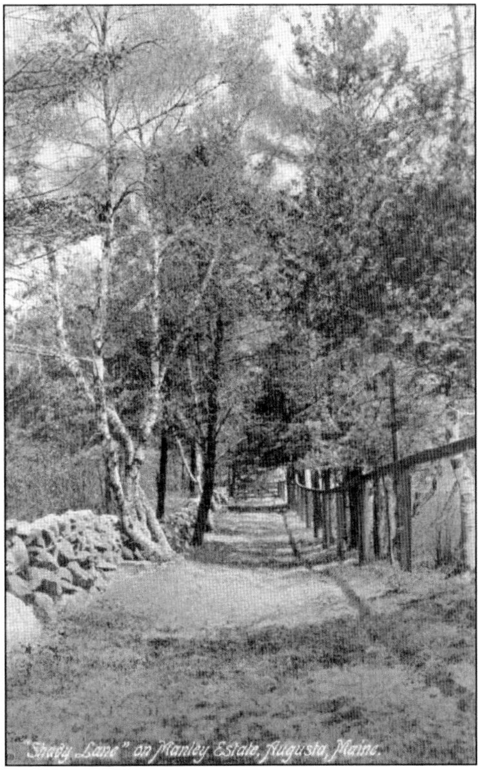

Tucked away between the Stone Street estates of Joseph Hartwell Williams, 27th governor of Maine, and Joseph H. Manley, postmaster, businessman, and political leader, lies "Shady Lane," connecting Manley's stable to several fields. Running about a quarter of a mile long, this grassy road is flanked by a stone wall to the north and a woven wire fence opposite, with a white birch (seen here) roughly halfway down the lane.

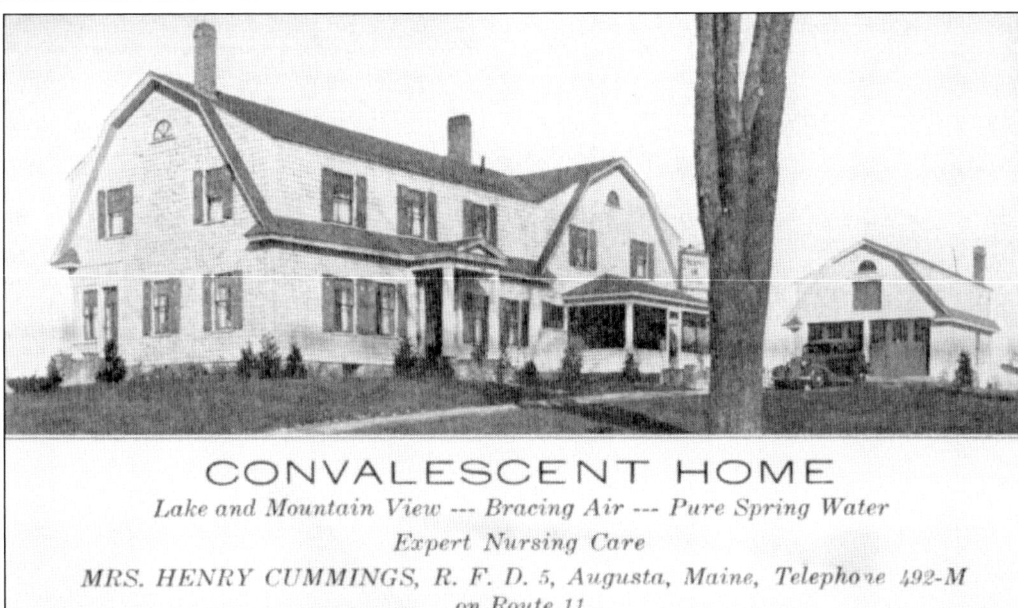

Lena Foster Cummings, the widow of Henry F. Cummings, operated the convalescent home through the 1930s and 1940s to care for the sick and elderly from neighboring communities. Although actually located in Manchester, the facility was able to offer fresh air and a quiet, restful environment not often found in a city. The home was the precursor to modern nursing home facilities, several of which are now found throughout Augusta.

Five

Industries

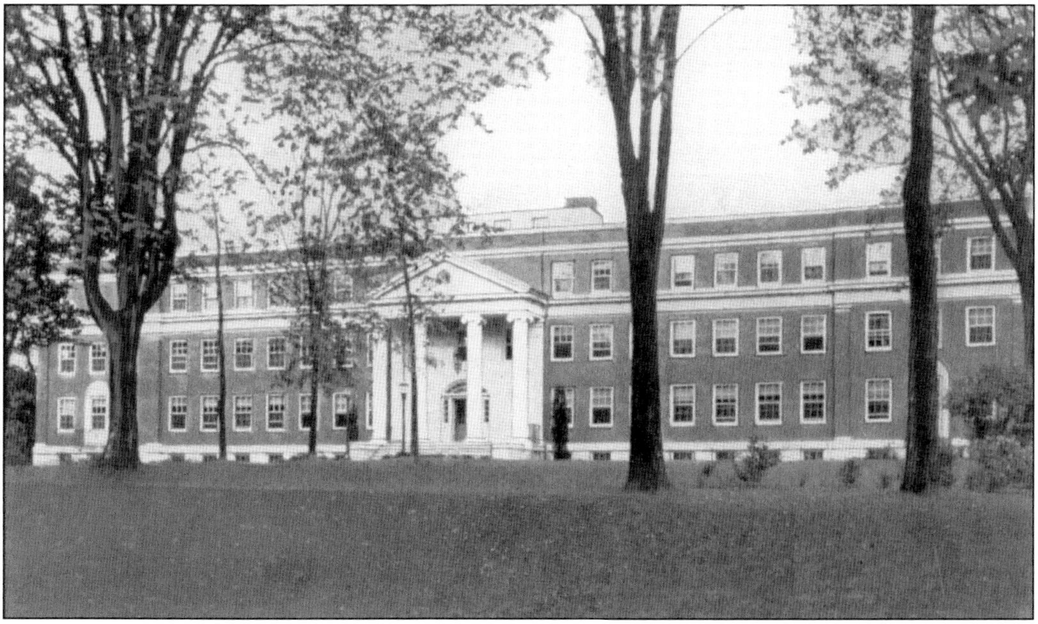

With selling controlling shares to Middle West Utilities in 1925, Central Maine Power outgrew its Water Street location. This grand structure, built in 1927, was owned by the New England Public Service Company, one of the many confusing corporate layers of Middle West Utilities. The parent company collapsed in 1933 amid allegations of stock fraud. Fortunately, Central Maine Power was able to buy back their stock and avoid any fallout.

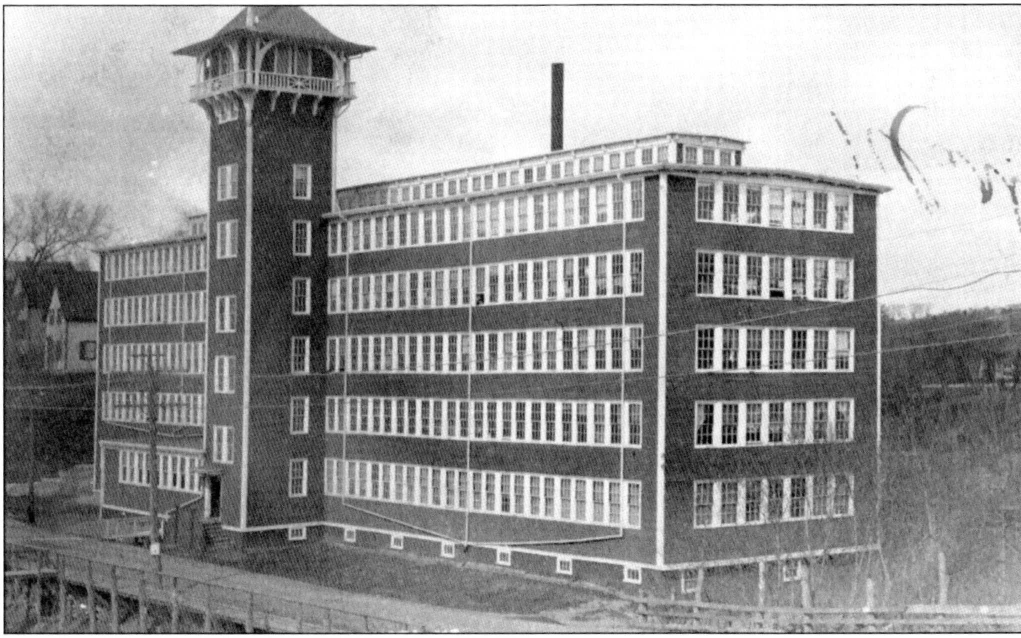

The Charles A. Eaton Company, based in Brockton, Massachusetts, reopened the former Augusta Shoe Factory located in the hollow of Gage Street late in 1902. Although the facility could accommodate 350 hands, the workforce was comprised of just over 100 workers, producing a meager 50 dozen pairs of shoes per day. These numbers would not stay low for long, however.

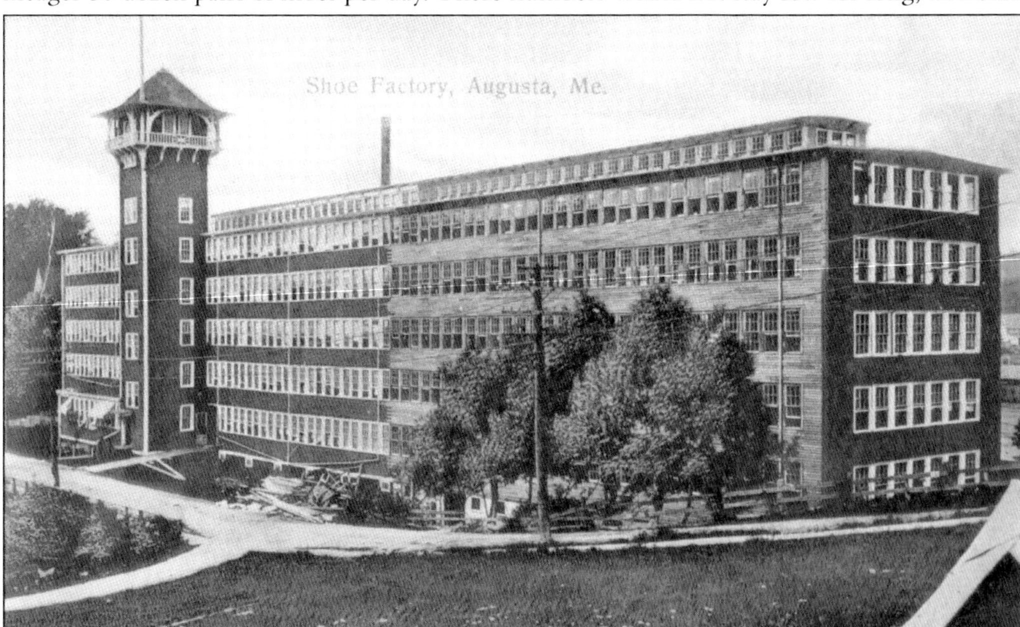

Seen here is a later postcard of the Eaton Shoe Factory after an addition was built on the southerly side. Constructed sometime between 1903 and 1910, the expansion likely occurred because of World War I, as Eaton had received several large army contracts during the conflict. One contract alone called for 550,000 pairs of shoes—100,000 pairs of welt shoes and 450,000 pairs of Pershing trench boots.

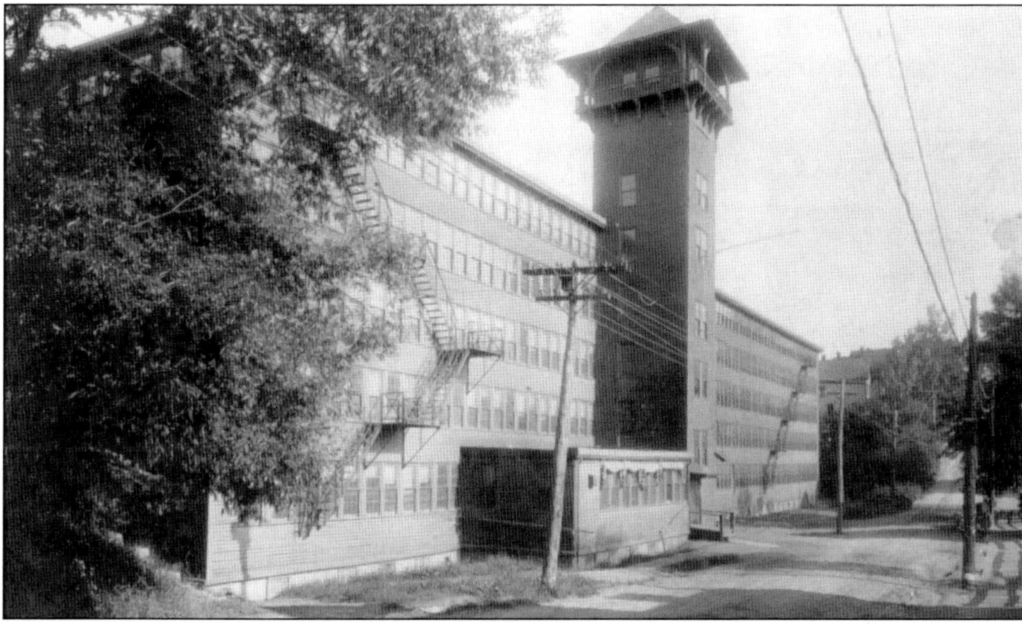

R.P. Hazzard Shoe Company arrived in 1928 and assumed control of the former Eaton Shoe Factory. Note that fire escapes were installed as employee safety awareness and working conditions were becoming better. Hazzard Shoe had operated until the early 1970s. In the years following, the building was gutted, stripped for salvage, and torn down.

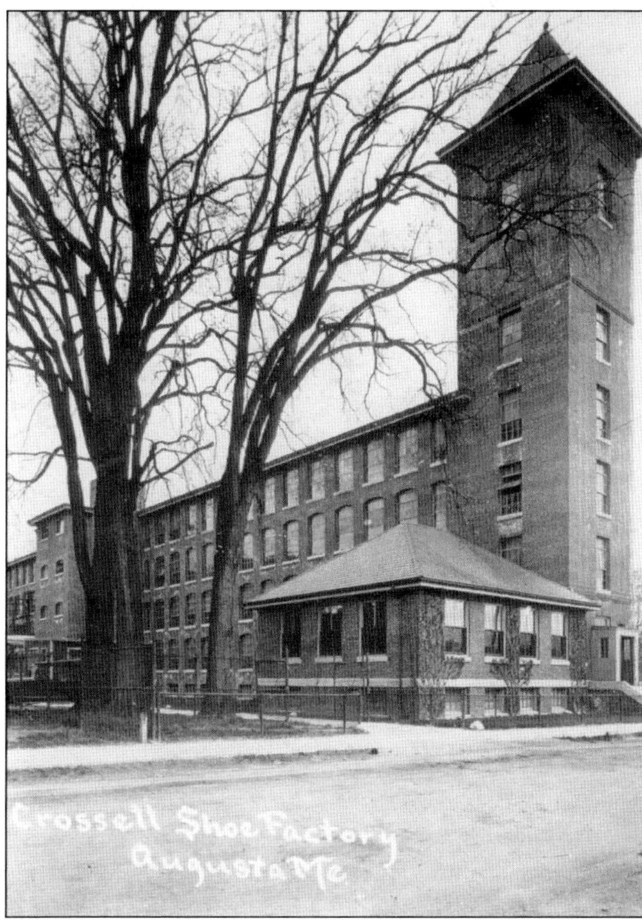

The Crossett Shoe Company of North Abington, Massachusetts, built a brick-and-granite factory on the former site of the Cushnoc Trading Post on Williams Street in the summer of 1915 and began producing 3,000 pairs of shoes per day. By 1937, Crossett Shoe had become defunct, and E.E. Taylor Shoe Company assumed control of the factory, where it remained until 1975 when it closed its doors and razed the building.

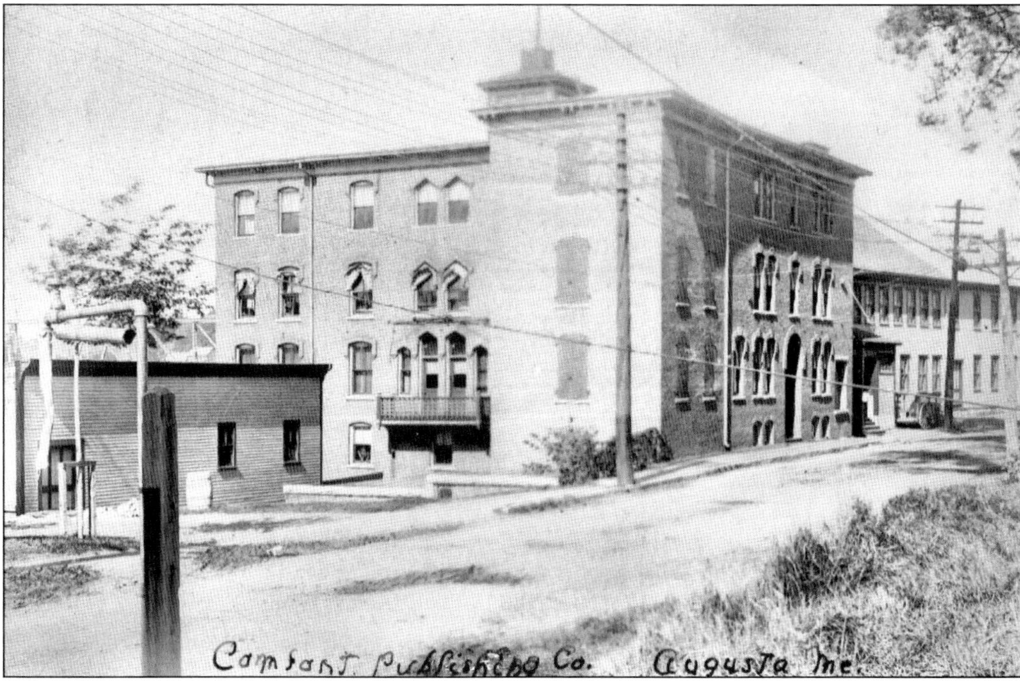

Published by the Gannett and Morse Concern, *Comfort* magazine had its humble beginnings in an attic loft on Water Street in 1888. Within three years, the publishing company had grown so large it prompted Gannett to build this five-story brick structure on Willow Street to house production. Published continuously until 1942, *Comfort* was one of the most successful periodicals of all time, with a peak circulation of three million.

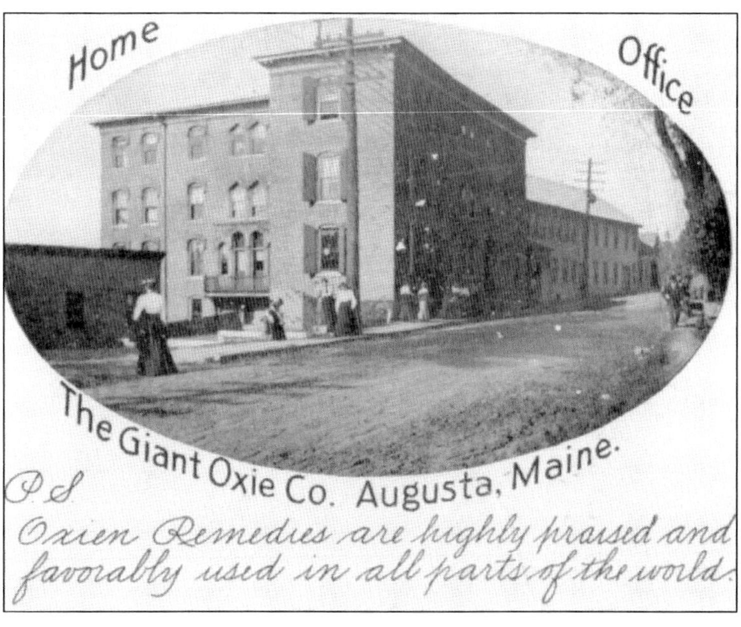

Comfort began as an eight-page folio to promote Oxien, a patented nerve tonic for women, and as the magazine grew, so did the Giant Oxie Company. Sharing the same headquarters as *Comfort*, Oxie employed about 60 people, some of whom were dedicated to the sale and promotion of the tonic, while several specialized clerks translated advertising into modern languages, as the cure-all was sold all over the world.

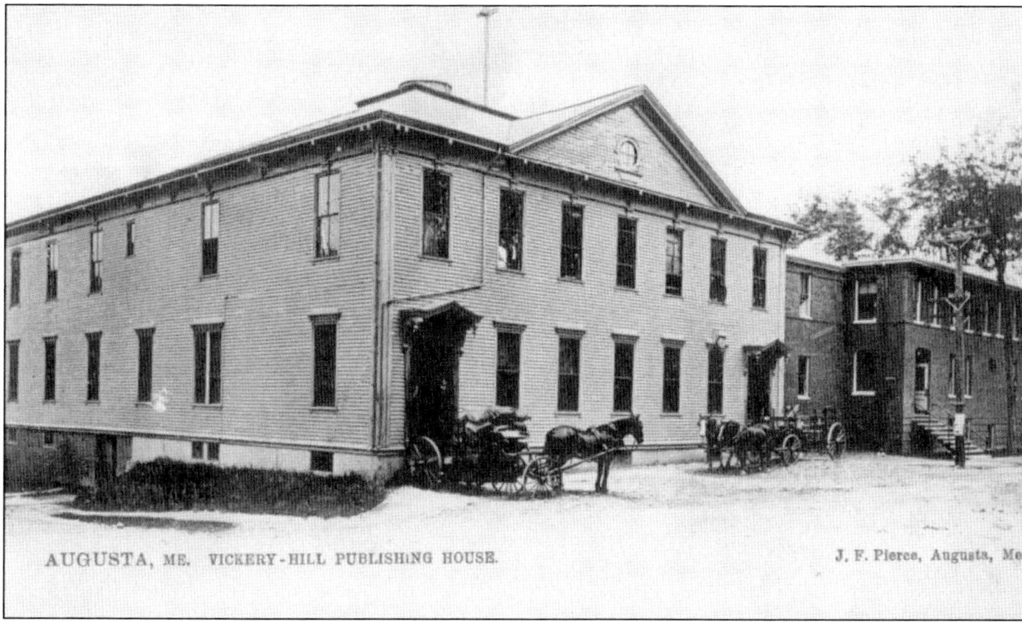

Peleg O. Vickery first began publishing *Vickery's Fireside Visitor* on Winthrop Street in 1875, then moved to this newly constructed building on Chapel Street in 1879 after outgrowing his original location. Dr. John F. Hill, Vickery's son-in-law, quit his profession and joined the publisher to form Vickery & Hill Publishing. Printing four periodicals by 1897, the publishing house employed 165 people with a monthly payroll of $5,000.

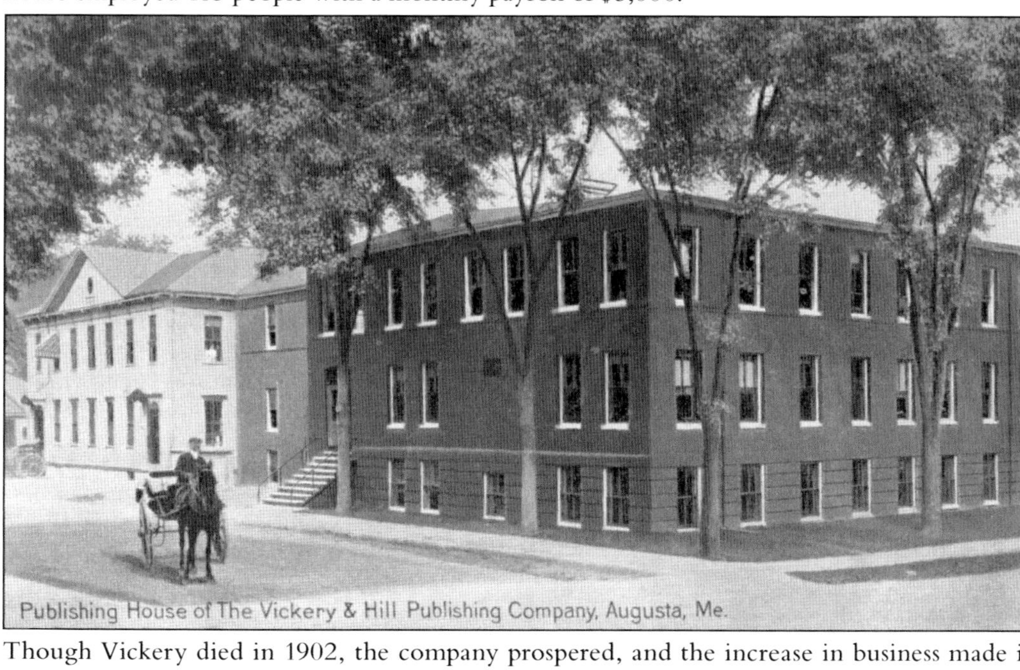

Though Vickery died in 1902, the company prospered, and the increase in business made it necessary to construct an addition to handle the volume. Built around 1900 on the Weston Street side of the publishing house, this brick structure added the much needed space for composition, mailing, and storage. Furthermore, Vickery & Hill Publishing had also expanded and maintained offices in New York, Boston, and Chicago.

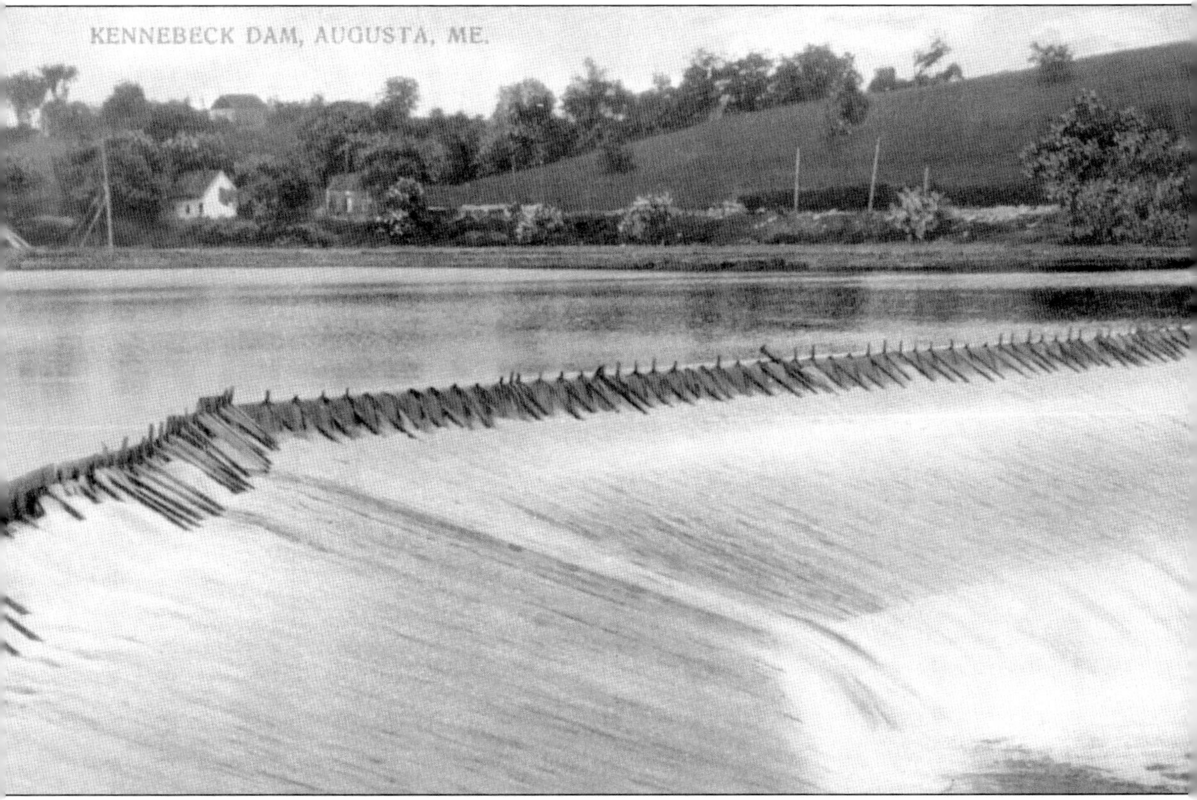

The Kennebec Dam Company, later called the Kennebec Locks and Canals Company, was incorporated in 1834 for the purpose of building a dam, locks, and canal. Consuming 2.5 million feet of timber, 75,000 tons of ballast, and 25 tons of steel, it took hundreds of laborers two years to complete the project. This impressive structure was approximately 475 feet long with a face of 22 feet high and could generate upwards of 7,150 horsepower. Over the next century, the dam was no stranger to disasters. With four floods before it, the worst occurred in 1870 when 160 feet of the dam was swept away. It was rebuilt and withstood the flood of 1896, another in 1936, and one in 1987. Although the fire of 1850 changed the aspect of the dam somewhat, the blaze that started on September 2, 1853, destroyed six sawmills, a flour mill, and a dwelling, among other structures. Even the locks could not escape misfortune. On May 22, 1847, the steamer *Halifax* exploded while preparing to exit the locks, killing six people instantly.

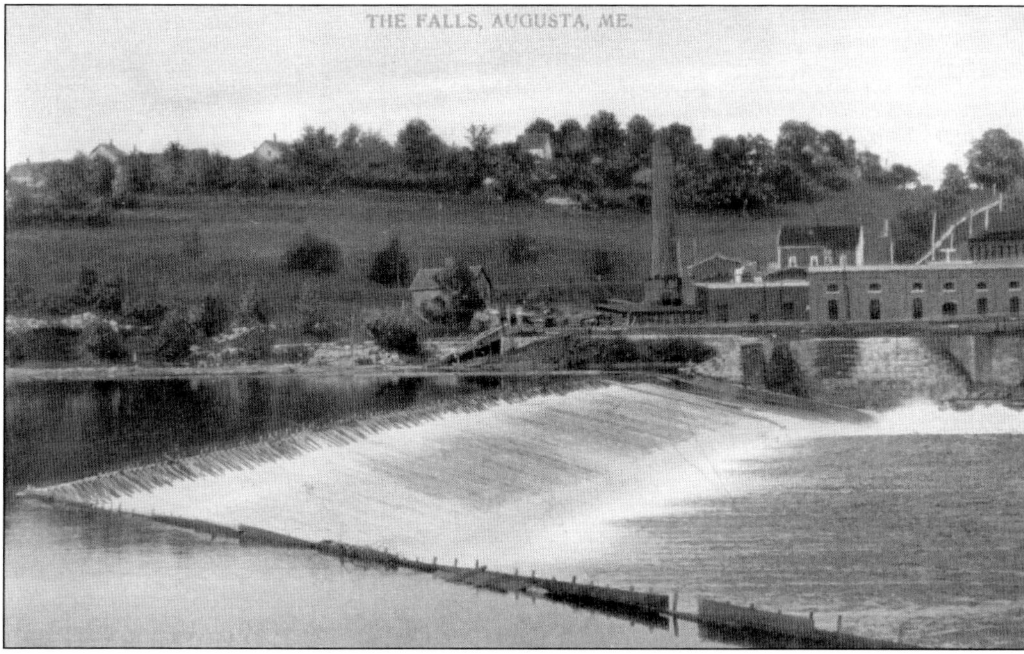

Upwards of a dozen sawmills, gristmills, and flour mills took an early foothold on the banks of the river near the dam. In 1846, a cotton mill, forerunner to the Edwards Mill, was constructed. Behind the locks on the east end of the dam is the building that the Kennebec Light and Heat Company erected to generate their electricity. Lock Street runs up the hill in the background.

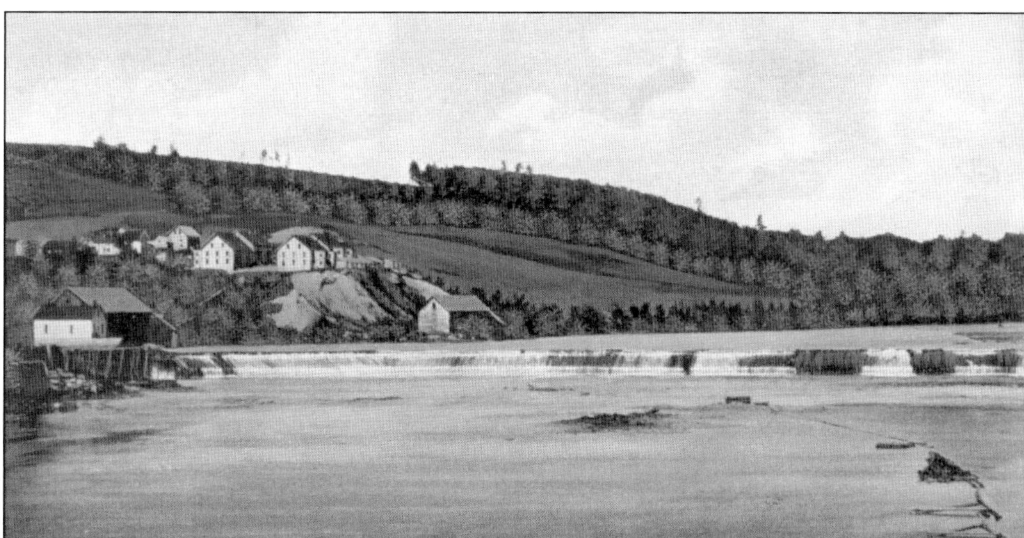

The small white building on the far left was the gatehouse. The larger building behind it and the structure along the water's edge farther upstream were icehouses of the Augusta Ice Company. Higher up on the hill sits the neighborhood of Cushnoc Heights. The largest buildings were part of the Greek Blocks tenement housing, constructed by the Edward Manufacturing Company in the late 19th century.

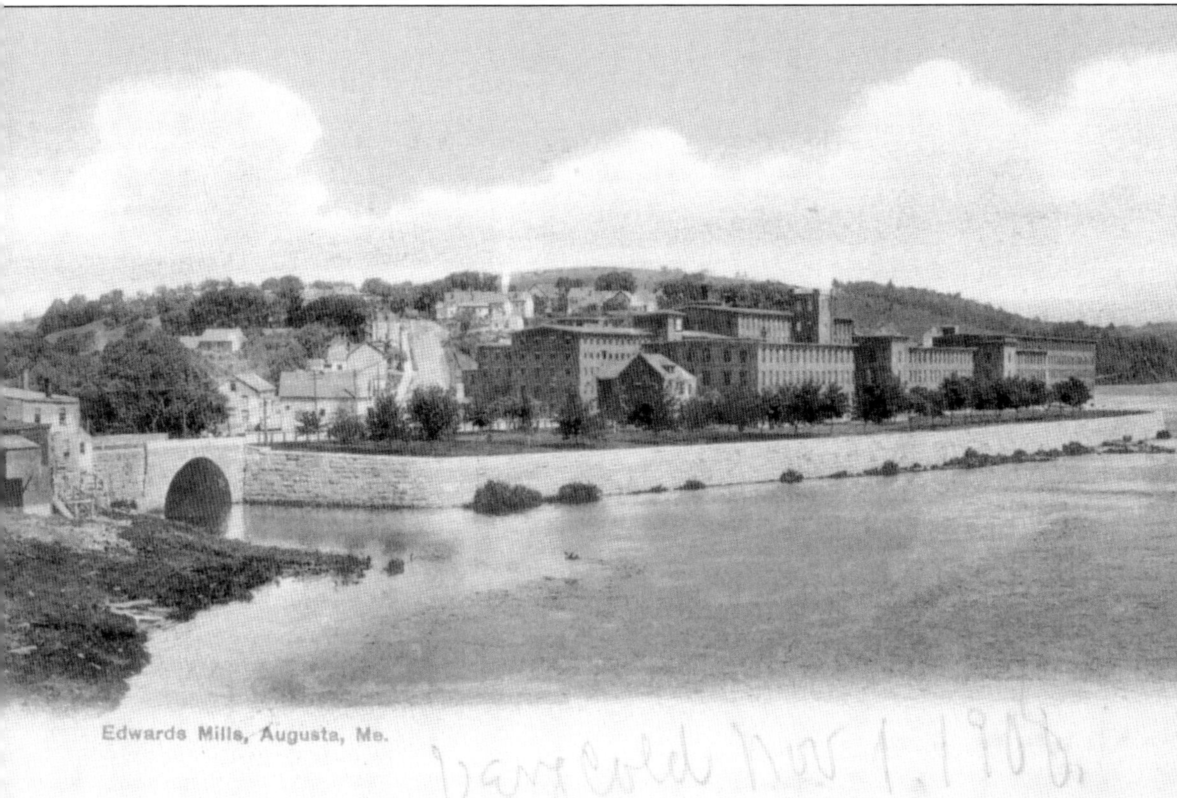

The completion of the dam brought industry, and in 1845, the Kennebec Company built the first cotton mill, operating with 10,000 spindles. By 1867, the Amasa and William Sprague Manufacturing Company of Rhode Island bought the property and, two years later, added a second mill, with more improvements to come over the next decade. Due to financial setbacks unrelated to the mill, Sprague went bankrupt, and in 1882, the property was operating as the Edwards Manufacturing Company. With an influx of French Canadians, the 1880s saw tremendous growth to the mill and the neighboring community; much of the housing in the area was built to accommodate laborers. Having added the No. 3, No. 4, and No. 5 mills and operating with over 60,000 spindles, the mill was producing 42 million miles of yarn, woven into 20 million yards of cloth, by 1889. By 1940, the mill employed over 1,300 workers and, in 1945, became the Edwards Division of Bates Manufacturing. Due to cheaper labor in the South, the mill closed in 1981, and the complex was consumed by fire in 1989.

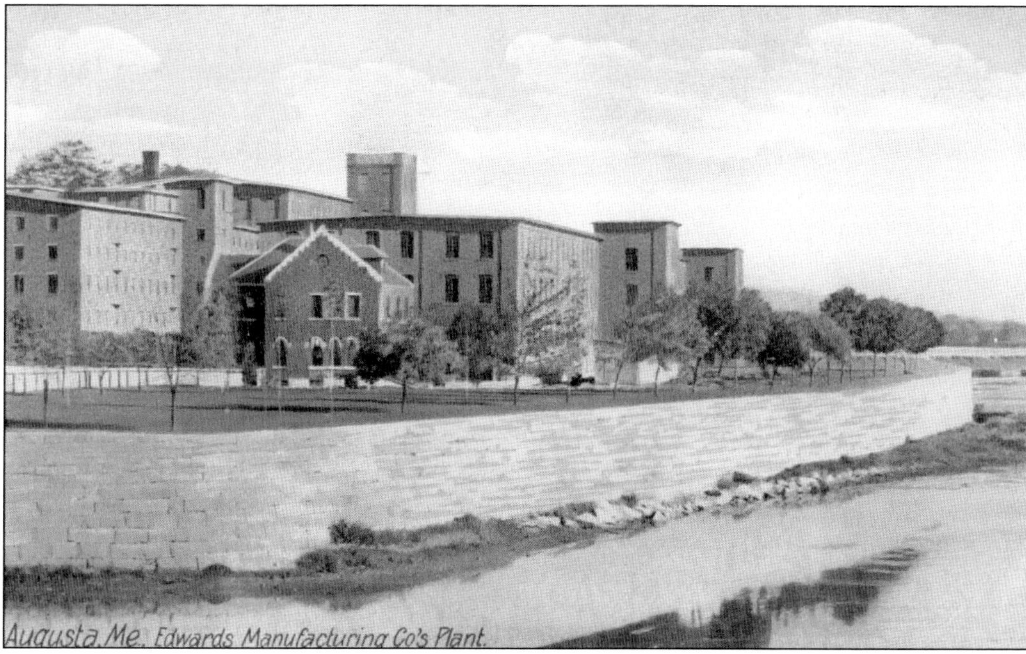

From the left, mill No. 1, used for carding, roping, and mule spinning, is seen in front of the taller mill No. 2, which was used similarly, as well as for frame drawing and ring spinning. The smaller building with the gabled end was the office. Behind that is mill No. 5, used for shafting and weaving. The stair tower of mill No. 3 is seen on the right.

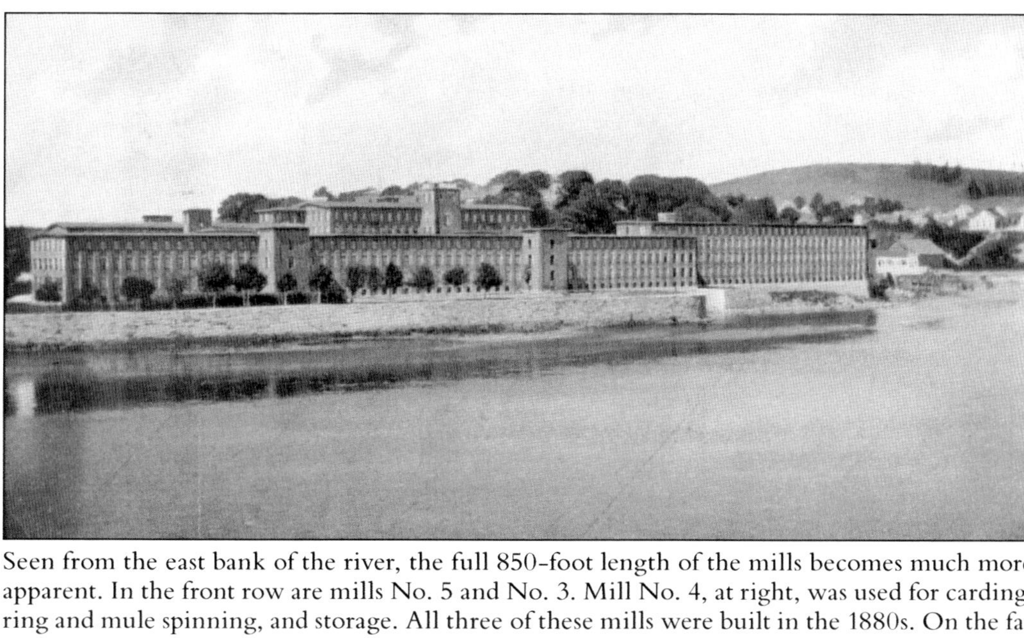

Seen from the east bank of the river, the full 850-foot length of the mills becomes much more apparent. In the front row are mills No. 5 and No. 3. Mill No. 4, at right, was used for carding, ring and mule spinning, and storage. All three of these mills were built in the 1880s. On the far right is Cushnoc Heights, a neighborhood that was, in part, developed for mill housing.

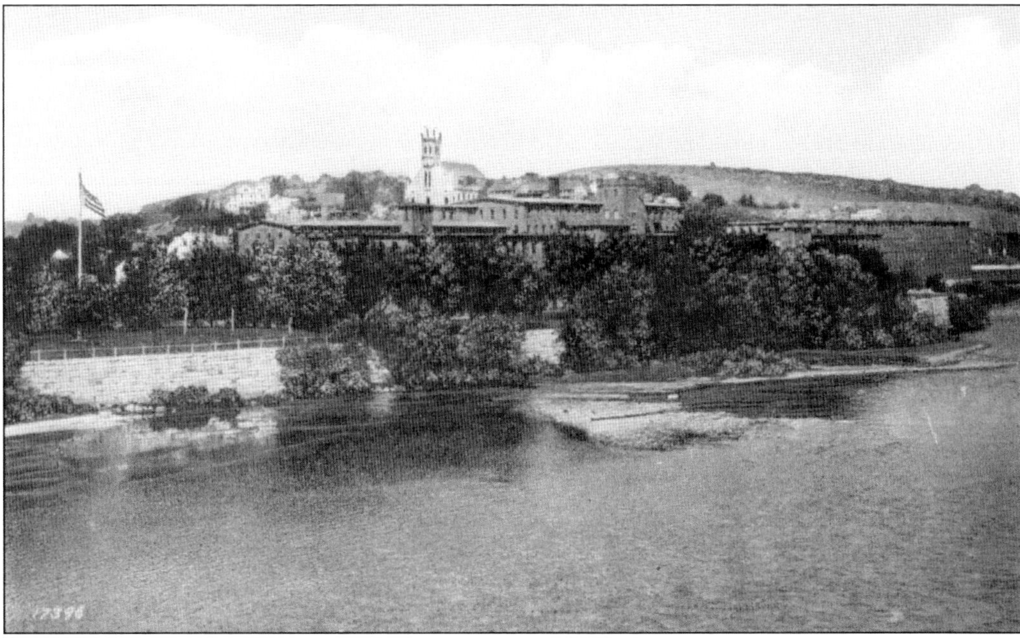

With immigrating French Canadians seeking work at Edwards Mill, the Cushnoc Heights neighborhood had grown significantly by 1916. Over 1,000 workers had found employment by this time and resided on the hill. Just north of the mill on Sand Hill lies the newly constructed St. Augustine's Church, considered the landmark of the neighborhood despite its lack of spire.

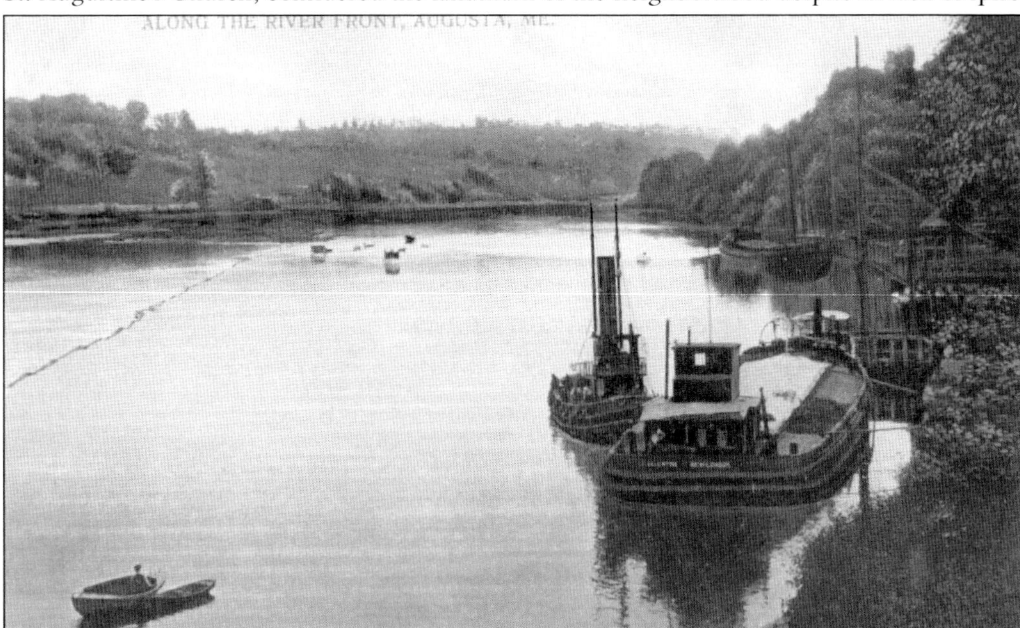

Seen around 1906, the steam tug *Charlie Lawrence*, which has been serving on the river since the 1880s, is holding fast to the barge *Valentine* of New London at a southern dock on the west side of the Kennebec River. After the *Valentine* had taken on her cargo, likely ice destined for New York, the tug would escort her downriver, where a larger vessel would haul the barge to its final destination.

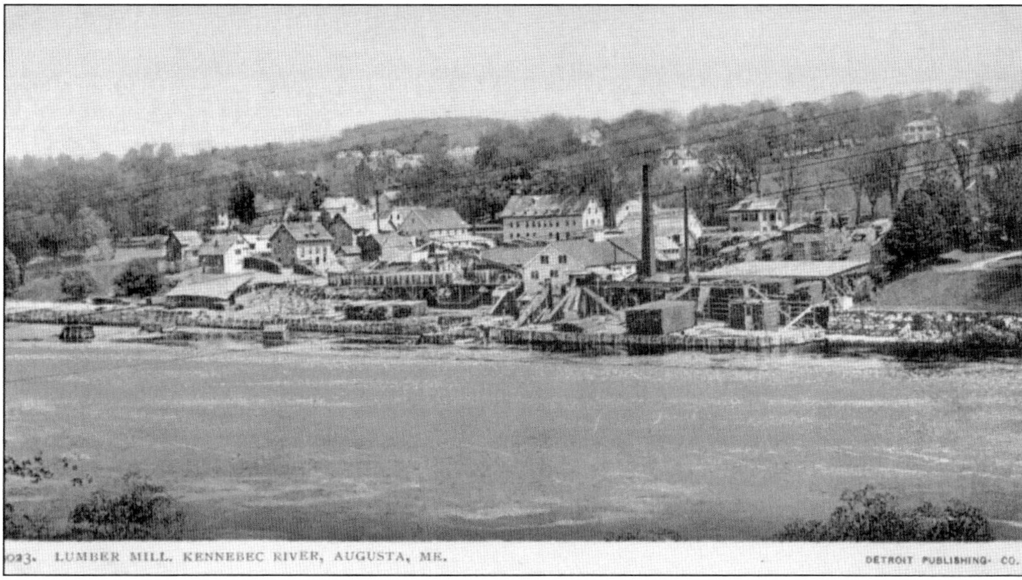

Established by Ira D. Sturgis and partner Albert Daily, the Kennebec Land and Lumber Company took a firm foothold on the east bank of the Kennebec River in 1866. After the lumberyard burned in October 1875, the sawmill reorganized as Sturgis, Lambard & Company the following year. The company later incorporated as the Augusta Lumber Company in 1889. By 1897, the mill was producing 50,000 board feet of lumber per day.

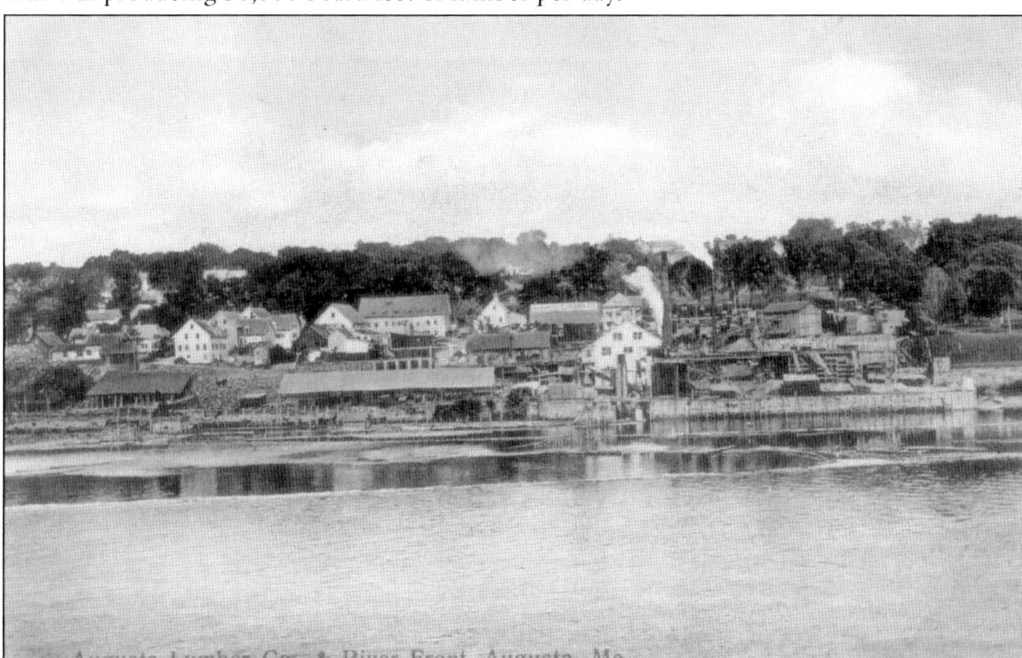

Sometime after 1903, the Augusta Lumber Company added several new structures. From the left, the two lumber sheds on the waterfront are the most obvious. Just above and to the right is the clapboard shop. Next, the mill with the large smokestack, containing the steam engine as well as the shafting and shingle machines, is diagonally connected to the chip house via the chain conveyor. The large lumber-filled wharf sits in front.

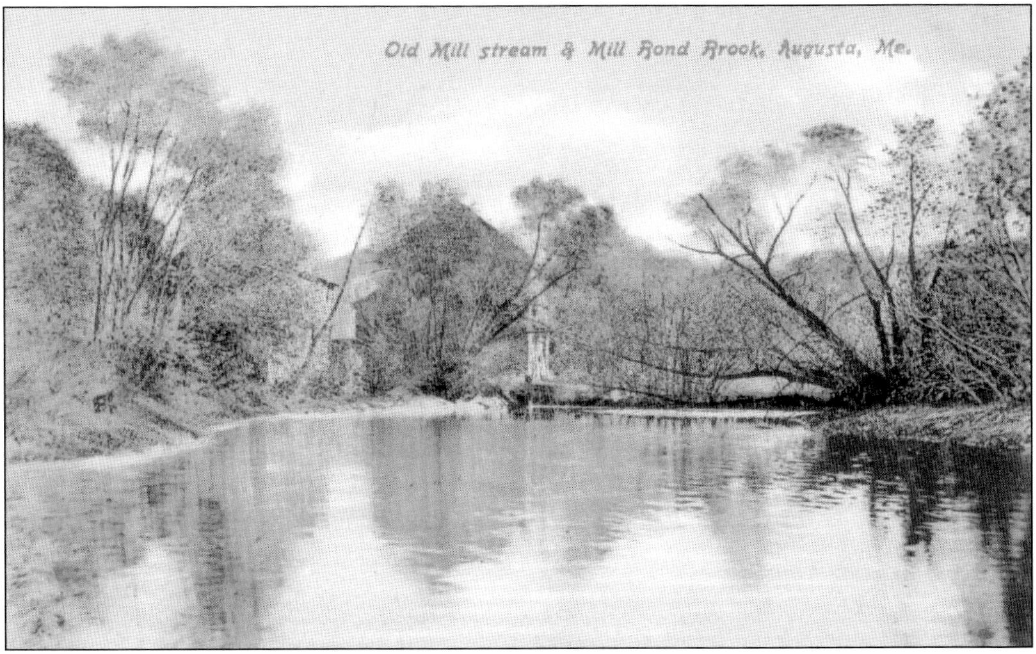

Though difficult to see here, B.F. Parrott Company's gristmill, which supplied wholesale flour, grain, and feed, was founded on Mount Vernon Avenue, near the base of Mill Street, in 1858. The Upper Mill Dam, seen just to the right, powered the mill. The dam formed a large pond to the north that flooded an area that is now a ball field.

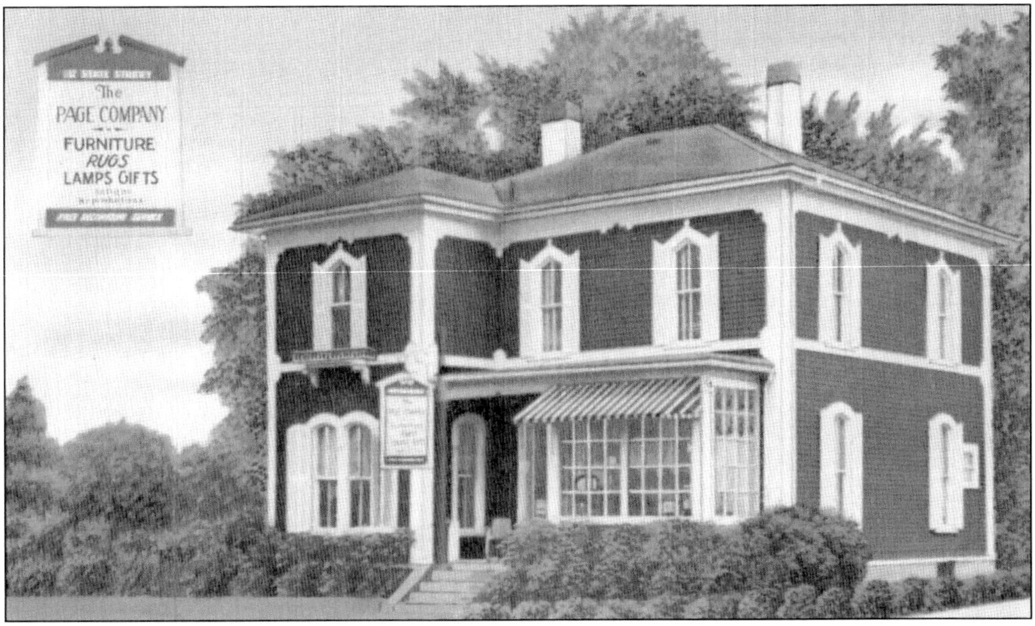

In 1949, Edward and Muriel Page purchased the first building of what was one of the Vickery Triplets—three identical houses built by Peleg O. Vickery in 1880. Located at the corner of State and Court Streets, it became the home of the Page Furniture Company, which remained there through the 1950s. Sadly, Edward passed away at a young age, and the building was sold in 1961.

Six

Transportation

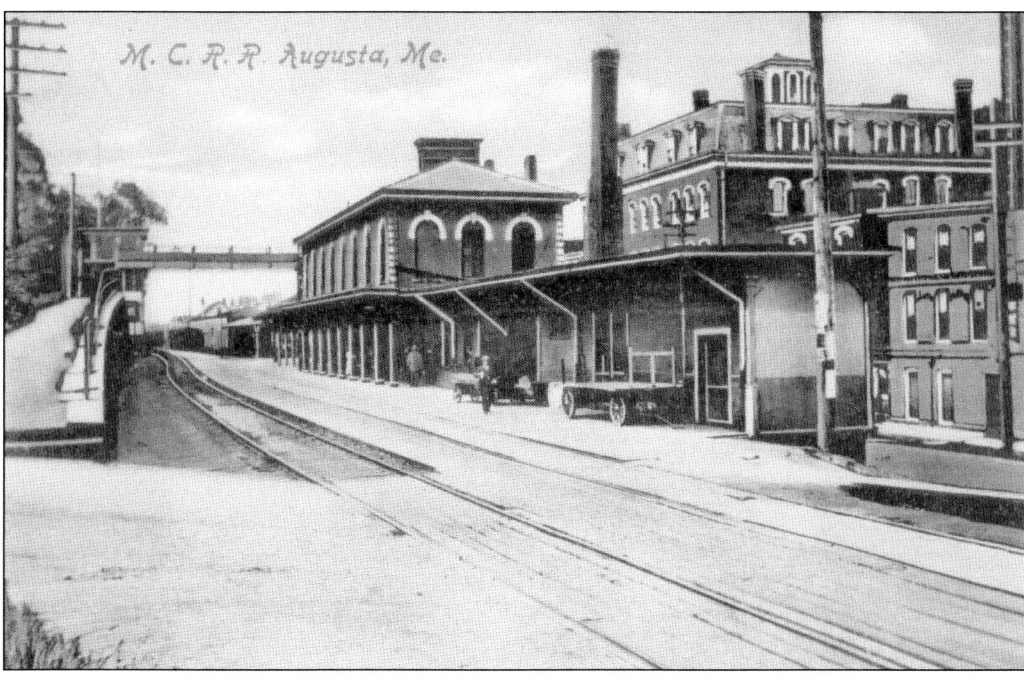

Built in 1866, this railroad station was constructed to replace the previous depot lost in the fire of 1865. Designed by Francis H. Fassett, it was a grand Italianate masonry structure located on Commercial Street, between Winthrop and Oak Streets. The second floor contained the local telephone exchange, servicing about 260 phones. In the early 1900s, a catwalk was added that connected the station to Dickman Street.

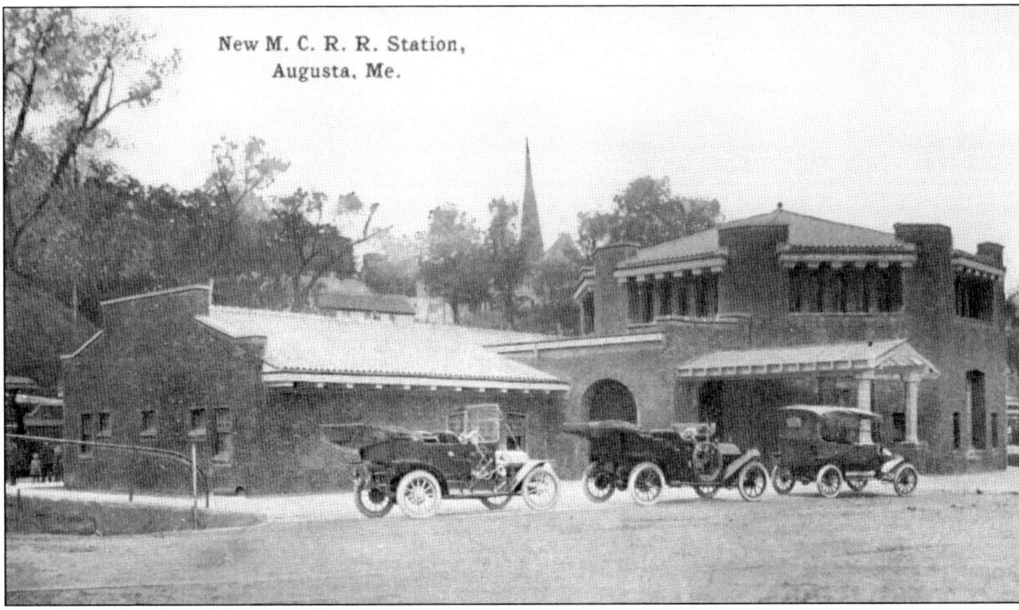

The Maine Central Railroad passenger station, built at the base of Rines Hill in 1913, was certainly one of a kind and worthy of its final cost of $100,000. Influenced by the Art and Crafts style, architect Robert C. Reamer designed the station with an octagonal waiting room, arched doorways, a porte cochere and canopy, and a variant of crow-stepped gables. The exterior was constructed with tapestry bricks and green tile roofing.

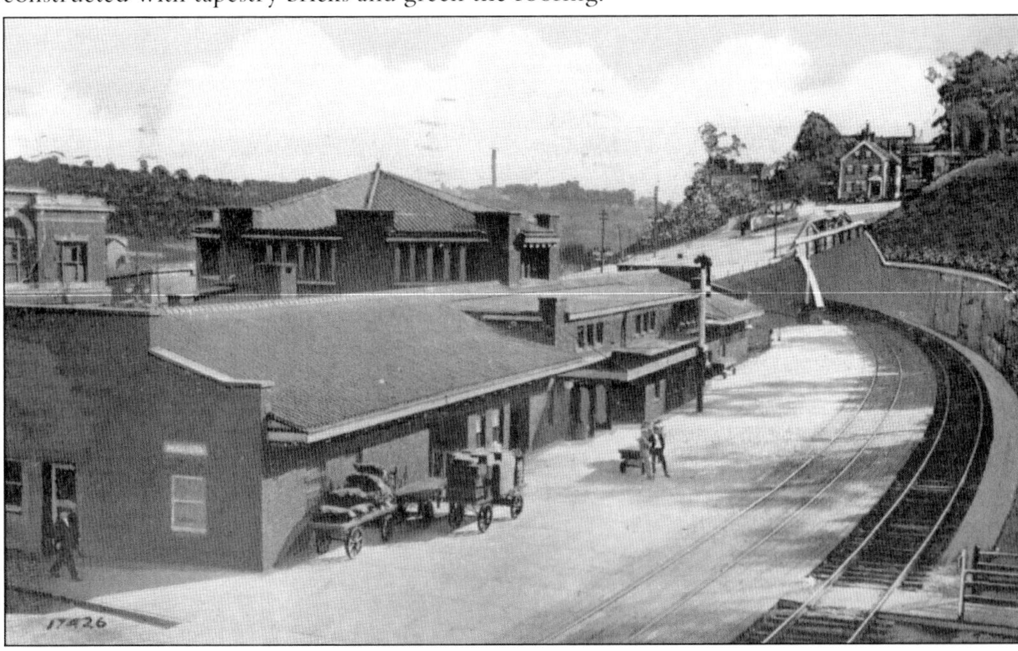

Located on the west side of the station is the ticket office between the two sets of doors under the canopy. The station was an impressive 187 feet long, and the actual platform reached 525 feet from Rines Hill to Winthrop Street, covering 12,000 square feet. The recently constructed Rines Hill Cut and bridge are seen in the back. A wooden walkway crosses the tracks to steps leading up Court Street.

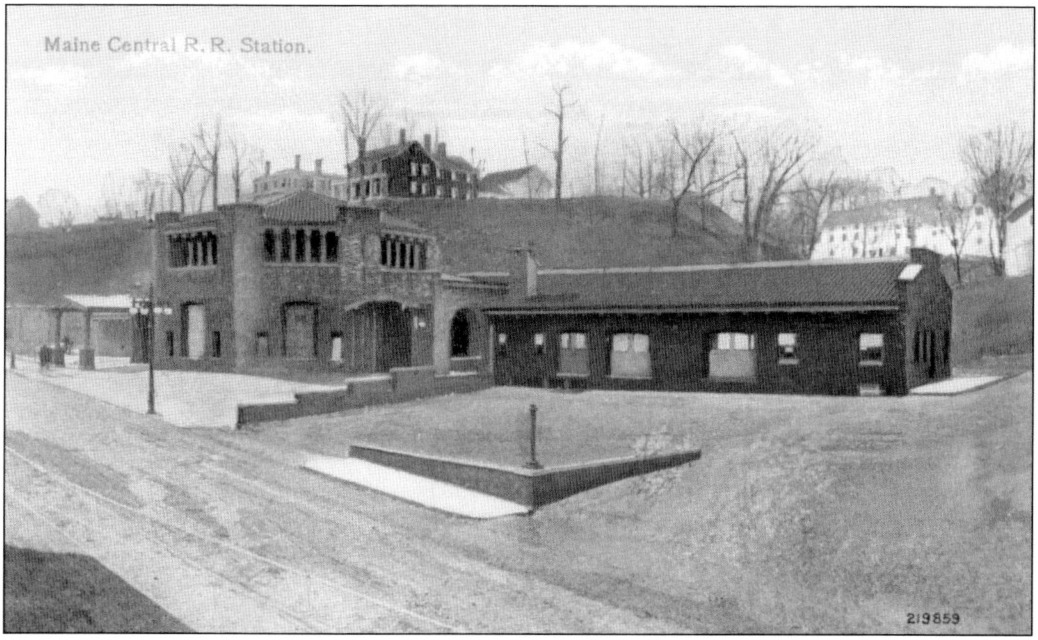

The old roundhouse, the Swift and Company plant, and two frame blocks on Water Street had to be razed for the construction of the Maine Central Railroad station. Though the grounds were sparse after its completion in 1913, a broad expanse of lawn would soon flank the south end of the building, while a flower bed would be planted at the north end on the Water Street side.

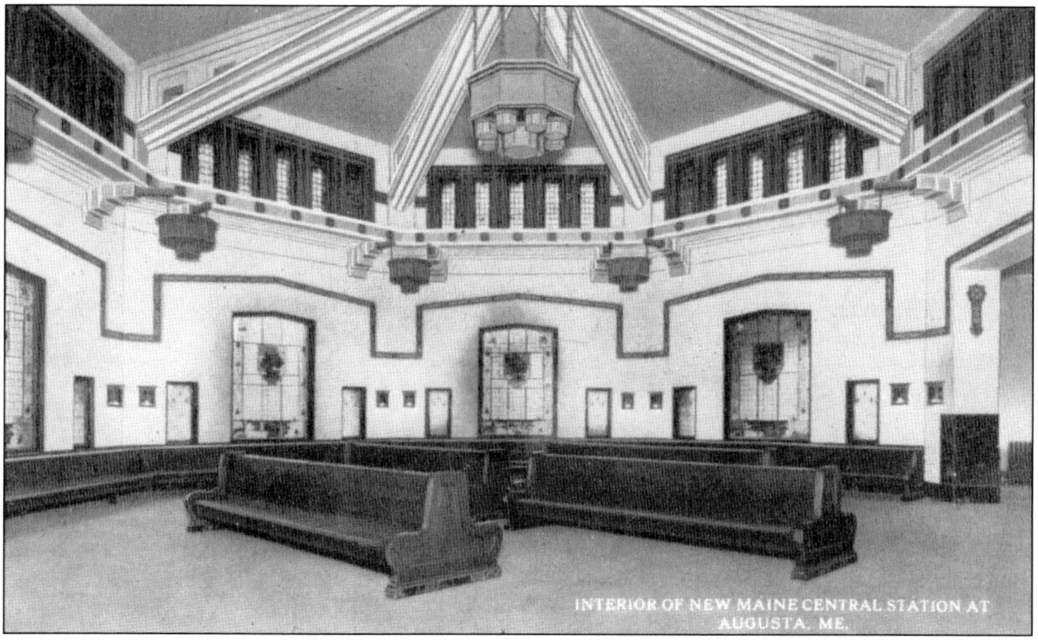

Perhaps the most remarkable feature of the station was the octagonal waiting room. The room had a terrazzo floor measuring 52 feet across, along with oak benches that could accommodate 100 people. The walls were made from imported Caen stone and trimmed with black Irish marble. There were 55 windows with large stained-glass panels inspired by the state seal, and octagonal lamps hung from the walls and ceiling, indirectly lighting the room.

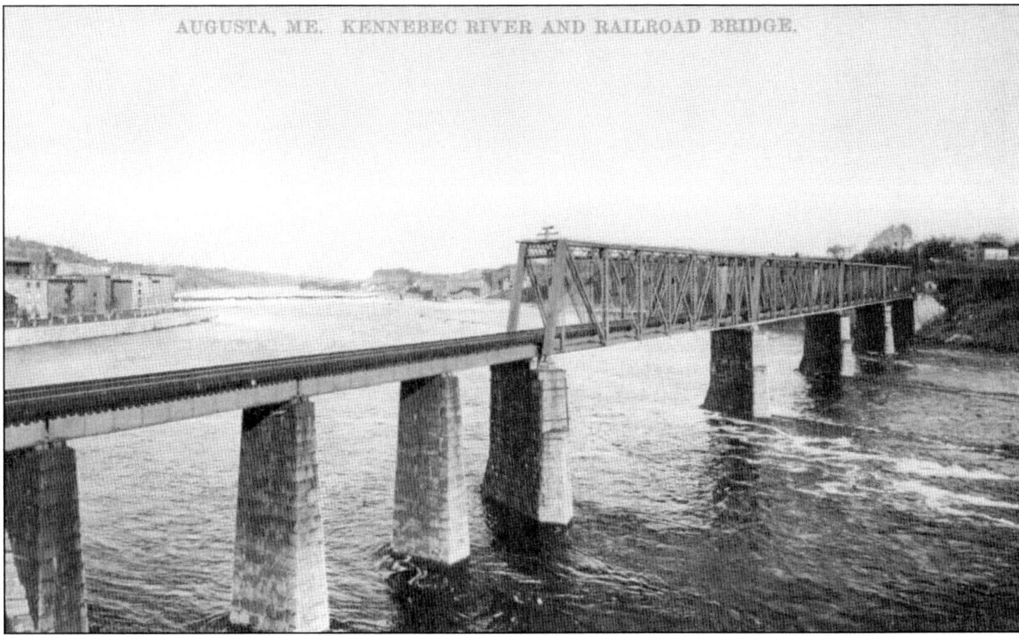

The railroad first came to Augusta from Brunswick on the west bank of the river in 1851 and from Waterville on the east in 1853, but it was another four years before the first railroad bridge was built to connect the two lines. Built from wood, it was destroyed by the great freshet in February 1870; it was quickly replaced with an iron Pratt truss bridge later that summer. In 1885, the bridge was partially swept away by a winter freshet; rehabilitation started later that year, then was completed in 1886. The iron columns were removed, and the original short stone piers were built higher. (The original height can be seen as a step about halfway up each pier under the spans.) The iron trusses also were replaced with more robust spans, which lasted for the next 25 years.

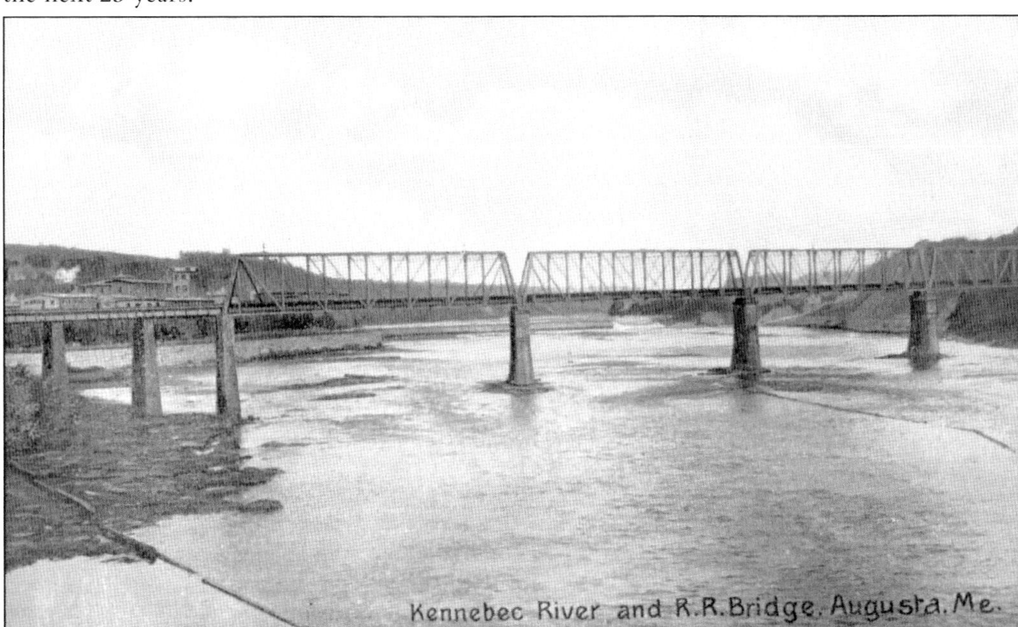

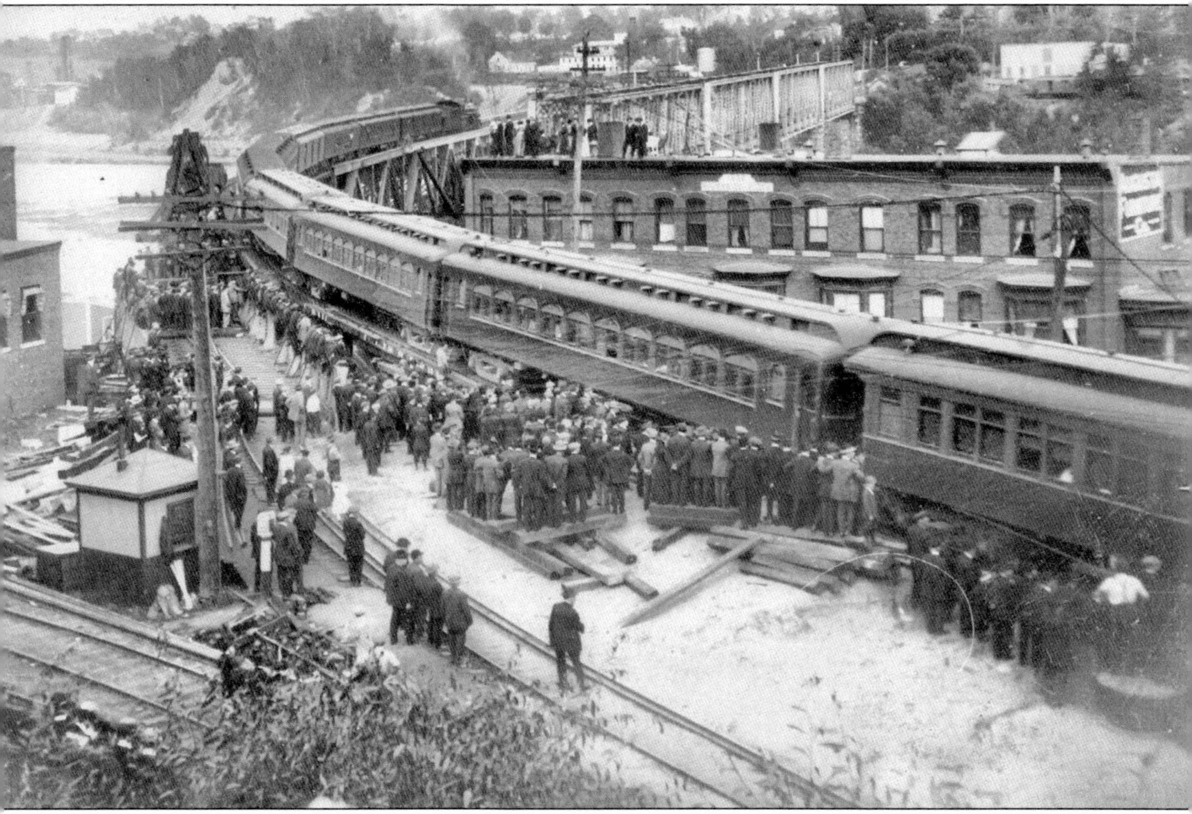

On June 29, 1916, over 15,000 people thronged Water Street and Market Square as the 2nd Infantry marched down Rines Hill to applause and fanfare. Hundreds of people packed the windows and dotted the roofs to watch the Maine soldier boys depart for their destination of Laredo, Texas. After much ceremony, the roughly 1,000 troops boarded three waiting trains. The second of three trains to depart, this one containing Augusta's Company M, pulled out of the station at 5:35 p.m. and is seen crossing the railroad bridge. Note that the train is crossing the new double-track bridge that was erected in 1914, while the truss bridge is used only for carrying the water main. Today, the structure has been removed, and only the masonry piers capped with the iron bridge footings remain as a testament to this old bridge.

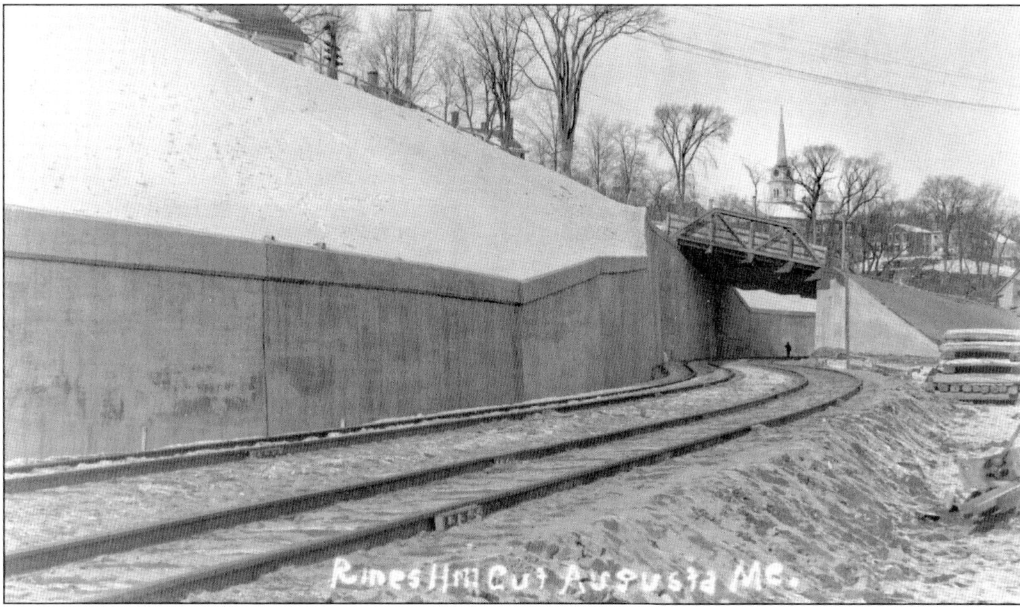

Trains crossed every 20 minutes and trolleys every 6 on a 12 percent grade, making Rines Hill one of the worst at-grade street crossings in New England. By cutting back southerly into the hill, building one of the largest retaining walls of the day in 1911, and installing a new bridge, Maine Central Railroad's tracks were rerouted under the now six percent grade to eliminate the dangerous intersection.

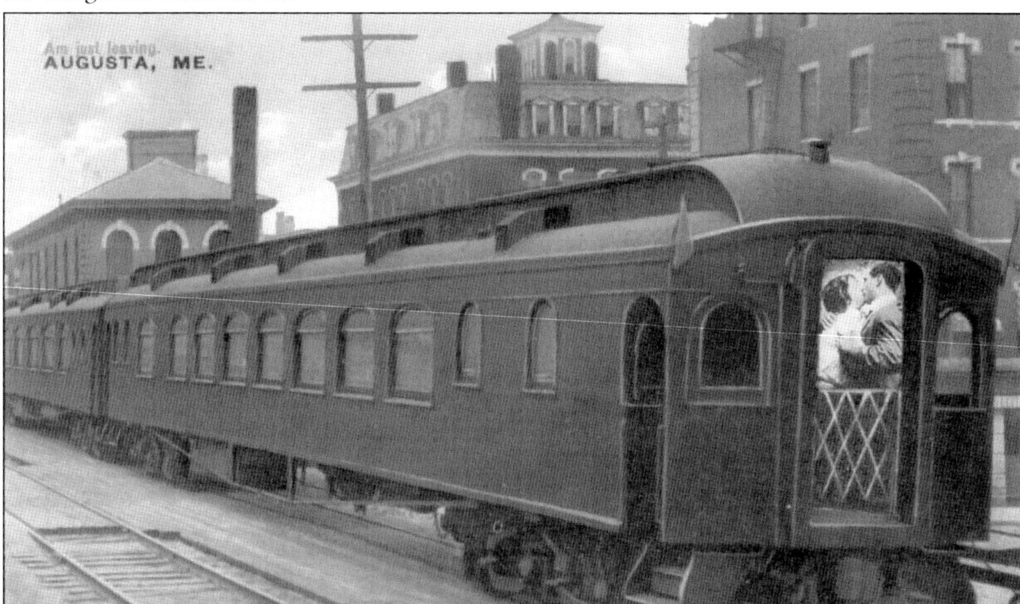

Though the backside of the old Portland and Kennebec Railroad station, the Hotel North's mansard roof, and the west end of the Augusta Trust Company are easily seen, the focus of this postcard is obviously the rolling stock of Maine Central Railroad's passenger service. That is not to say that one's eye is not still drawn toward the risqué whimsy of the kissing couple aboard the Pullman.

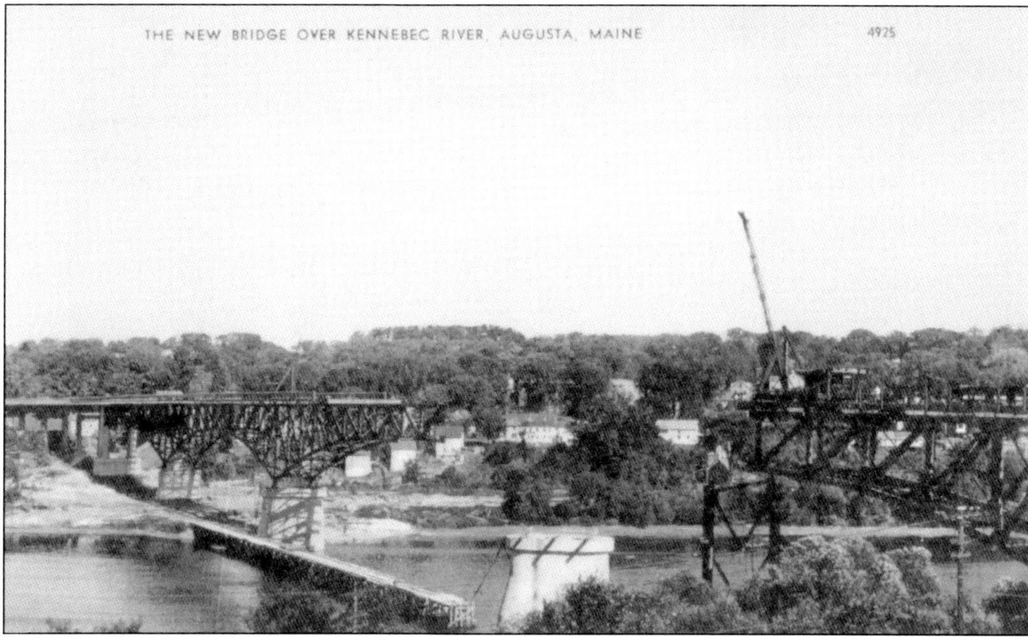

Construction on the Memorial Bridge officially started on May 24, 1948. Not long after, two American Bridge Company travelers were hoisting beams and girders into place from atop either end of the steelwork. A trestle runs alongside the piers where cranes with clamshell buckets excavated the river bottom, and a falsework bent can be seen on the near end that is temporarily supporting the steel while the span is completed.

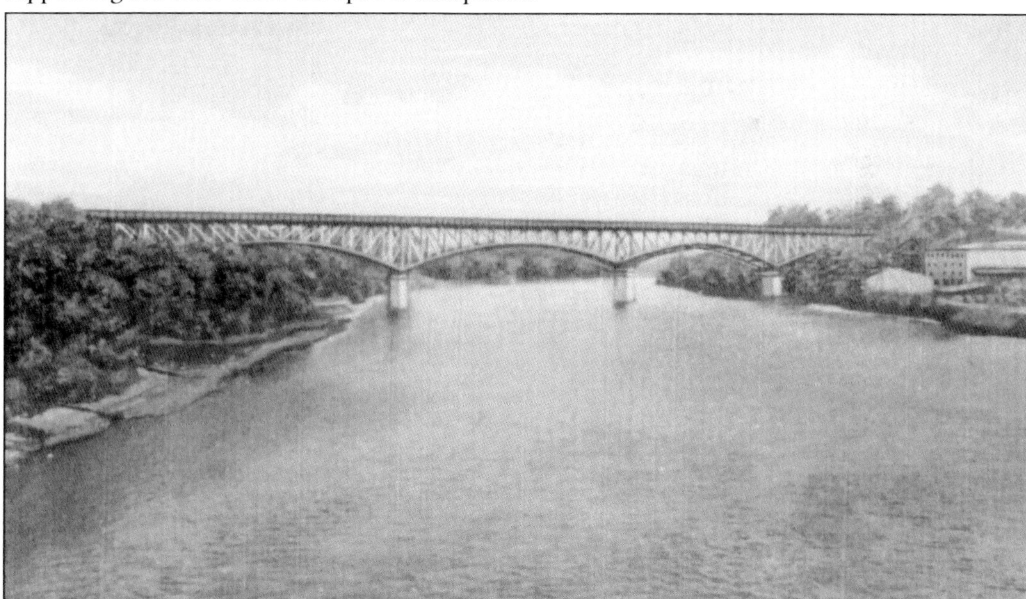

After two years of work, and consuming over 3,300 tons of steel for the structure, wooden forms containing over half a million feet of lumber and 46,000 bags of cement for the piers, Memorial Bridge and the two rotaries were completed at a cost of over $3.2 million in November 1949, amid much celebration. But it was not without growing pains, as 19 buildings were destroyed, moved, or altered in some way.

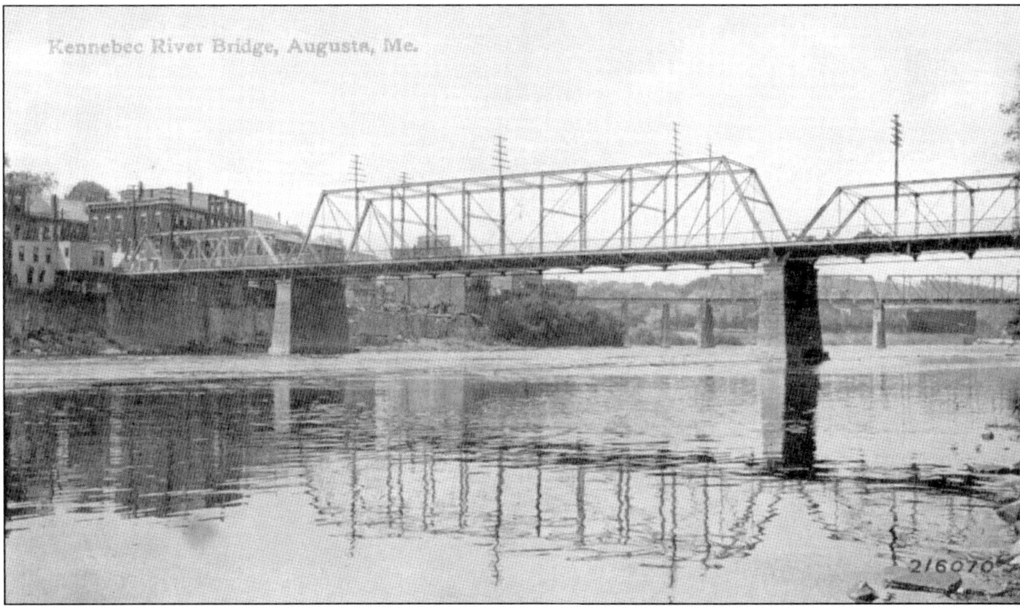

The Kennebec River Bridge has always held a special significance for the city. Now on its fifth incarnation, the first bridge, built in 1797, was the catalyst for the separation of Hallowell and Augusta. The original arch bridge was followed by a covered bridge in 1816, which burned 11 years later, and another covered bridge was erected in 138 days. The truss bridge of 1890 was the fourth in line.

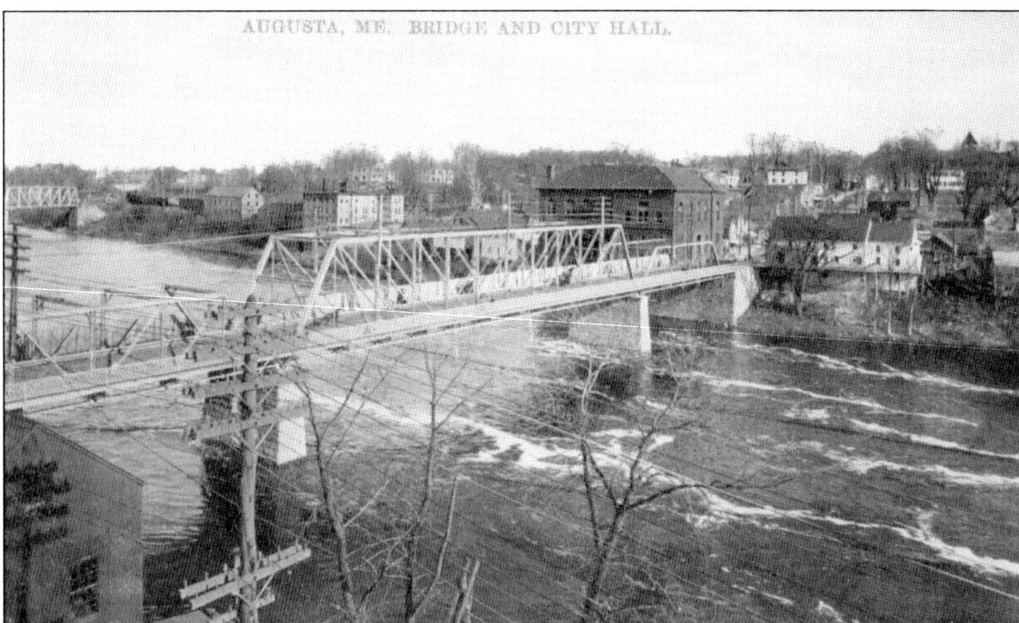

With Shanahan of Portland as the stonework contractor, the single stone pier of the covered bridge was removed from the center of the river, and two smaller ones were erected closer to the shores. Coffrode and Sailor of Pottsville, Pennsylvania, built the bridge, which was completed for $59,000. Surprisingly, travel had only been suspended for one day during the construction, and the bridge was opened for use in April 1890.

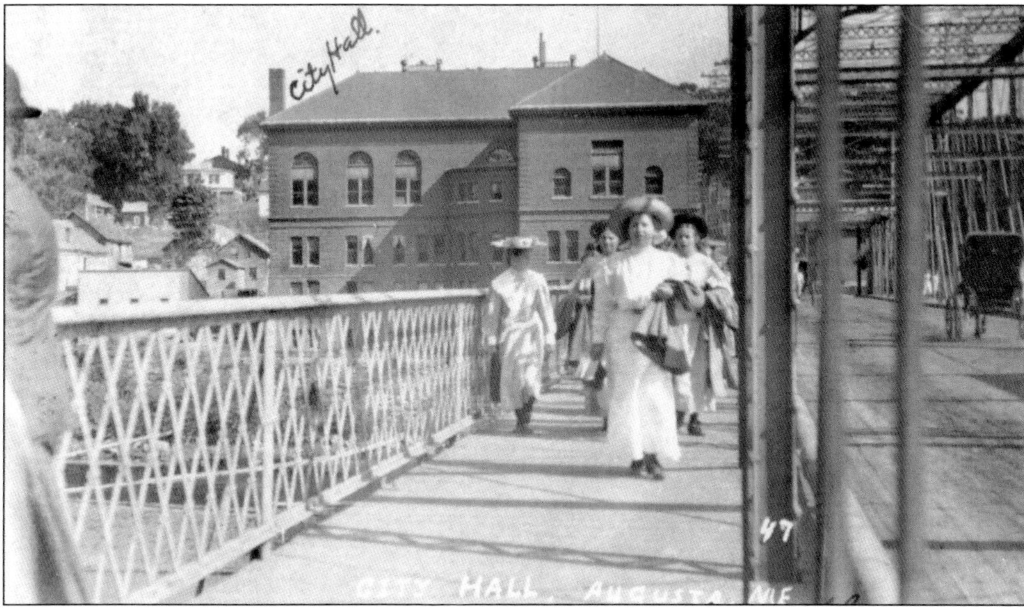

The Kennebec River Bridge was used by many modes of transportation. Trolley tracks crossing the bridge united both halves of Augusta with inexpensive local public transportation. Horses and buggies were also quite common, and later, the automobile. But the most popular form was simply walking, as seen by this young woman escorting a group of girls, quite possibly from Cony High School, across to the west side.

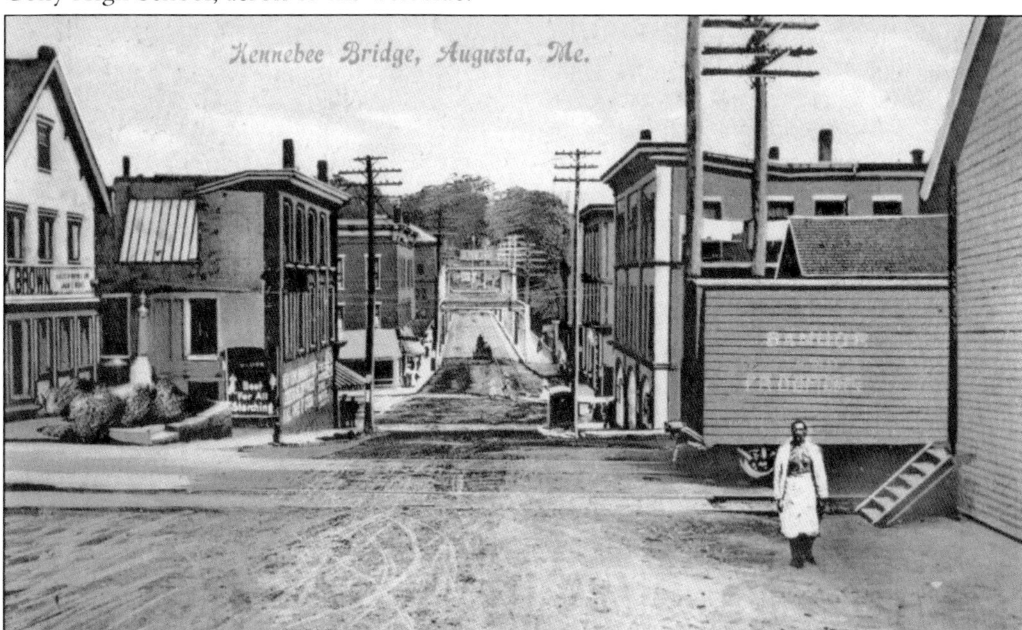

This view shows the importance of the bridge to the commerce and businesses of Augusta. In the front, railroad tracks lead to the passenger and freight station off to the right, with Commercial Street directly behind the boxcar. In the middle is the intersection of Water and Bridge Streets—the epicenter of the retail and banking district. Just on the other side of the bridge is the Augusta City Hall.

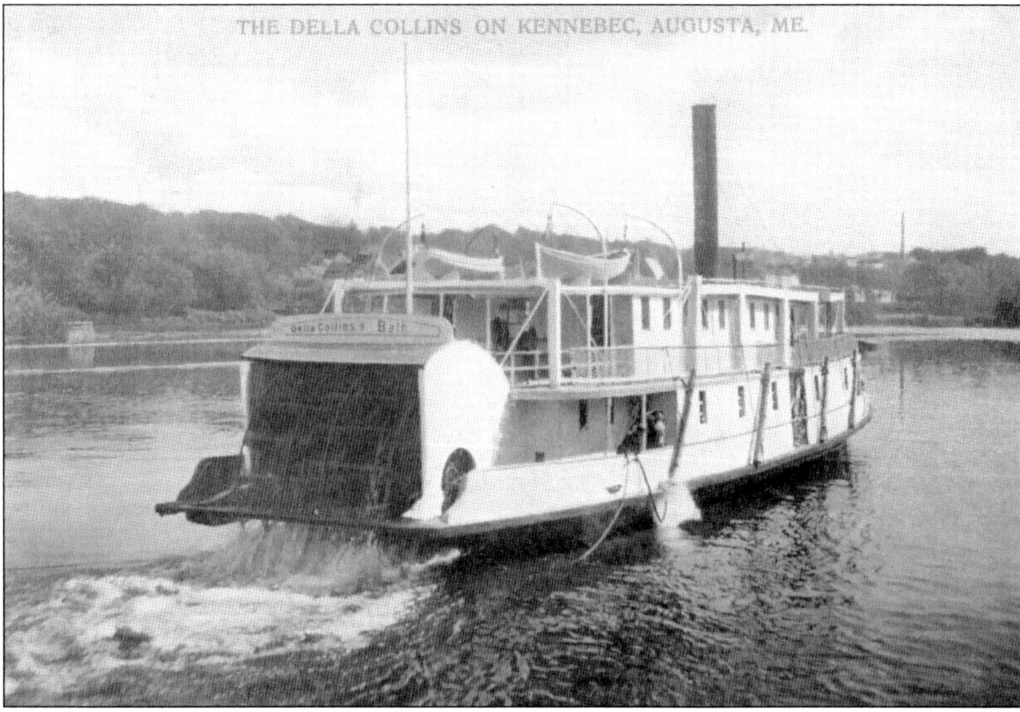

The stern-wheeler *Della Collins*, named after the daughter of Capt. Jason Collins, was built for the Kennebec Steamboat Company to replace the *Clarian* in 1879. She was used as a transfer boat for freight and passengers from Augusta and Hallowell to Gardiner, where a steamer to Boston was docked. She had once been sunk during a storm in December 1900 but was raised, repaired, and sailed on for another six years.

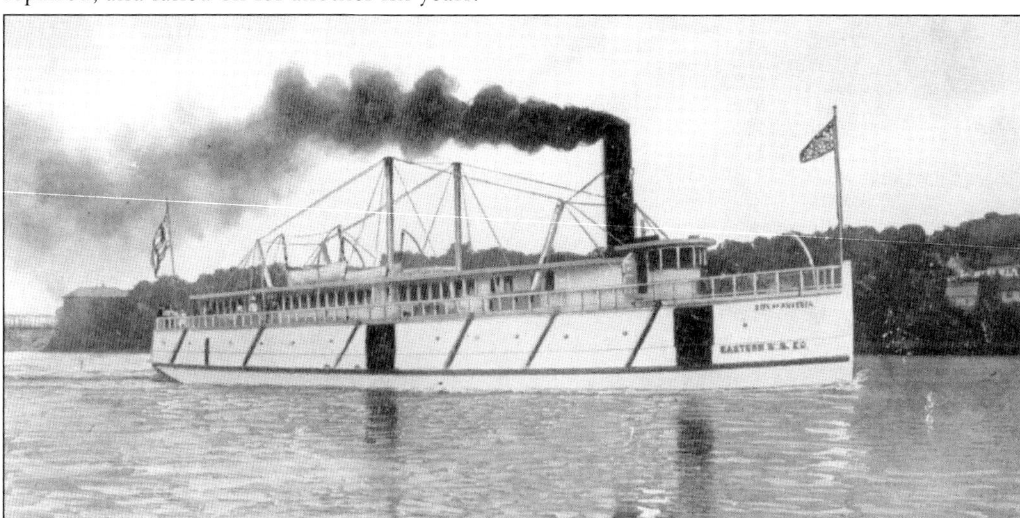

The Eastern Steamship Company bought out the Kennebec Steamship Company in 1901 and later added the steamer *City of Augusta* to replace the aging *Della Collins* in 1906. With the exception of Sunday, the ship would depart daily from the southern wharf, bound for Hallowell and Gardiner. Having just left its mooring, the steamer passes the Kennebec Bridge and the Augusta City Hall, the roof of which is seen at left in the background.

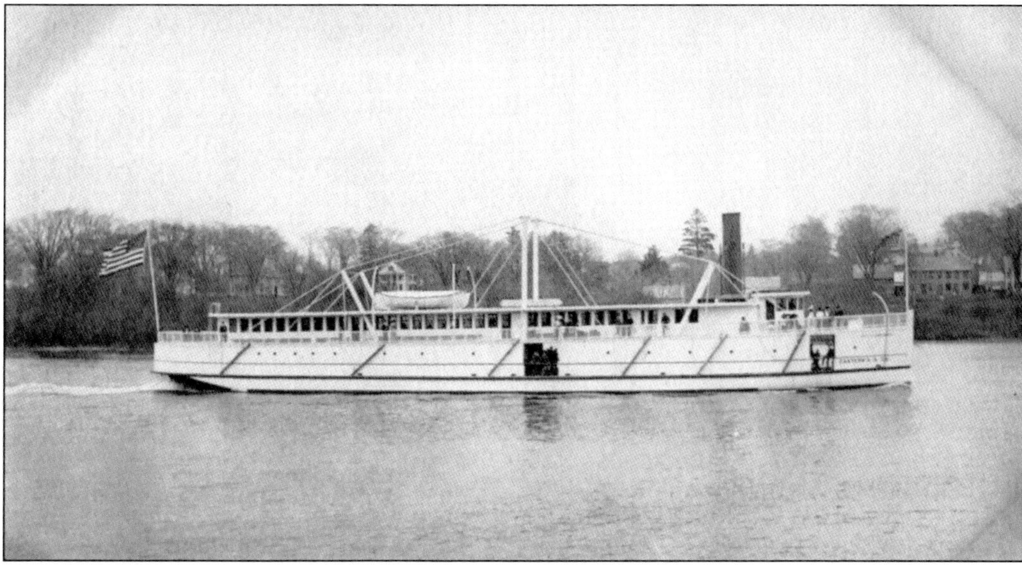

Piloted by Captain Lewis and a crew of 20 hands, the *City of Augusta* navigated the Kennebec River for 21 years. Although rumors abound as early as 1913 that the steamer was going to be sold, it was not until 1917 when this actually came to pass. She was sold to Jacksonville, Florida, and renamed *St. John*. She was lost to fire while at port in Savannah.

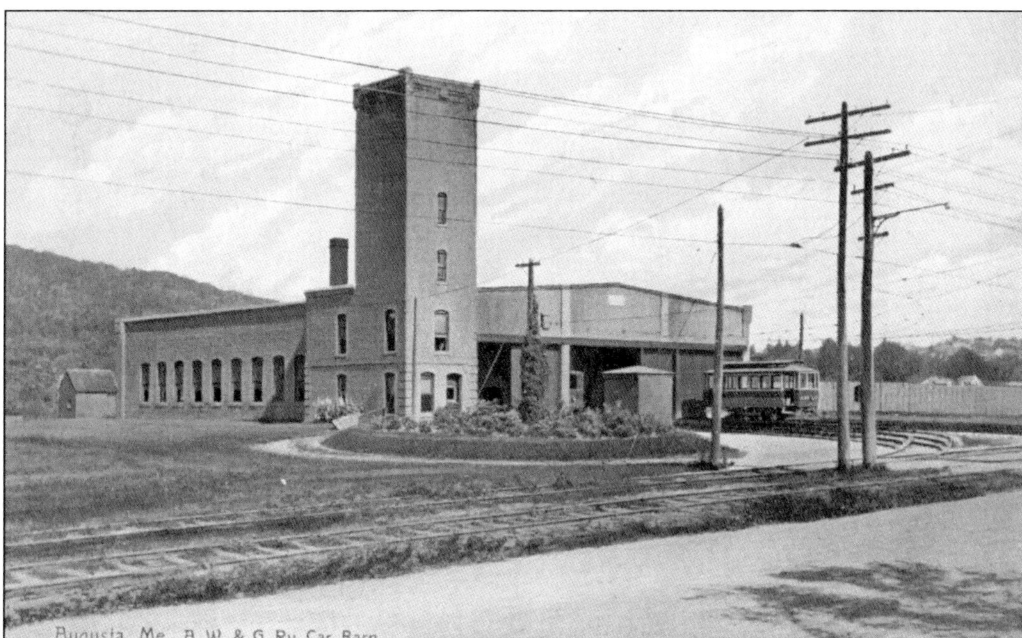

The Augusta car house was built on State Street in 1901 as the operating center for the Augusta, Winthrop & Gardiner Street Railway. The first two tracks had pits and were used for inspections and repairs, while the remaining three tracks held active cars. With the decline of the trolley system, a Studebaker dealership had begun using the car house by the 1930s. The structure still stands to this day.

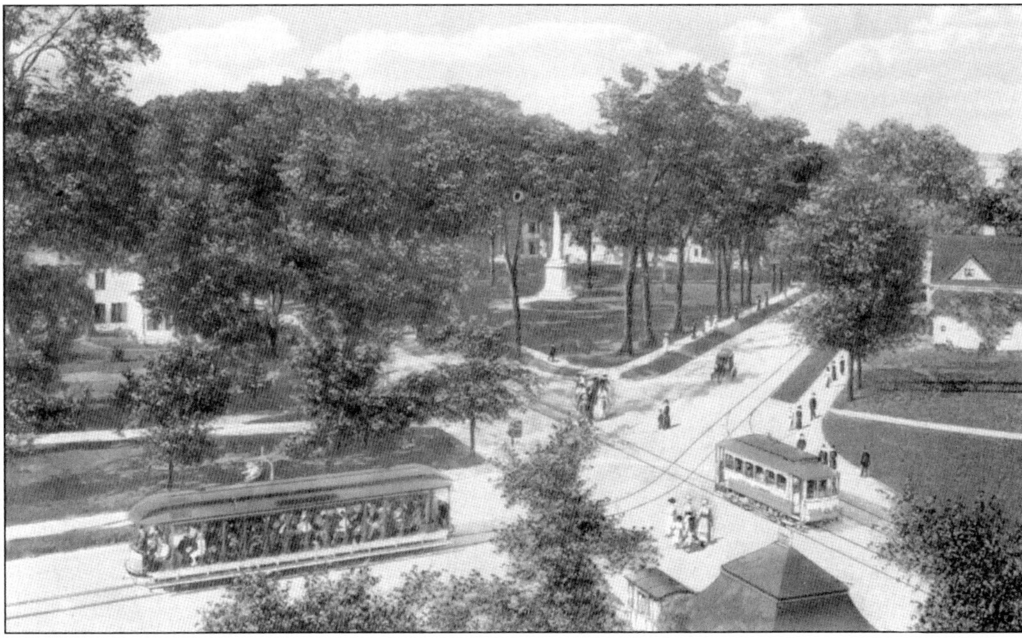

From high atop the Augusta House, an open trolley, at left, can be seen traveling up Western Avenue, possibly heading toward Island Park, a popular social destination of the day, while the State Street shuttle car traverses past Grove Street, which disappears behind the trees toward Water Street. This intersection was reconfigured with a rotary when the Memorial Bridge was constructed in 1949.

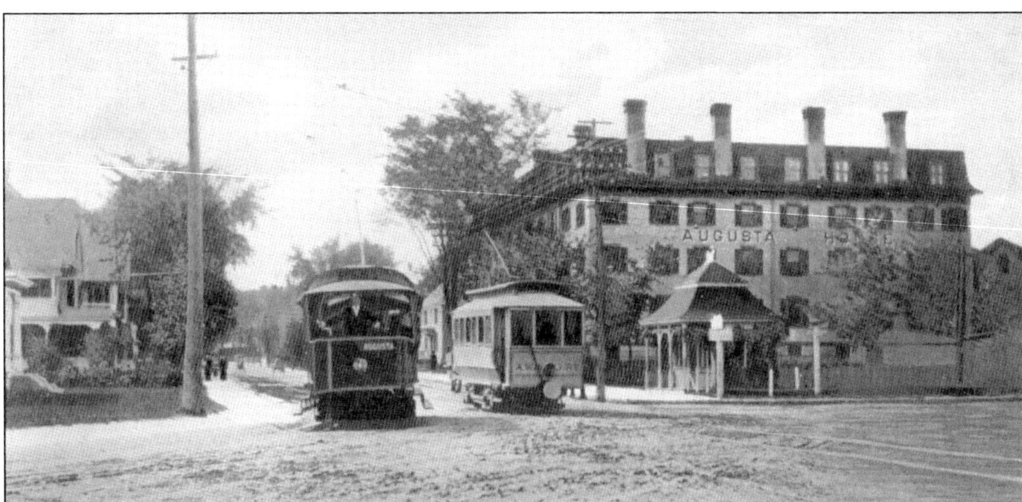

The State Street shuttle car, at right, began operation in August 1890 and ran a local circuit every half hour from right in front of the Augusta House, where the trolley connected with the Augusta-Gardiner lines, to just north of the railroad bridge via Bond Street. Due to the steepness of Gas House Hill, the line was truncated to six-tenths of a mile at Crosby Lane in 1892.

Seven

HOTELS

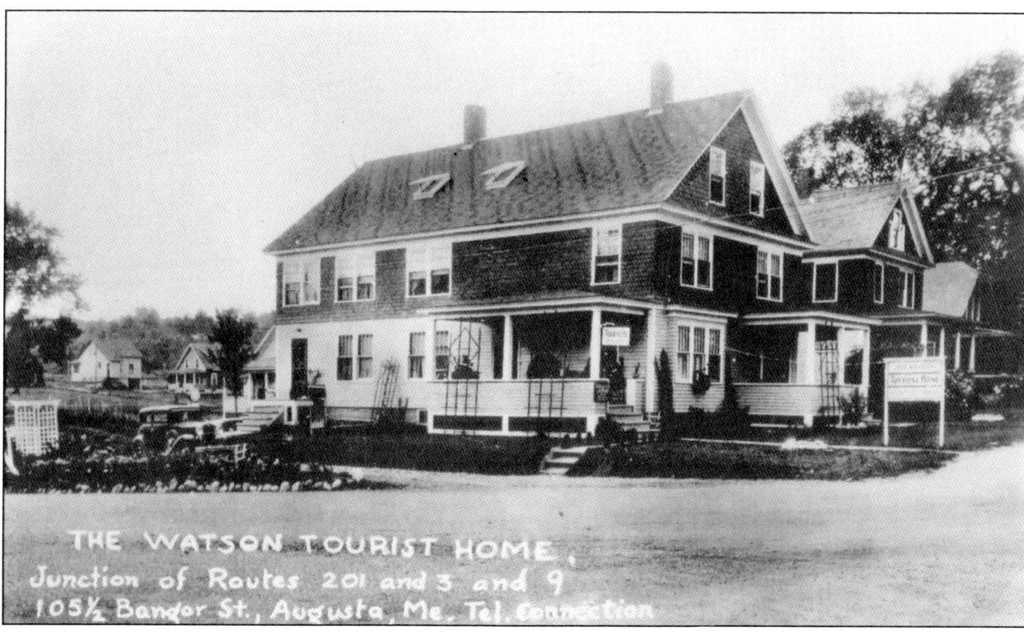

With the advent of better cars and even better roadways developed during the 1930s and 1940s, roadside bed-and-breakfasts were coming into fashion. The Watson Tourist Home had a prime location at the intersection of major routes that lead to Belfast, Bangor, and through Augusta to all points south. The tourist home and the two houses behind it are now gone.

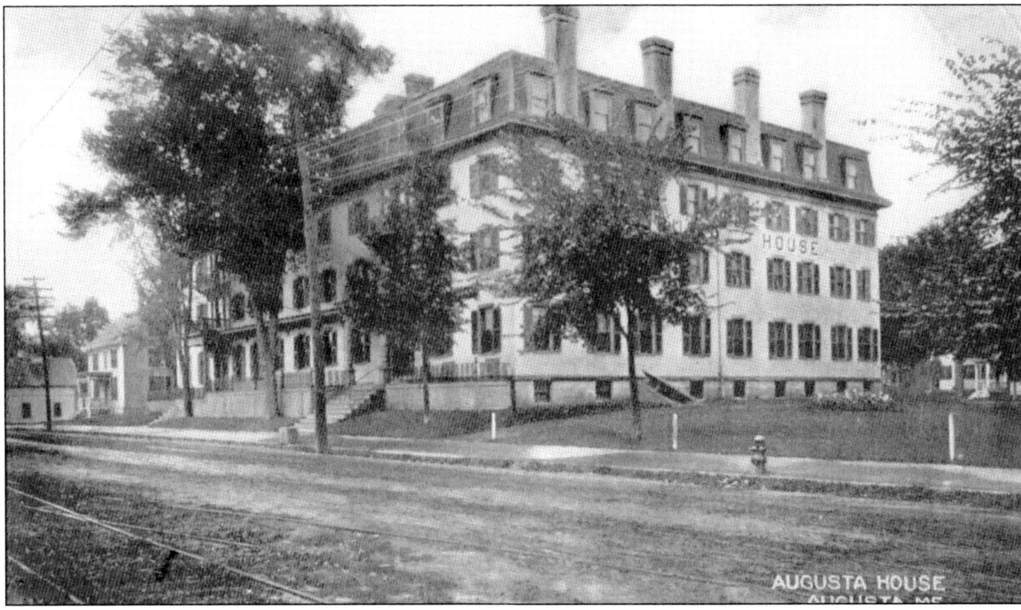

Anticipating the housing needs with the pending move of the legislature to Augusta, a group of businessmen led by Reuel Williams formed a corporation that built the Augusta House in 1831. The four-story brick hostelry was situated on a parcel of land over an acre in size and cost $26,000 to build. The doors opened the last day of that year, and in hotel tradition, the key was thrown away.

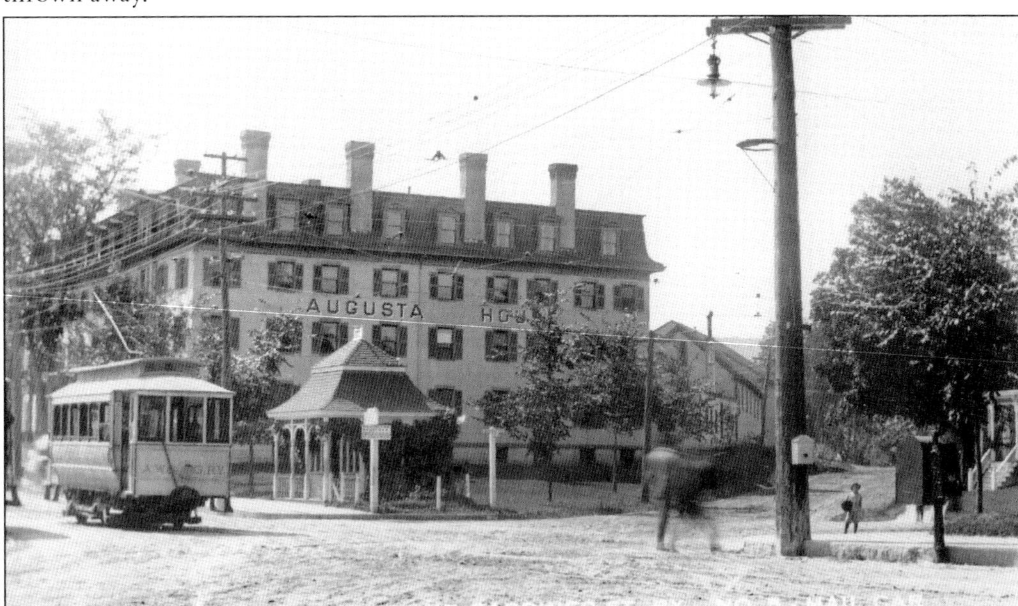

With throngs of people arriving in Augusta during the Civil War, the hotel was expanded in 1864. The $65,000 expansion, designed by Francis H. Fassett, not only increased the accommodations to 120 rooms but also included large parlors, reading rooms, and a telegraph office. Now quite popular by politicians, it has been said that more legislation has taken place in the lobby than in the capitol itself.

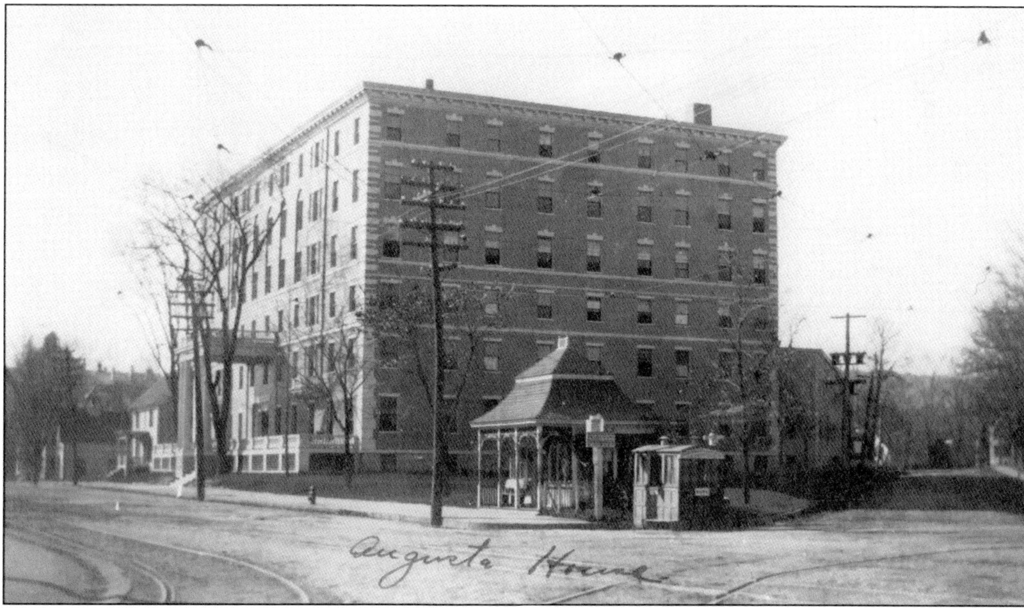

The Augusta House expanded again in 1910 with the passing of legislation that made Augusta the permanent seat of government. The hotel was increased to six floors, bringing the room count to 200. The ornate waiting station, built at least a decade prior, was busier than ever, serving trolley passengers at the bustling intersection of State and Grove Streets.

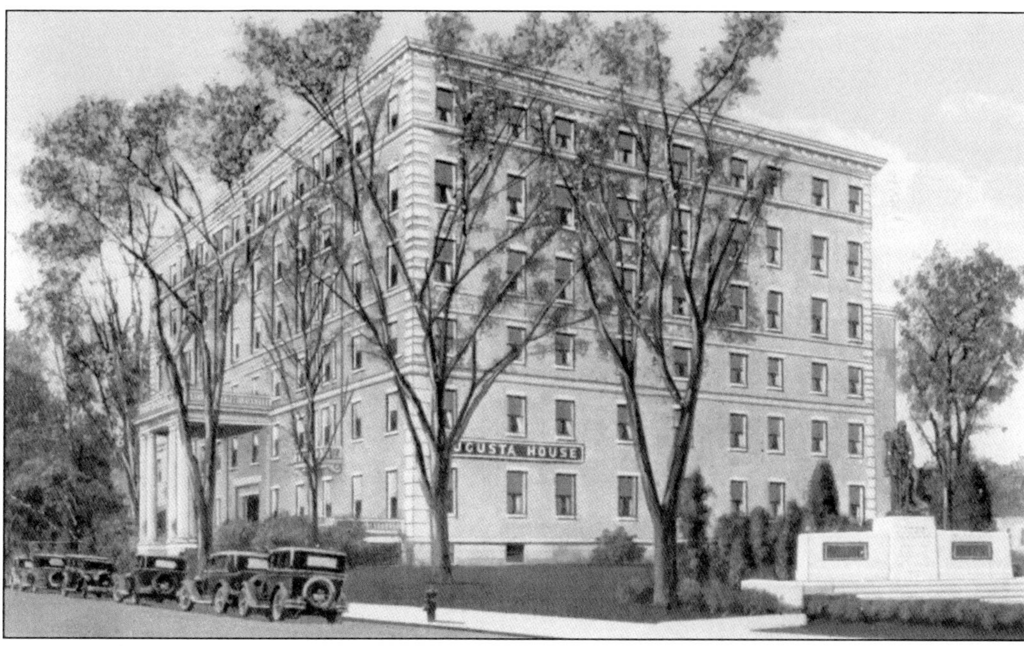

The year of 1939 brought extensive projects to the Augusta House, including a complete renovation of the lobby, construction of a new cocktail lounge and garden, and remodeling of both dining rooms, all designed by J.C. Stoner of New York City. Along with 5,000 yards of carpet that was installed throughout, extensive plumbing and lighting upgrades were made. The World War I monument was located in front of the hotel in 1929.

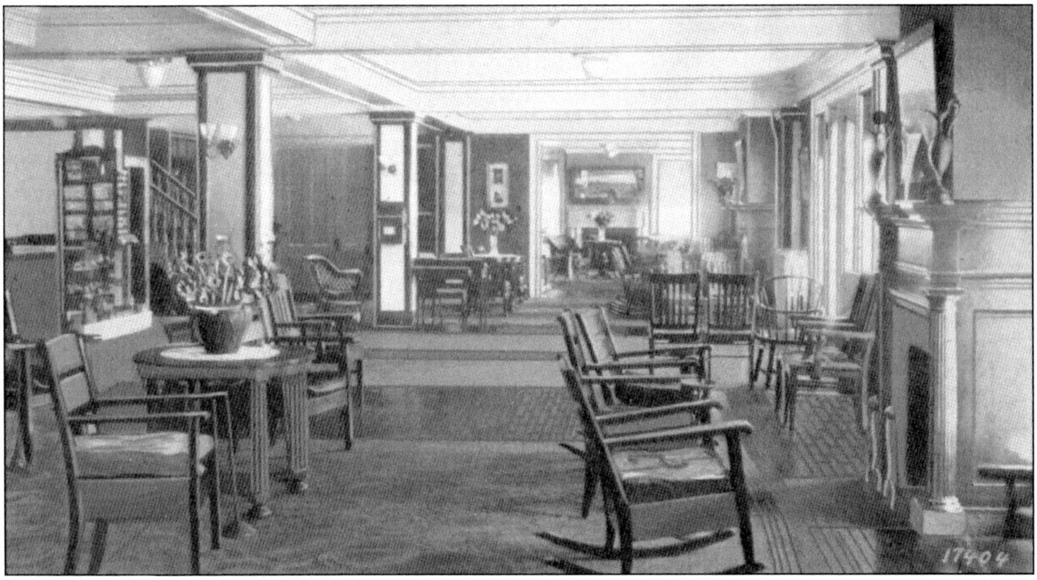

The Augusta House lobby was updated completely during the 1939 renovation, with new carpet replacing old rubber mats, the furniture being replaced or refinished, and painting done throughout. The massive fireplaces had been well preserved and continued to be a favorite gathering spot. Decorating the walls were items of the hotel's past, such as menus for state dinners and invitations to legislative assemblies dating back more than a century.

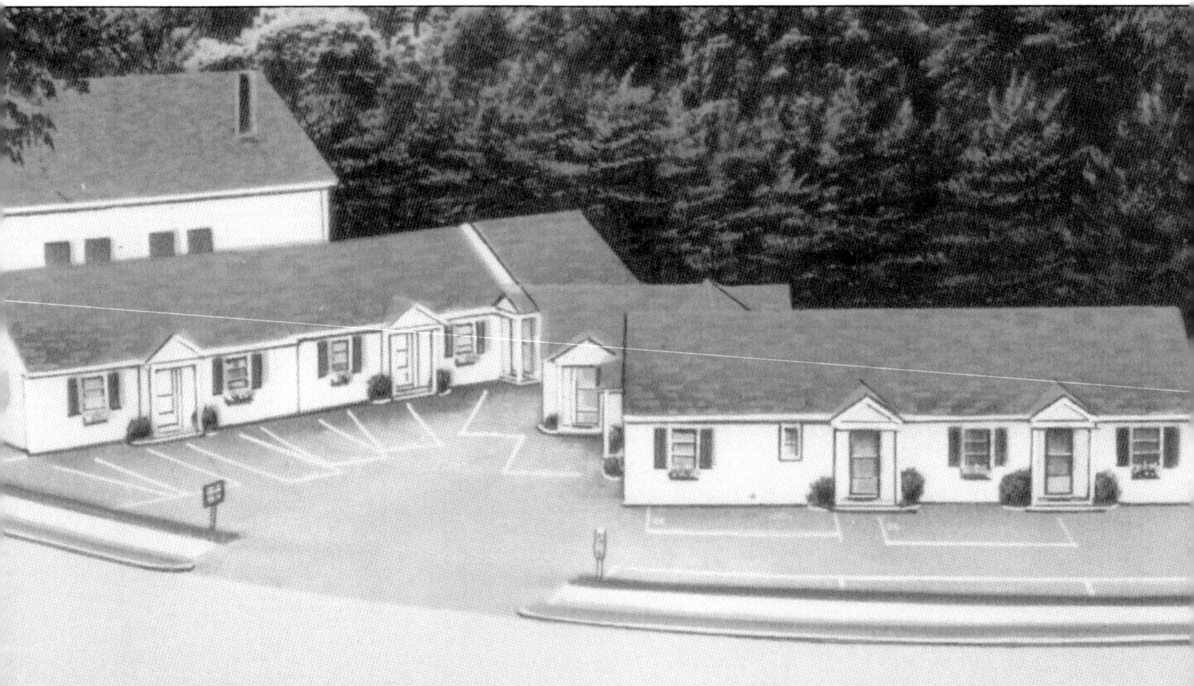

Built in the early 1950s, the Memorial Bridge Motor Court opened shortly after the completion of the Memorial Bridge. Perhaps one of the best descriptions of the motel comes from the message on the back of a postcard from a couple who stayed here the night of September 30, 1964: "Motel better than the picture. We had room 18—every comfort one could ask. Twin

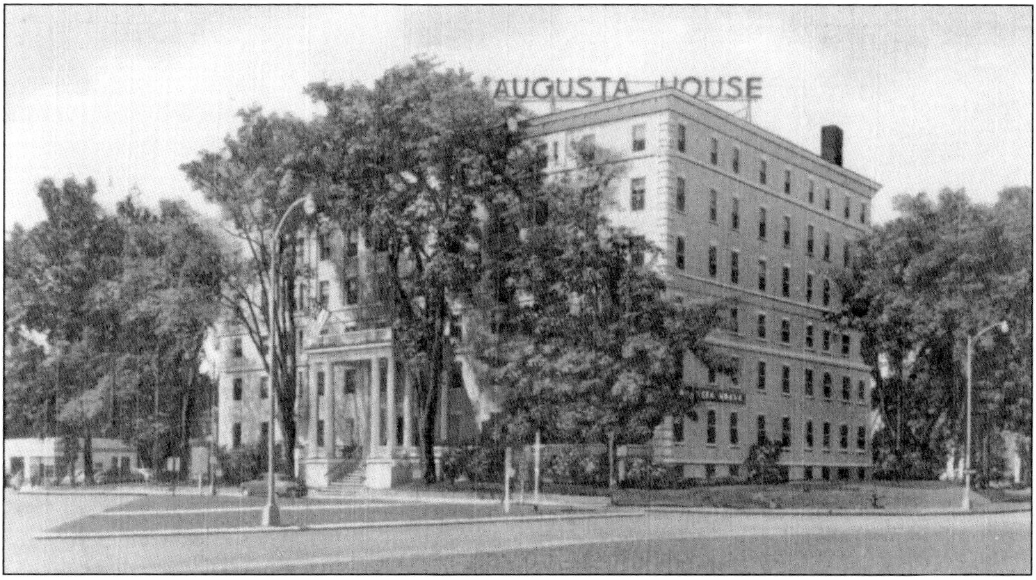

The Augusta House had many distinguished visitors over the years. Movie stars Dorothy Lamour and Faye Emerson were guests, and in 1951, Richard Nixon held a reception in the hotel during his presidential campaign. But the need for such a grand hotel waned, and it went bankrupt in 1971. Three years later, despite much public outcry, the proud 143-year-old Augusta House was taken down.

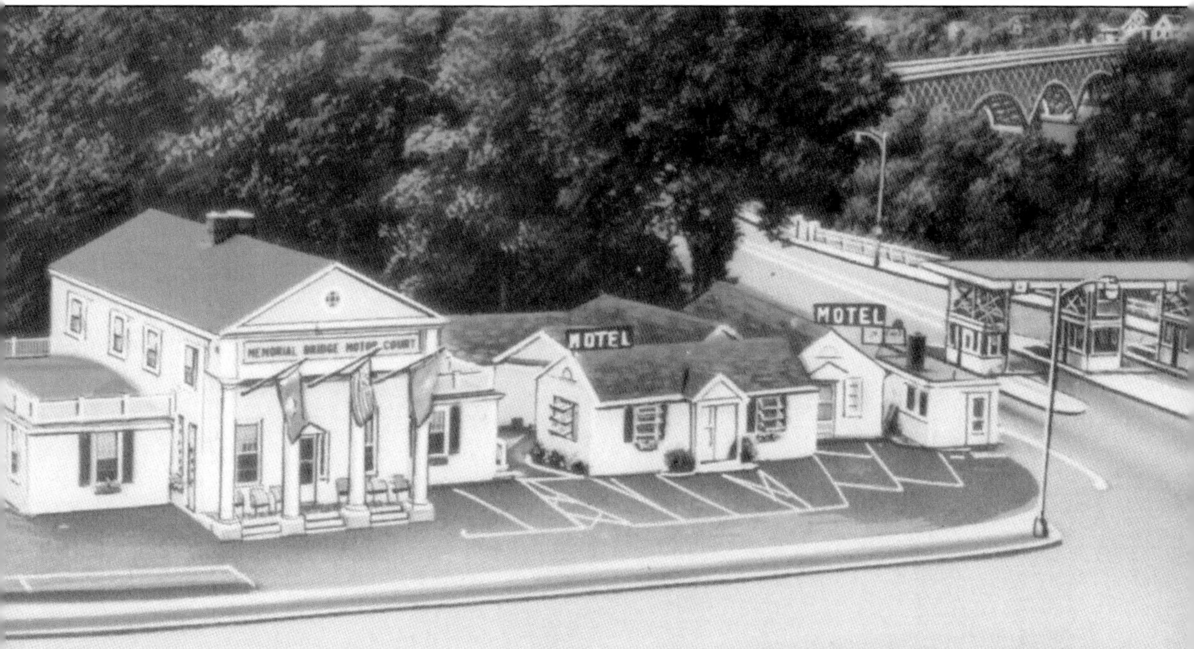

double beds, maple furniture—perfect but not cheap—$14.00." The tollbooths, seen on the right, were removed when the toll was rescinded in October 1967. The toll of 10¢ was collected from more than 8,000 cars during the first 12 hours of the opening of the bridge.

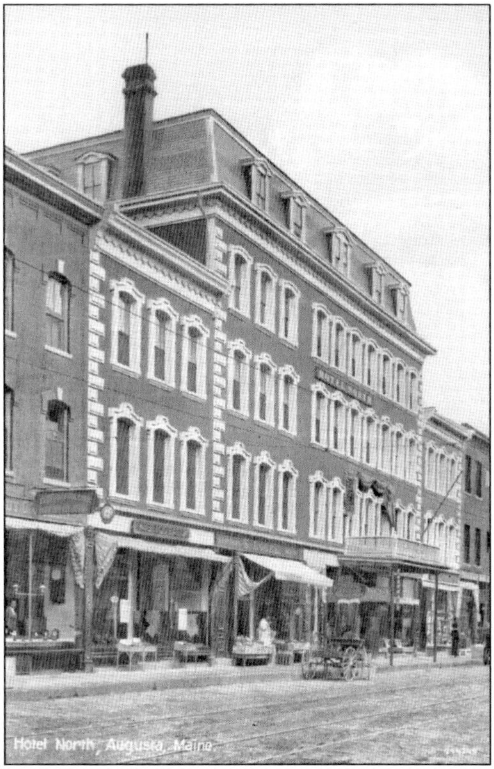

In 1877, James W. North built the Hotel North on the same site that his uncle Gershom North had built the Franklin House, which burned in the fire of 1865. Flanked by three-story wings, the main Italianate-style structure consisted of five floors, the first being occupied by upwards of nine retailers. The hotel had a kitchen, dining room, lounge, and more than 80 rooms.

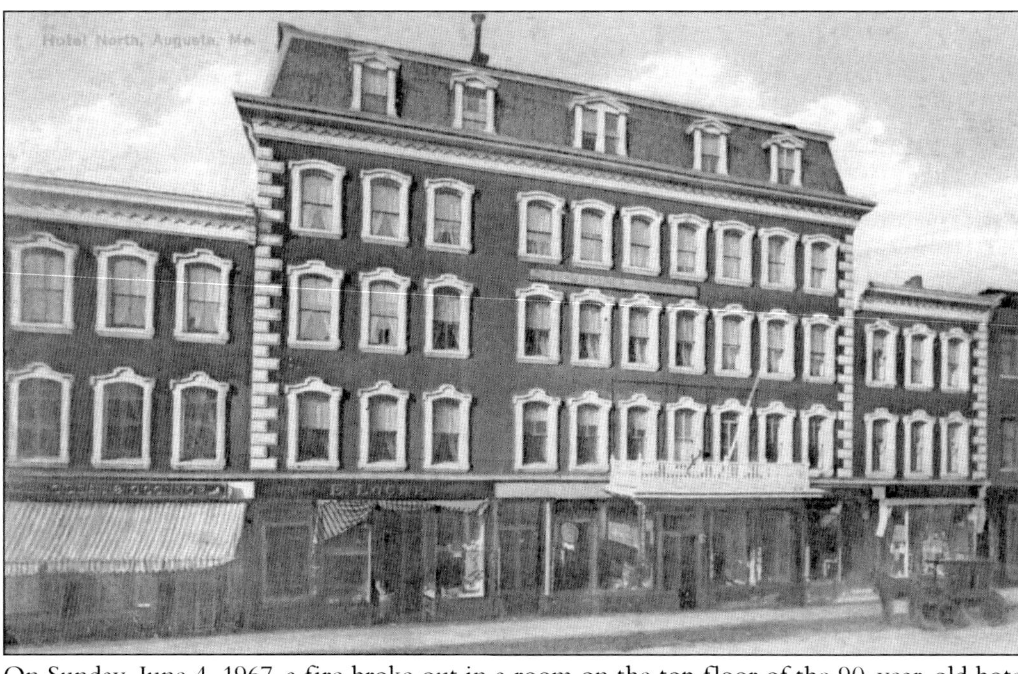

On Sunday, June 4, 1967, a fire broke out in a room on the top floor of the 90-year-old hotel and drew a crowd of about 1,000 spectators. Although the fire was contained to three rooms, there was extensive damage, estimated at $100,000, to the top three floors and furnishings. Torn down shortly after, only the north wing remained until the entire block was razed in 1986.

Eight

Parks and Monuments

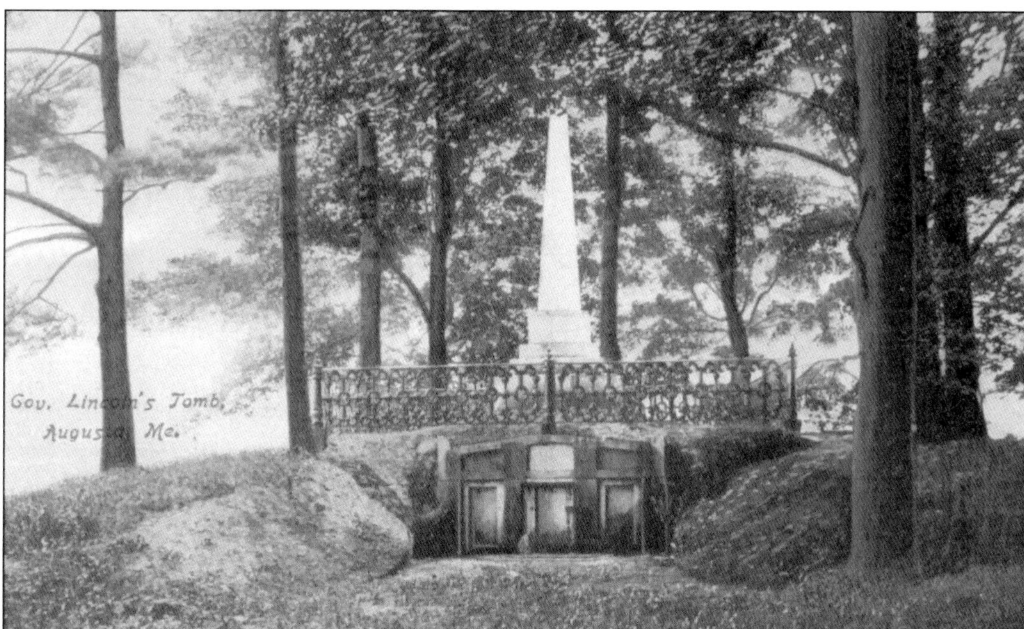

Gov. Enoch Lincoln, elected in 1827 as Maine's sixth governor, moved the capital from Portland to Augusta while in office. He came to Augusta on October 5, 1829, to deliver an address and fell ill. He died at Samuel Cony's house three days later at age 40. Buried with honors, Lincoln's tomb lies in the northeast corner of Capitol Park at the end of a long avenue of trees.

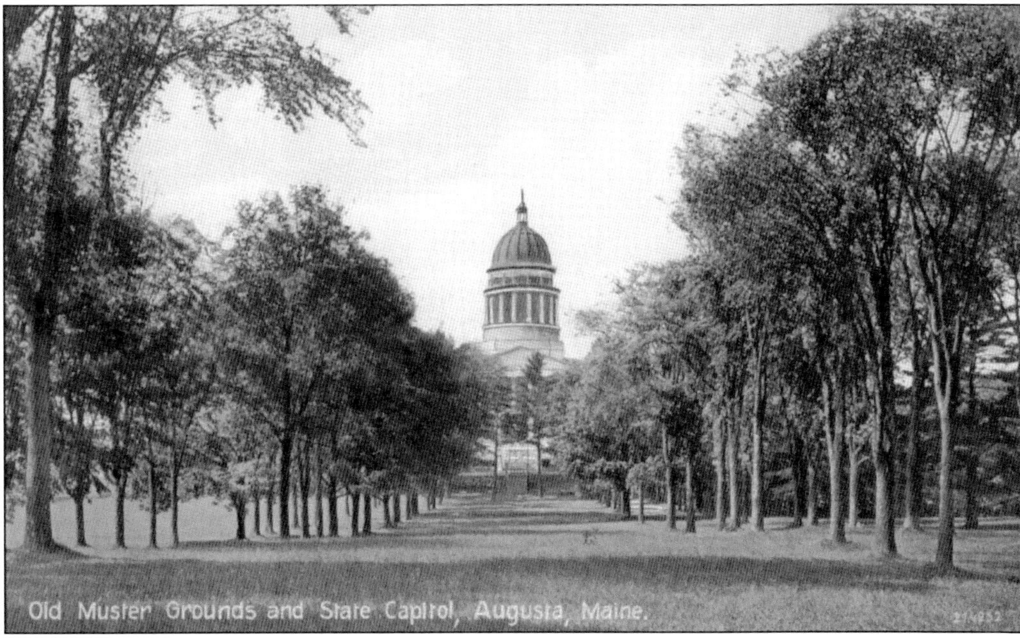

When Weston's Hill was chosen as the site of the State House after Augusta became the capital in 1827, the 20-acre tract of land in front, from State Street to the river, became Capitol Park. Initially, it was planted with two single rows of trees, which were doubled in 1857. During the Civil War, several Maine regiments were encamped here before being mobilized to the South.

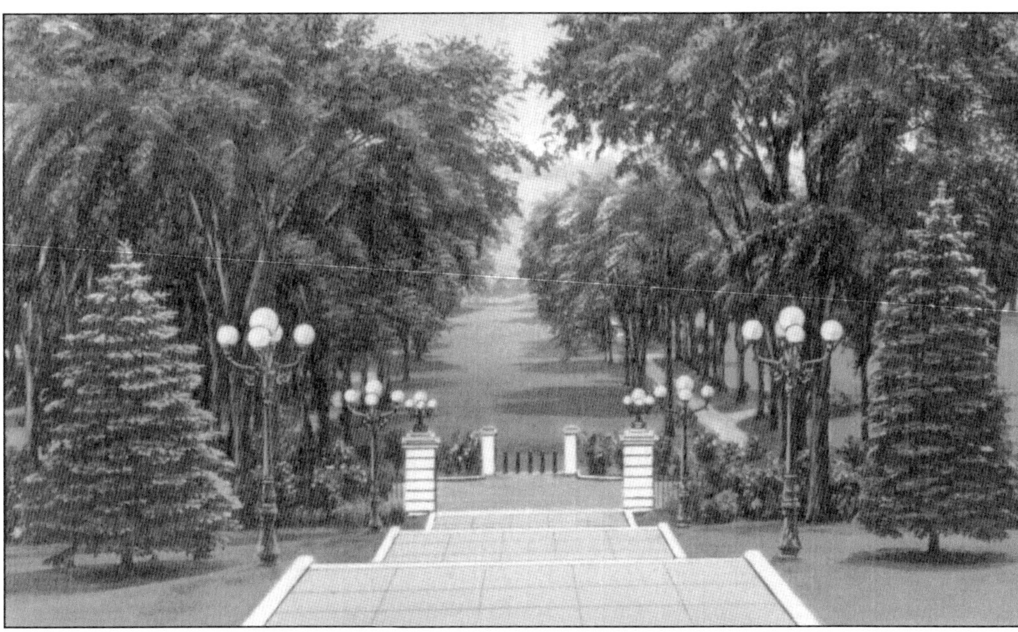

The view of Capitol Park from the steps of the State House was breathtaking. Carl Rust Parker, a Portland landscape designer, nurtured the park into an arboretum during the 1920s. There were about 100 species of native and exotic trees, even more types of shrubs, and over 30 varieties of ferns. In addition to an artificial pond, rustic seats and benches dotted over a mile of paths.

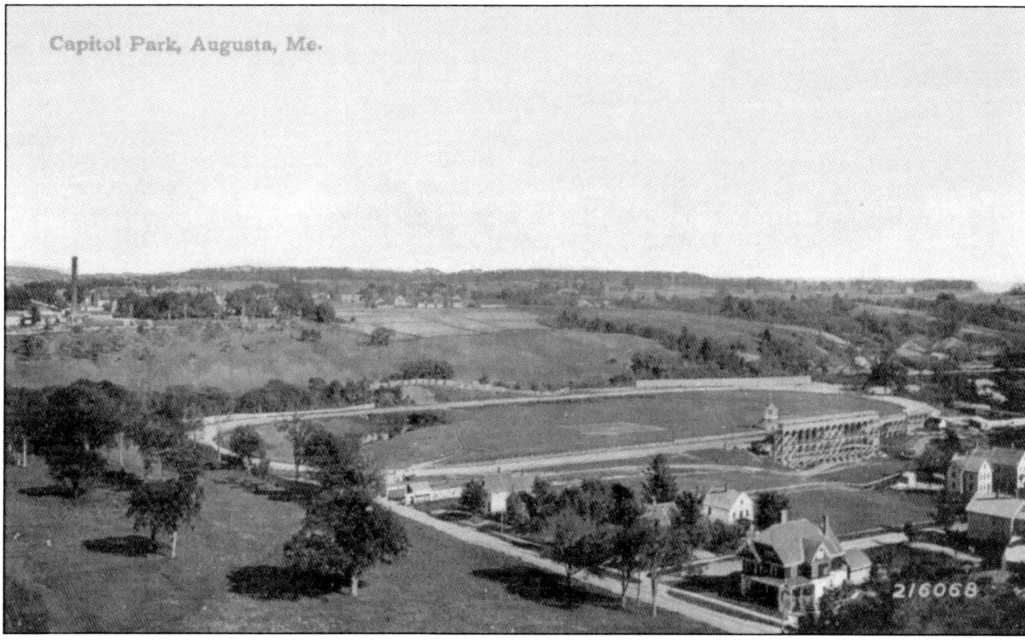

The 22-acre trotting park, just south of Capitol Park, had been a fixture in Augusta since as early as the 1870s. It was used for racing, agricultural fairs, circuses, sporting events, and on one occasion, an airstrip for Augusta's first-ever glimpse at an airplane—St. Croix Johnstone's Moisant monoplane in 1911. The grandstands were added the following year and could seat 2,000 people.

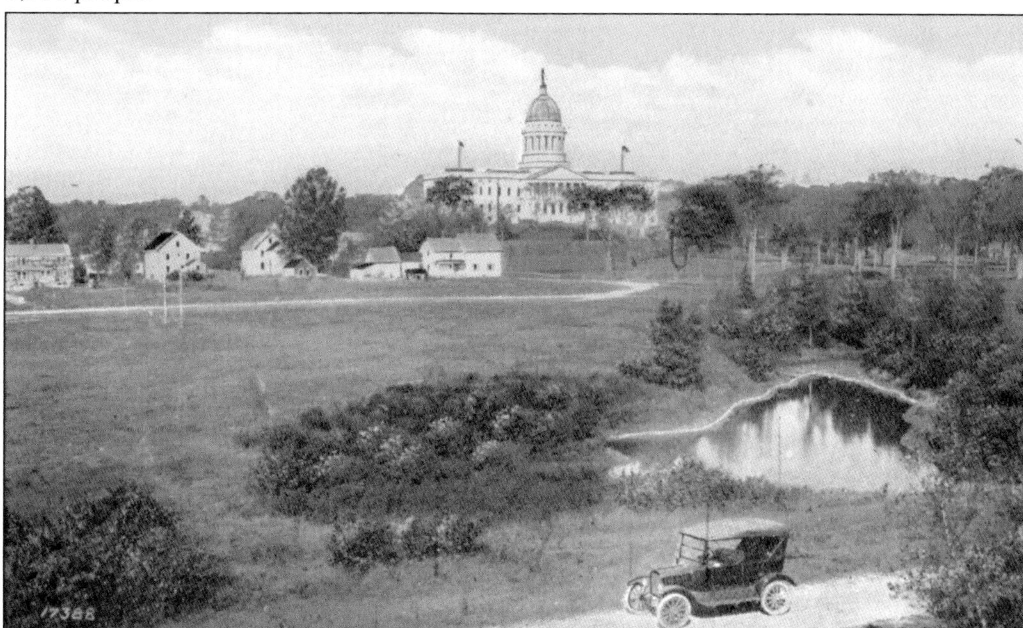
The Maine State House can be seen far in the distance from the easterly edge of the half-mile racetrack at the trotting park. To the left is the Columbia Street neighborhood, and Capitol Park lies to the right. The pond and racetrack in the foreground are gone, and the YMCA and the Augusta Police Department now occupy the site.

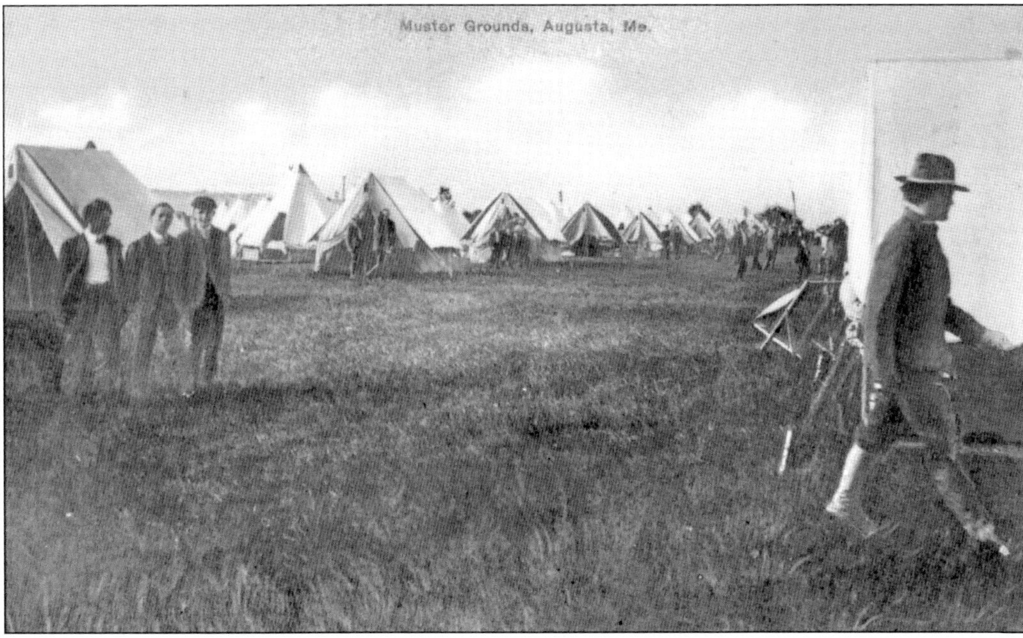

Although used as muster grounds since 1862, Camp Keyes, named in honor of Gen. Erasmus Darwin Keyes, did not receive its current designation until 1882. During the latter portion of the Civil War, the only federal hospital in Maine was operating on this site, treating upwards of 3,000 sick and wounded soldiers. By 1866, the Civil War Veterans home had been established in Togus.

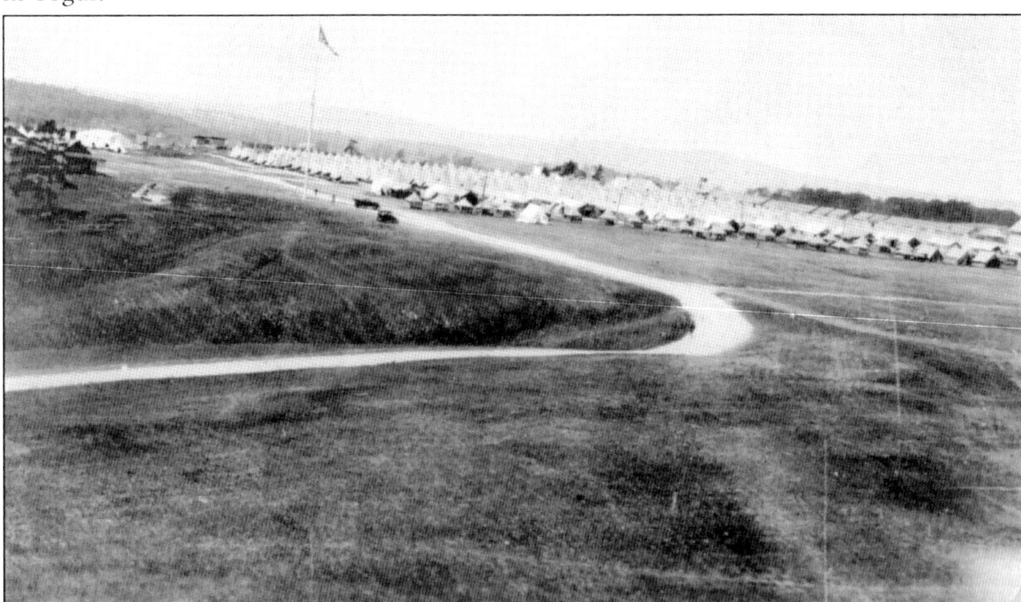

Camp Keyes contained approximately 70 acres of land on a plateau atop Winthrop Street. On the far left of the field, permanent buildings were erected for officers' quarters and supply depots. Barely visible in the background are the mess halls and kitchens. The road in the foreground winds its way toward Western Avenue. In 1934, construction of the Augusta Airport began, forever changing the composition of the camp.

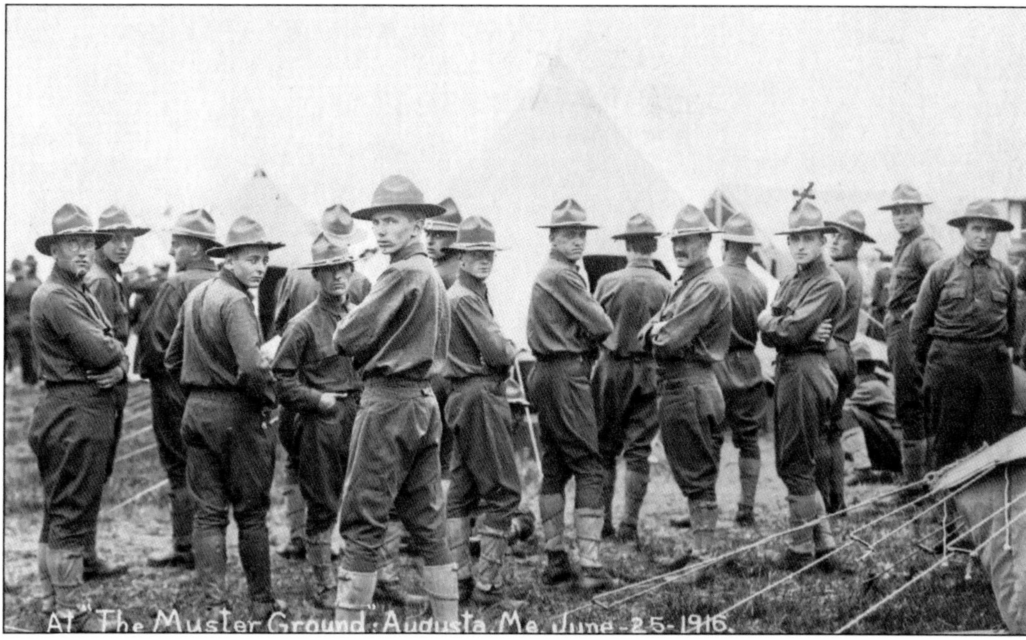

On March 9, 1916, during the Mexican Revolution, Pancho Villa attacked the American border town of Columbus, New Mexico, igniting the Border Campaign. In response, Pres. Woodrow Wilson called upon 110,000 National Guard soldiers for border service on June 18. One week later, this candid moment captured soldiers waiting for the deployment order. After four days, the order came, and the regiment marched to the waiting trains on Water Street.

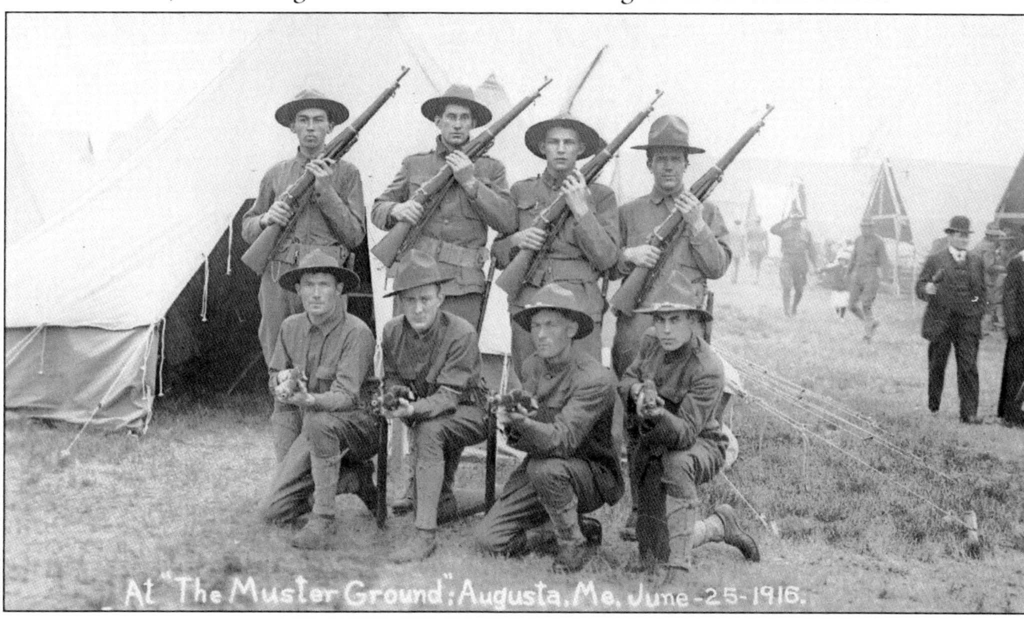

The activities of June 24, 1916, included federalization of the 2nd Infantry of the Maine National Guard, with a formal ceremony attended by at least 1,000 people the following day. About 5,000 visitors came to Camp Keyes to, according to the *Daily Kennebec Journal* on June 16, 1916, "personally inspect the manner in which our citizen soldiers are living," two of which are seen at right. Gov. Oakley C. Curtis walked the grounds, visiting every part of the field.

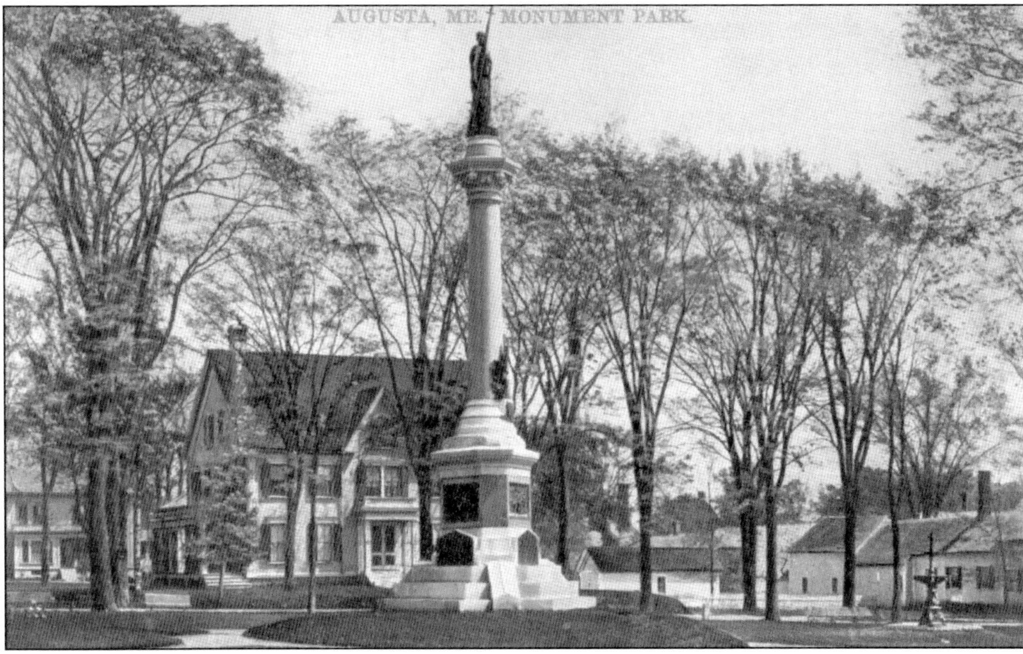

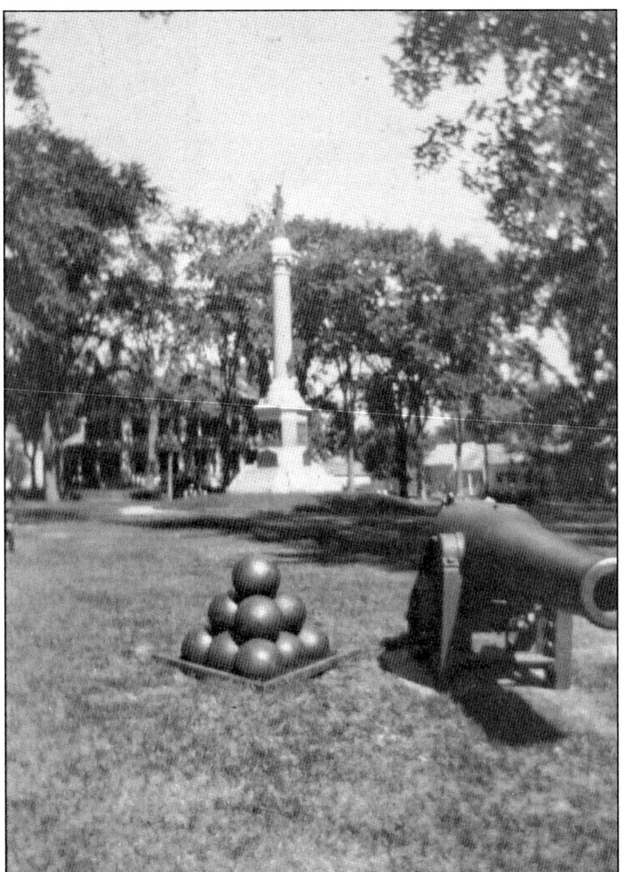

Maurice J. Power of New York designed the Civil War Memorial, erected in November 1881. It was constructed of Hallowell granite and reaches a towering 45 feet. The monument is topped with a bronze figure based on Nike, the Greek goddess of Victory. The base bears the names of 36 officers and 120 enlisted men from Augusta who served in the Civil War.

It is believed that the cannons in the three corners of Monument Park were introduced shortly before the Spanish-American War, but little else is known. The cannonballs, much larger than the bore of the cannons, were added later. With favorable public opinion, the cannons and cannonballs were removed in October 1942 to support the scrap metal drives of World War II.

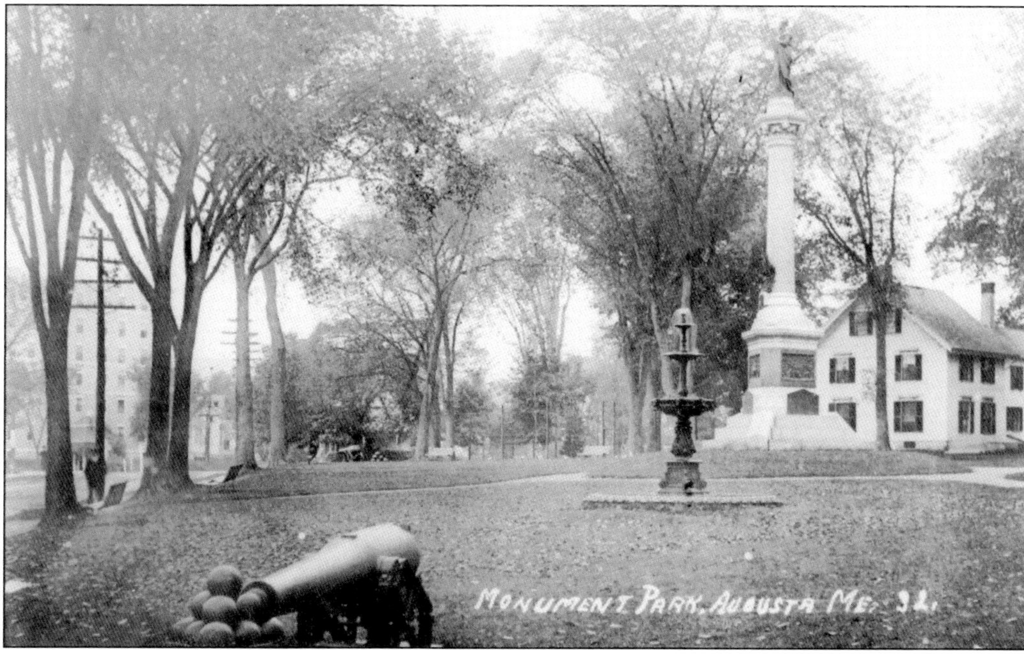

The parcel of land that became Monument Park had once been used as mustering grounds during the Civil War. Acquired by the city in 1879 for use as a site for a memorial, it became a favorite location for civic and social events, having once contained a bandstand that was later removed in 1900. Though gone now, the water fountain was installed in 1887 at a cost of $400.

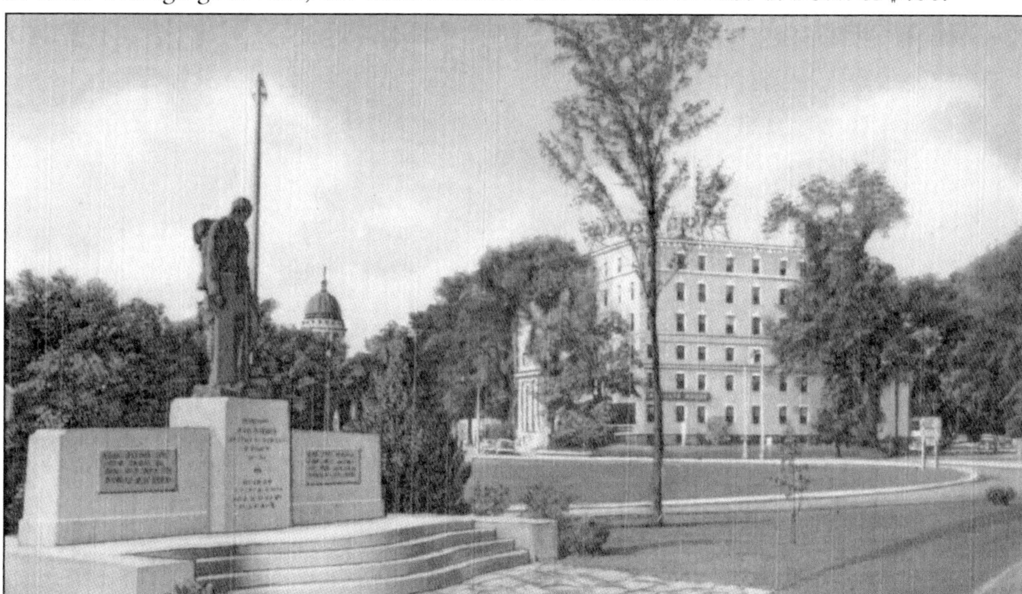

In 1929, George E. Macomber and his wife, Laura L. Macomber, presented the City of Augusta with a memorial dedicated to the soldiers and sailors of World War I. Originally located in front of the Augusta House, it was moved to Monument Park, as seen here, when the rotary was constructed in 1949. On the front are the names of the fallen, and on the reverse are all the Augusta men who served.

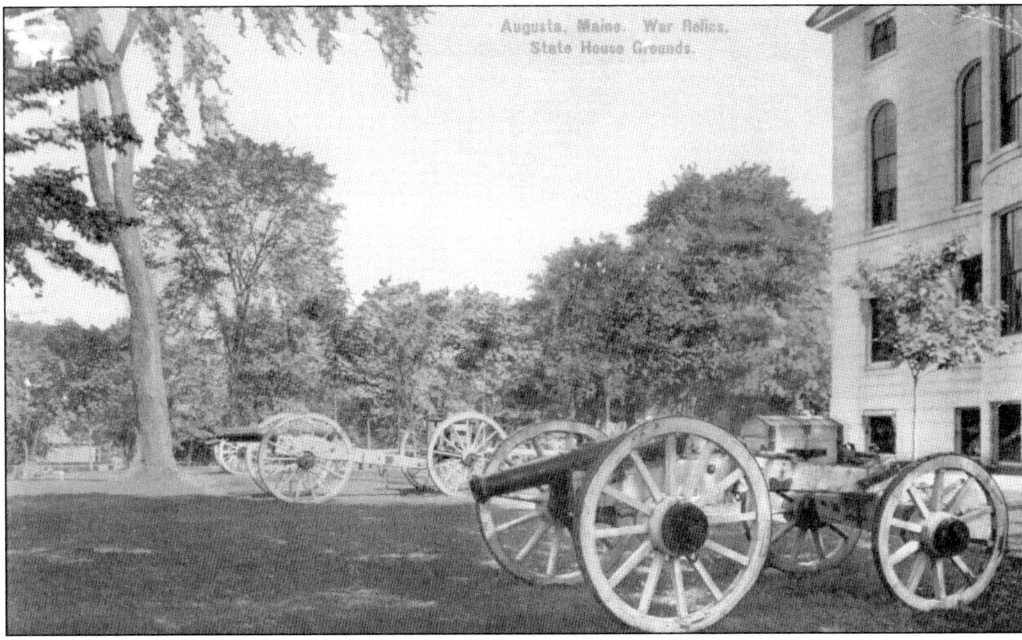

In 1817, Massachusetts sent these cannons to East Machias, Maine, to replace the two the British had captured in 1814. Later, in 1838, they were called into service for the bloodless Aroostook War. For several years, they sat unused, except for Fourth of July salutes, until they came to Augusta in 1905 and were placed on the State House grounds. Because of disrepair, they were moved to the museum in 1912.

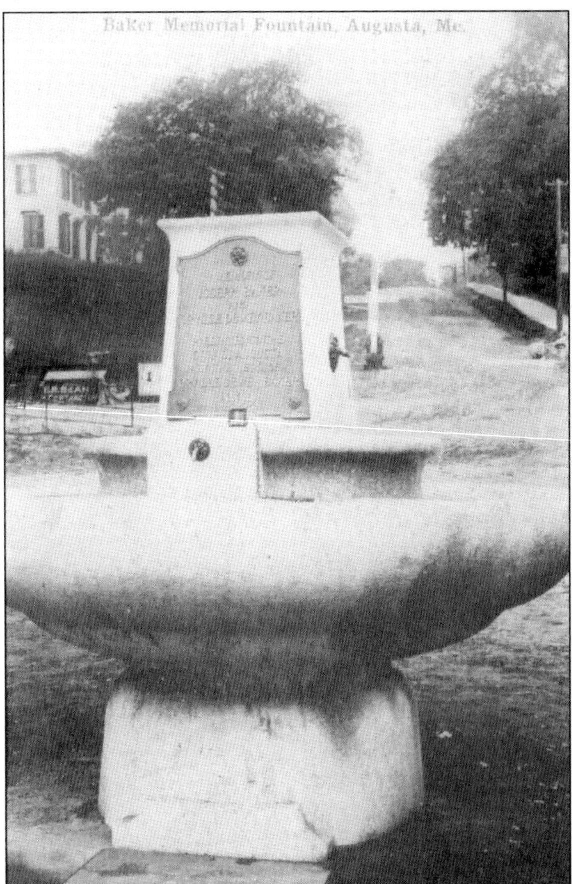

Joseph Baker and his son Orville Dewey Baker were two prominent lawyers in Augusta from the mid- to late 19th century. Joseph had also served in the state senate and House of Representatives, and Orville was Maine's attorney general for two terms. The Baker heirs memorialized the father and son by gifting this fountain to the city in 1909.

Nine

Street Views

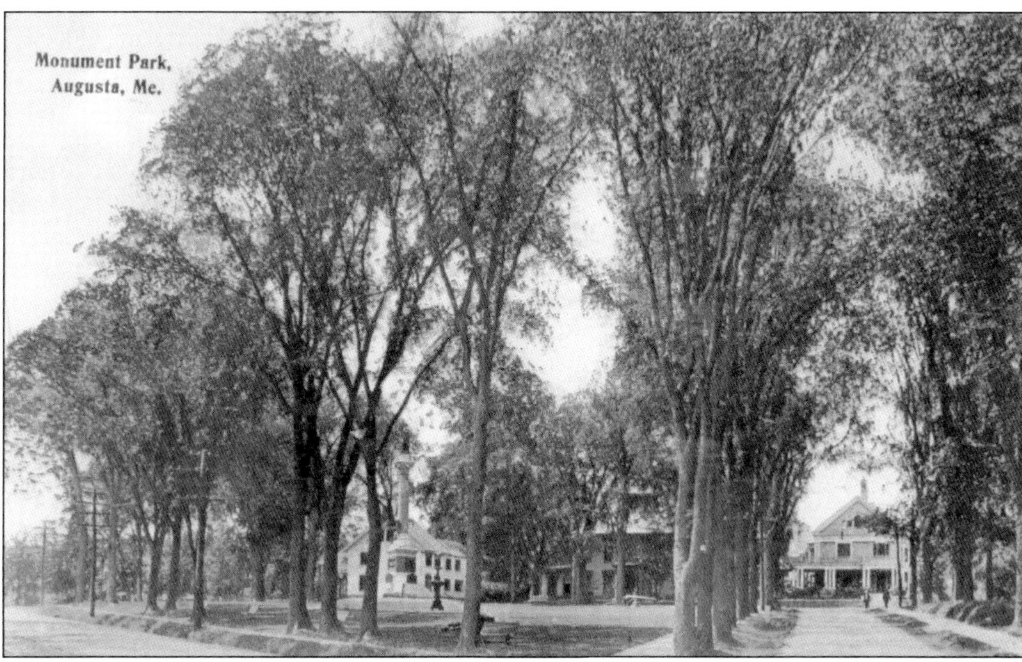

Bordered by stately elms, the original triangular shape of Monument Park was bound by Grove, State, and Chandler Streets. At the end of Chandler Street, at right, is the home of George W. Macomber, mayor of Augusta from 1886 to 1888 and benefactor of the World War I Memorial added to the park in 1929.

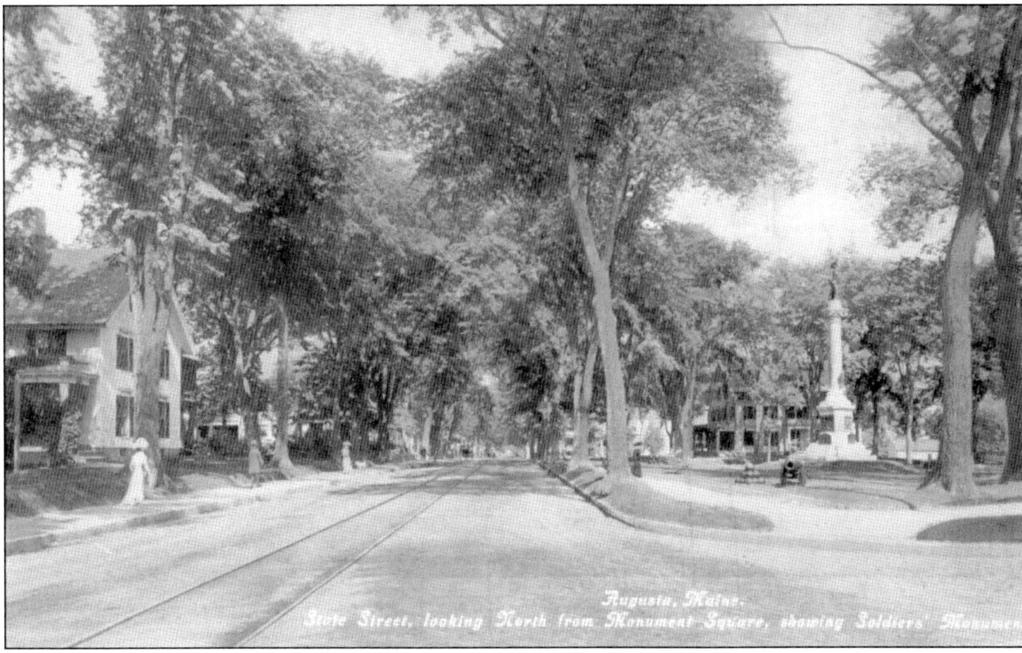

From the intersection of State and Grove Streets, it is easy to see the 19th-century splendor of Victorian urban life in Augusta. The majestic elms formed a canopy that enveloped the entire avenue, affording the traveler a shaded and pleasant journey. Monument Park was a frequent gathering place for social events, and it was quite common for people to pose for photographs with the cannons.

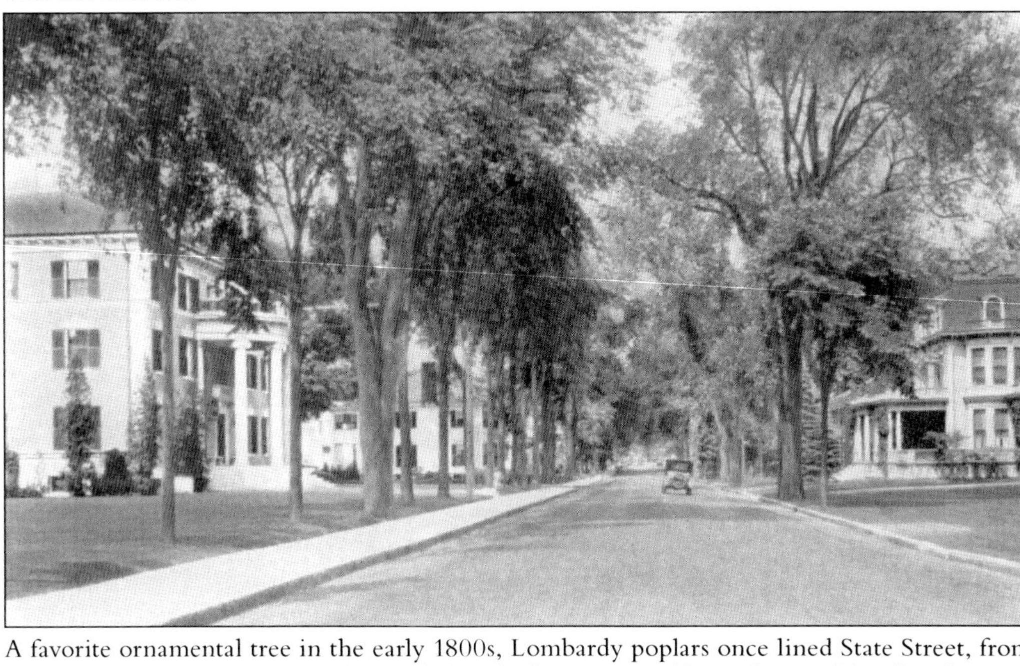

A favorite ornamental tree in the early 1800s, Lombardy poplars once lined State Street, from Bridge Street to Grove Street. They only lasted a few years, and later, the much hardier elm trees were planted. Sadly, Dutch elm disease decimated these trees during the 1950s and 1960s. Governor Hill's residence is visible at left, with the Honorable Herbert M. Heath's home at right.

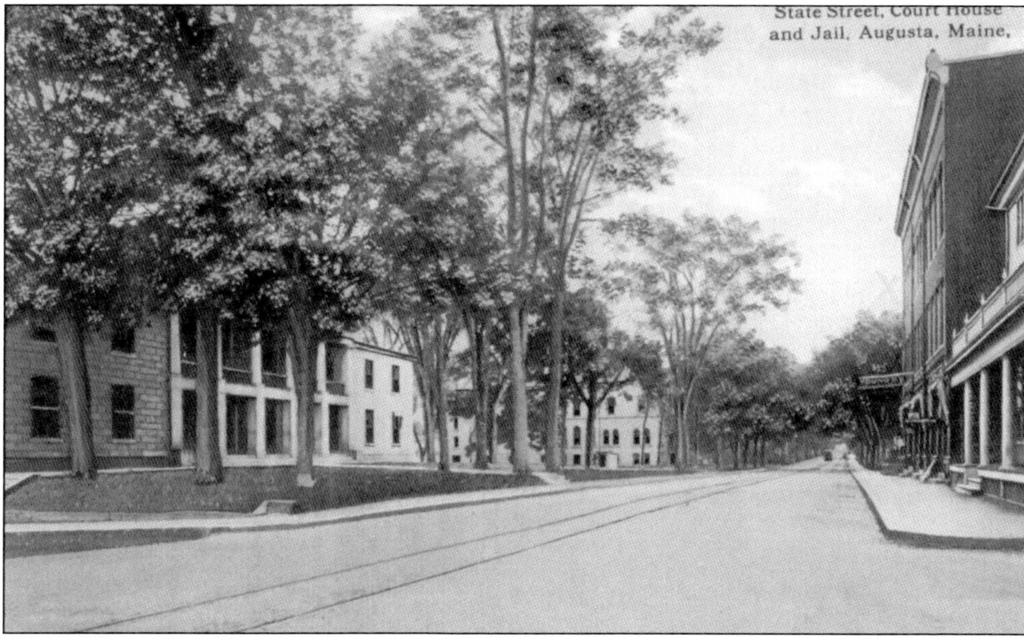

In 1800, the city paid Samuel Titcomb the sum of $112.37 to construct a framed bridge across the steep gully located just south of the courthouse, making State Street (then called Court Street) passable to the south. The gully under the street was filled in completely sometime between 1895 and 1903, and the bridge is now gone.

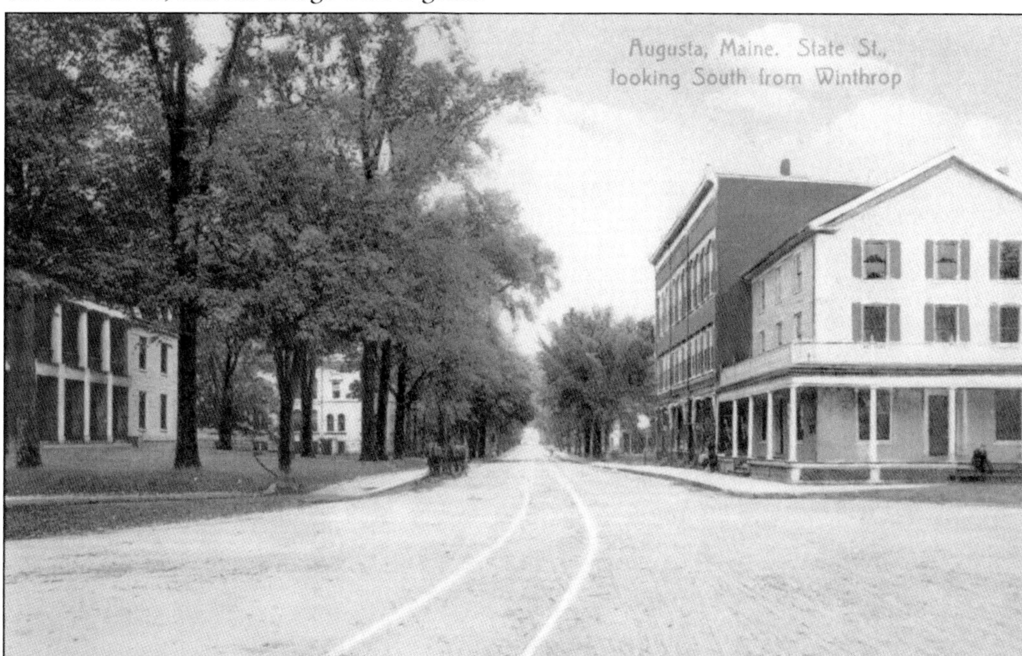

The brick building on the corner originally was built on the present site of the jail as the Kennebec County Courthouse in 1801. When the new courthouse was built in 1829, this structure was used as a meeting hall and church. It was relocated to this site in 1857 when the jail was constructed. Known as the Concert Hall, it held many important meetings during the Civil War.

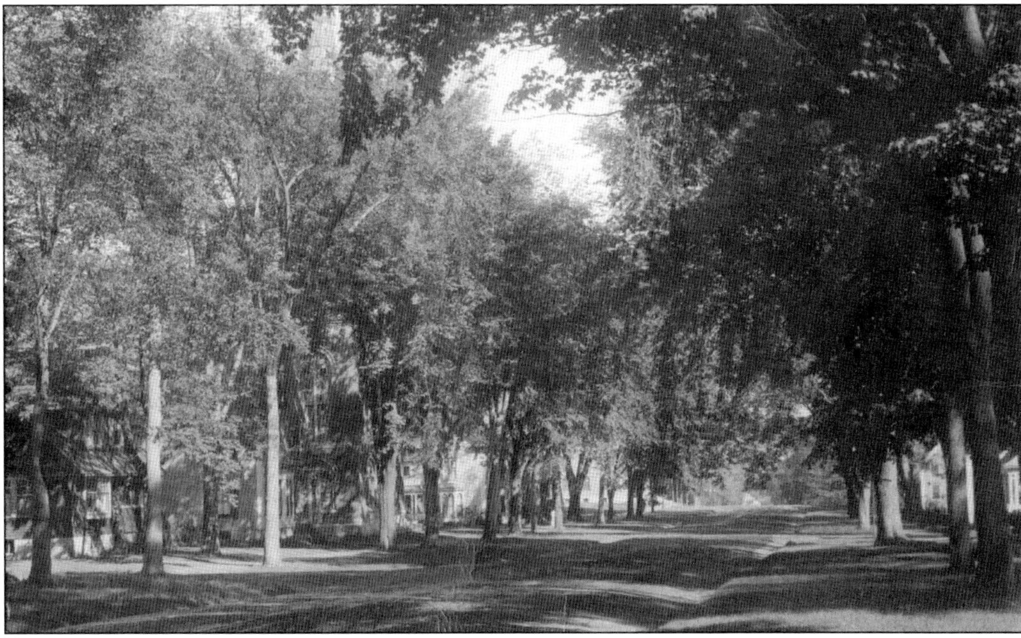

Winthrop Street was laid out on March 1785, just 12 days after Water Street. Known as Augusta's "grand old avenue," it served as the main road to Winthrop. During the 1850s, the residents planted elm trees 15 feet from the road and 40 feet apart. Obscured by the greenery, the Universalist Church is just left of center, and the YMCA is at the left of the intersection with State Street.

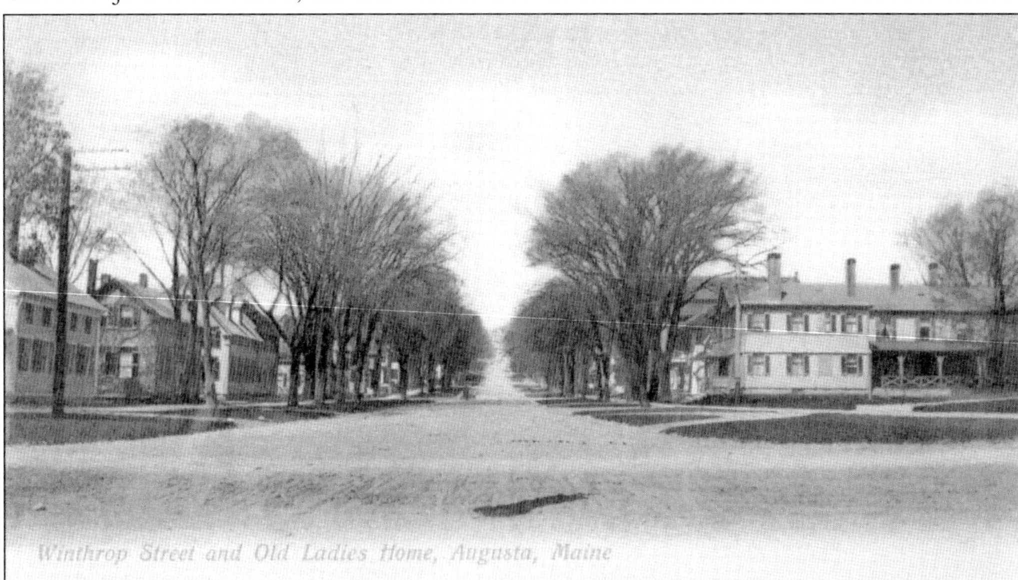

Looking west on Winthrop Street, the first house seen at left was built on the corner of State Street around 1851, then moved here to accommodate the Concert Hall. In 1934, it was converted into a restaurant, which burned in 1966. The Greek Revival home behind it was likely moved here for the Concert Hall and has since been torn down. St. Mark's Home for Women is at right.

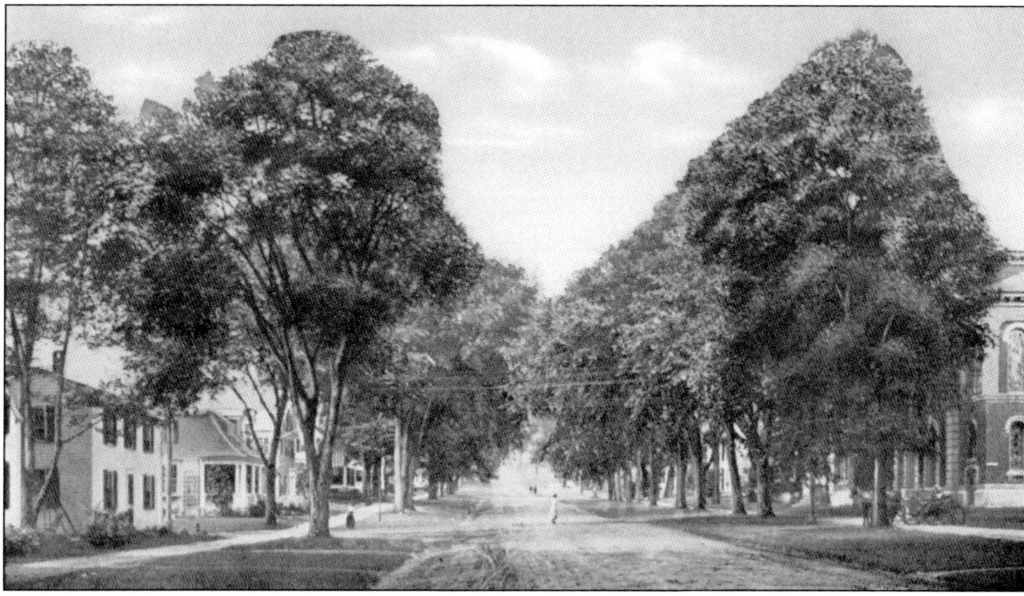

The Young family built the Federal Revival–influenced home at left, on the corner of Chapel and Winthrop Streets, around 1835. Just beyond it is the Shingle-style house built by Charles S. Hichborn in 1893. Hichborn was the mayor of Augusta in 1905, as well as a member of the committee organized to rebuild the State House in 1909. The Universalist Church is behind the trees at right, and Winthrop Hill lies straight ahead.

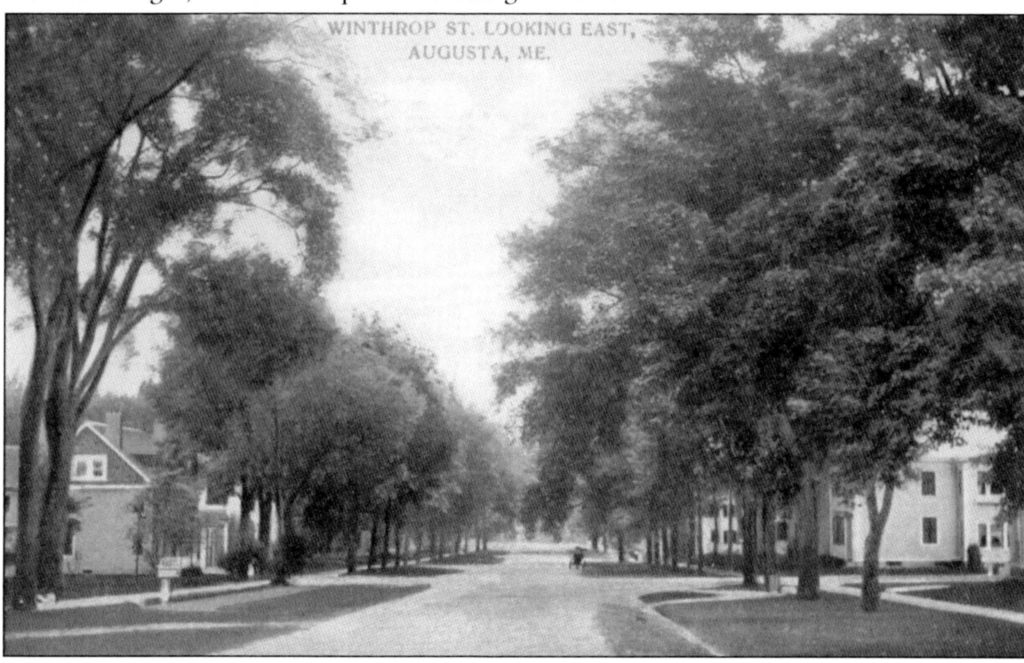

Though it is unclear who built the five-bay Greek Revival home on the corner of Winter Street, it is known that Frederick G. Lyman, president of Cushnoc Paper Company, bought the house in 1894. On the right is the Greek Revival home built by Loyal Lovejoy in 1851. Later, it was owned by Gustavus Robertson, the superintendent of schools and the 1903–1904 mayor of Augusta who died in office.

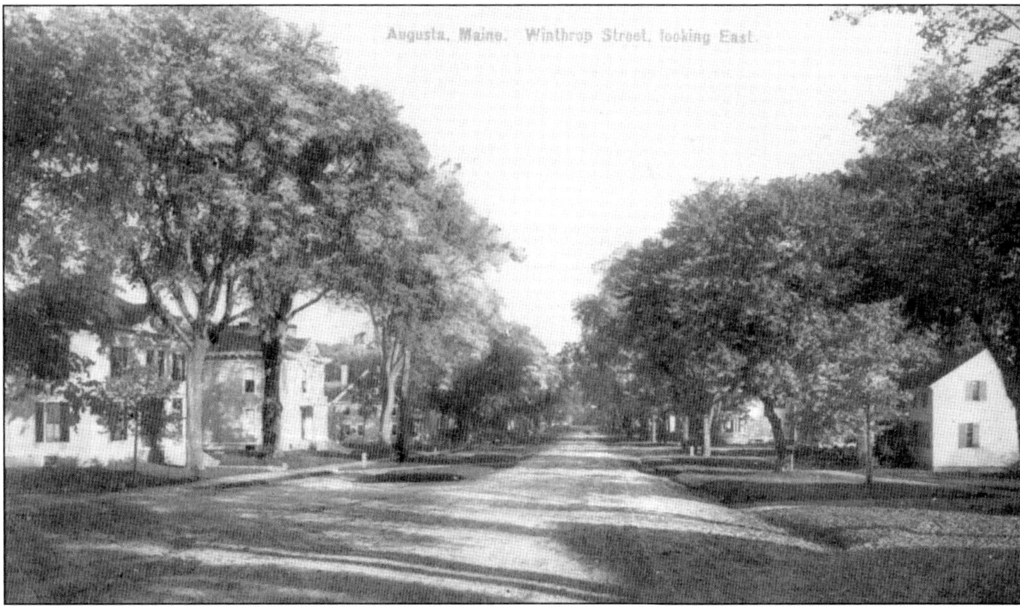

Francis H. Fassett designed the Italianate home at left, with details similar to the Vickery & Hill building, for Peleg Vickery in 1878. William Badger, postmaster, had built the Victorian house farther down in 1877. It was later owned by Fred L. Hersey, who operated a shoe store on Water Street. Olive Partridge commissioned the Greek Revival house at right, built between 1838 and 1851.

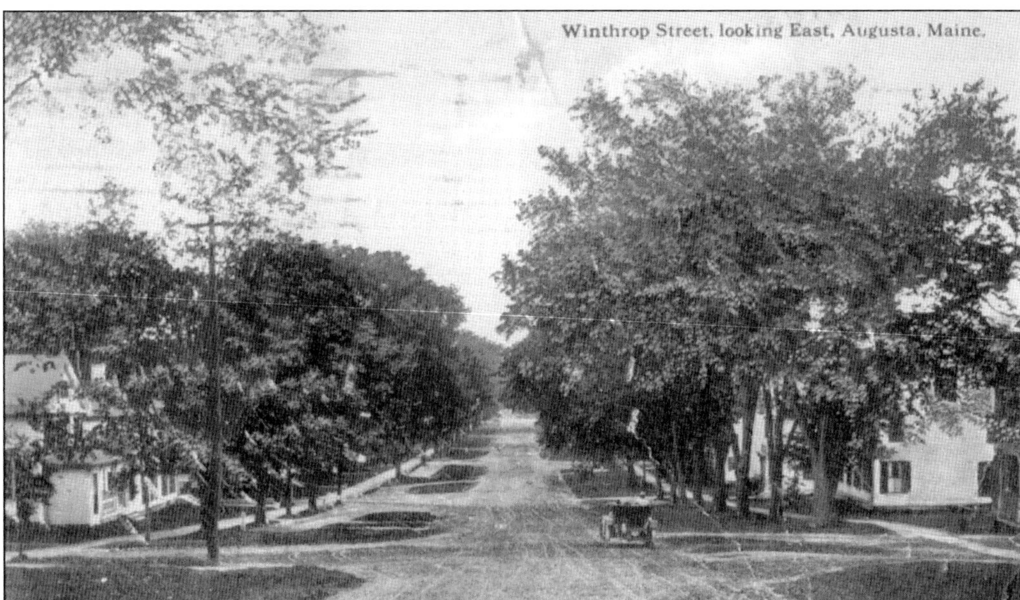

Viewed from the intersection of North and South Chestnut Streets, the Greek Revival house of Daniel Fairbanks can be seen at left. It was built between 1820 and 1838 and later became the residence of city solicitor Melvin Sawtelle. The construction date of the Greek Revival house at right is unknown, but it predates 1838. At one point, Willis Swift, mayor during World War I, had come to live here.

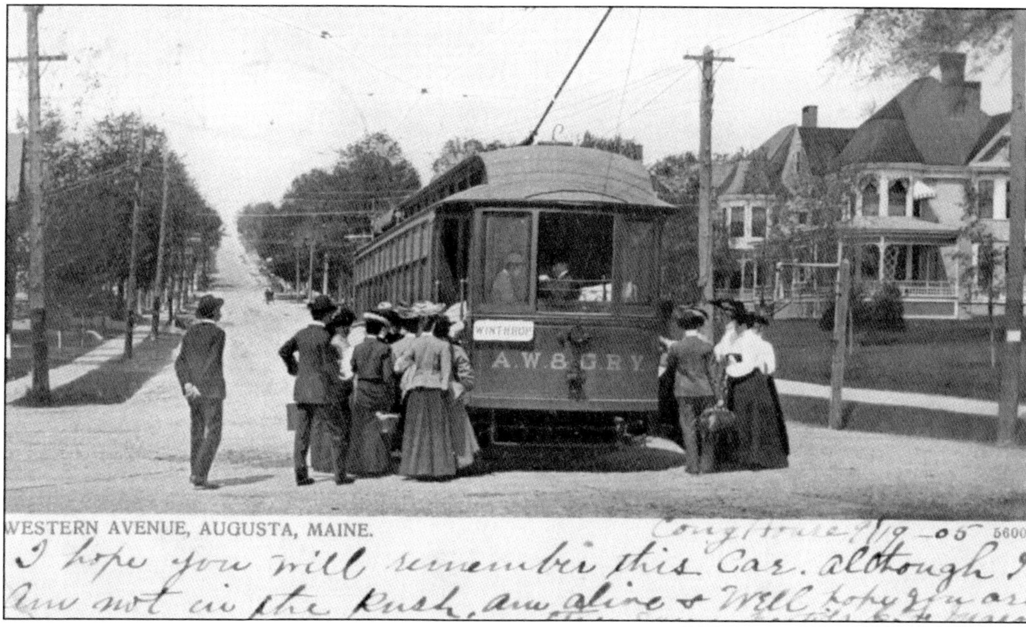

Viewed from the base of Western Avenue, passengers can be seen boarding train No. 20, the "Cobbosseecontee" of the Augusta, Winthrop & Gardiner Street Railway, for their destination of Island Park or Winthrop. Taken around 1903, this image shows two of the many opulent homes that could be found on the avenue. Unfortunately, the identical stately homesteads seen on the right are now gone.

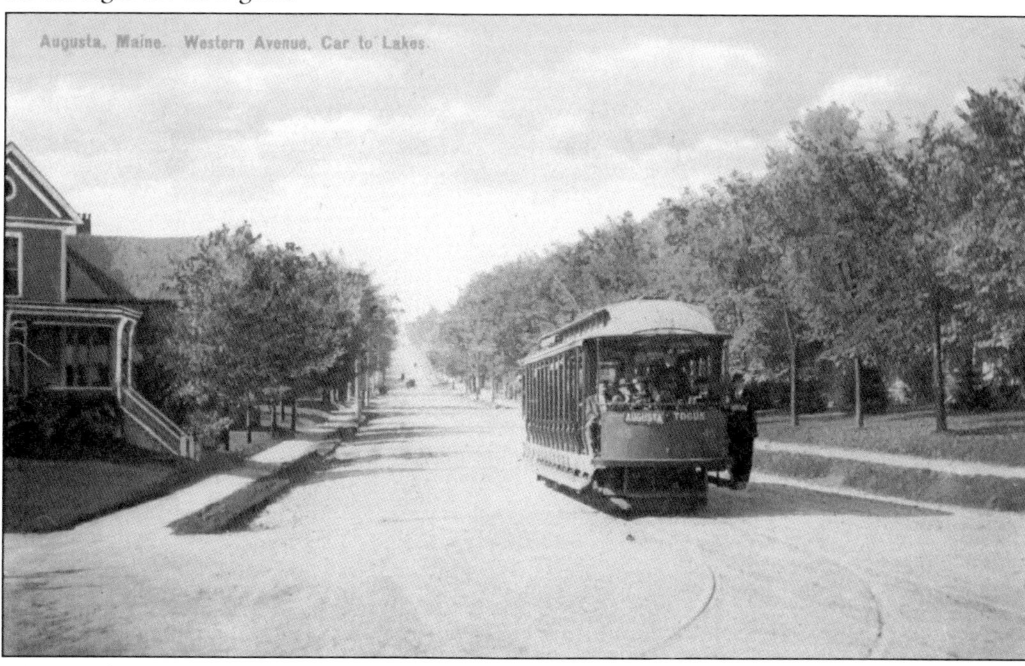

Inbound from Winthrop, open car No. 45 of the Lewiston, Augusta & Waterville Street Railway approaches the intersection of State Street. The composition of Western Avenue was much different in the early 1900s; the road was gravel and only a modest 42 feet wide, with handsome shade trees standing over the esplanades that lined either side of the thoroughfare.

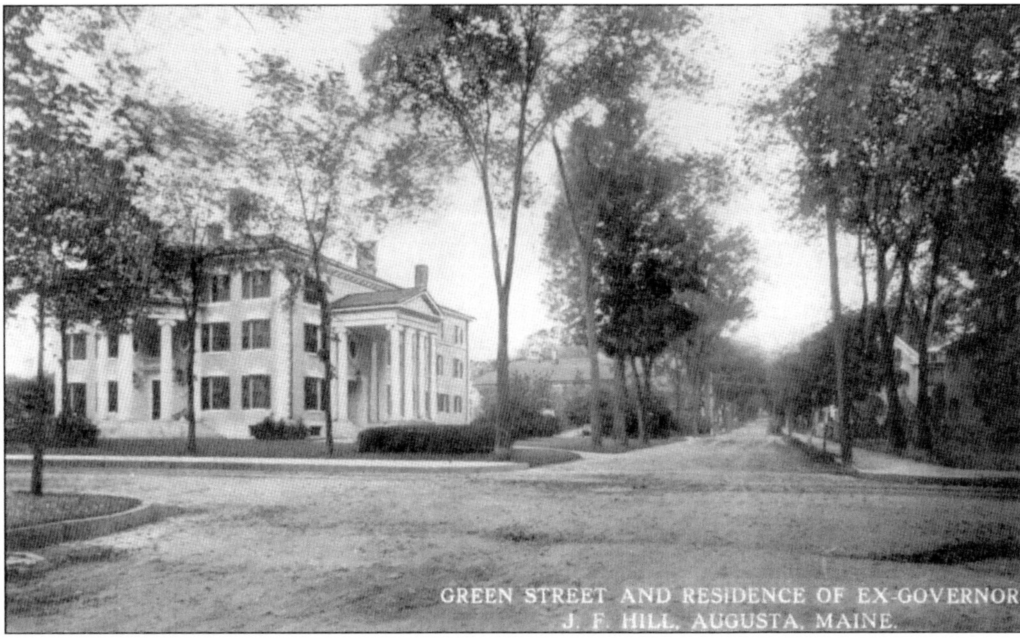

In 1796, Matthew Hayward built a home for himself and his family on Hartford Square, at the easterly end of what had recently been named Green Street. He owned 40 or 50 acres west of his house, and over the course of a century, what had started as a small farm was cultivated into this compact residential neighborhood.

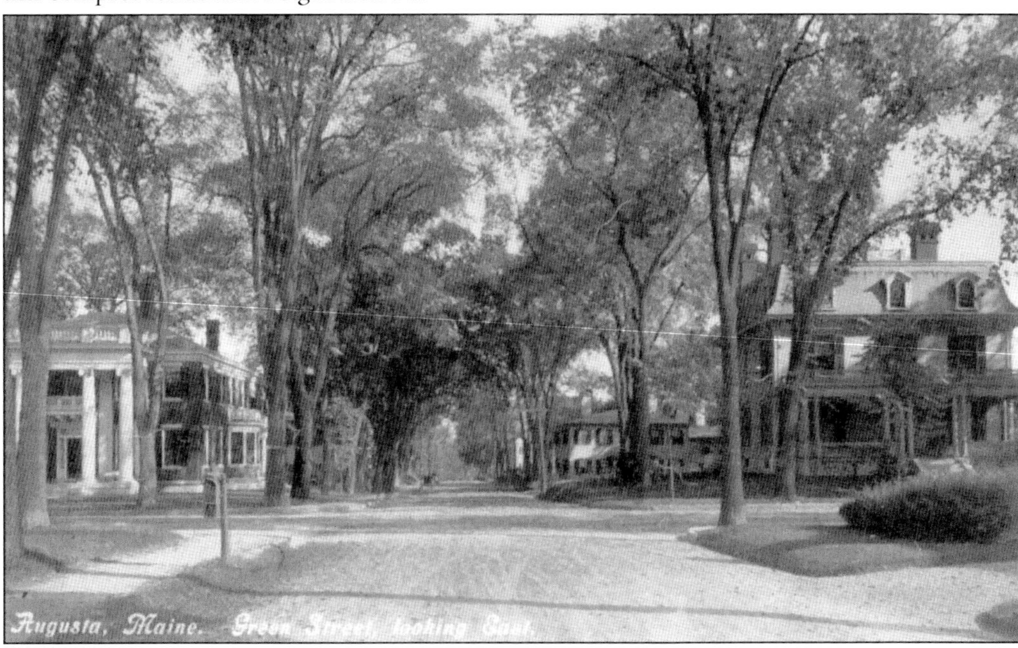

Looking through the intersection of Green and State Streets, the Honorable Herbert M. Heath's house is seen on the right. Heath twice served in the Maine House of Representatives and equally as long in the state senate. Farther down Green Street is the 1805 home of prominent lawyer Benjamin Whitwell. The grand brick building on the left was constructed by a local dry goods merchant, Johnson Lunt, in 1838.

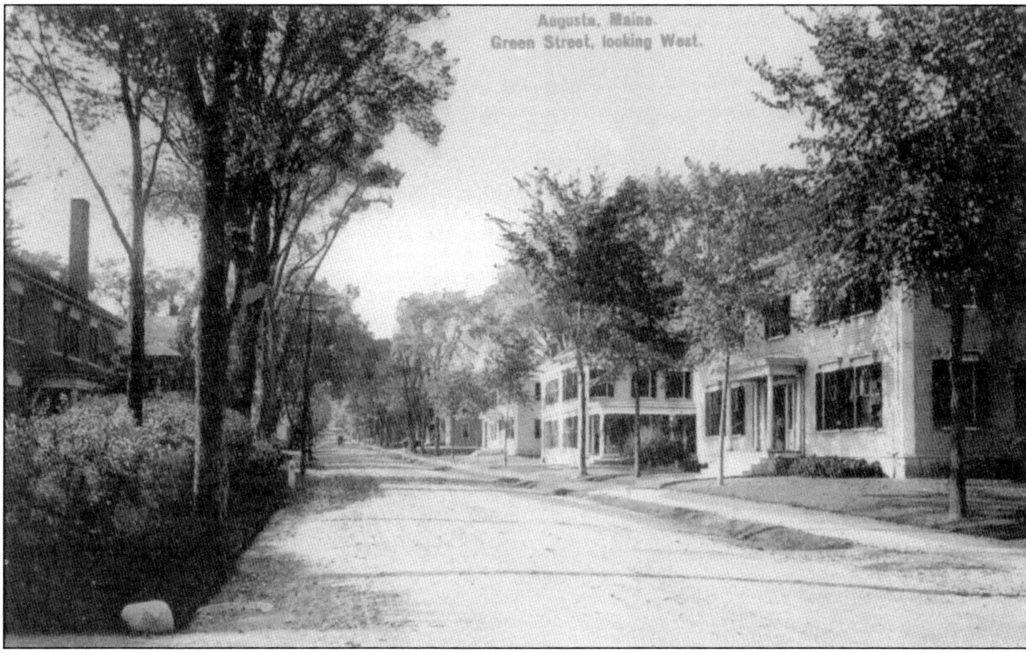

The house on the right, built in 1842, was the home of Vassal D. Pinkham. In 1853, Pinkham sold the city 12 acres of land at the top of Burnt Hill to be used for Mount Pleasant Cemetery. Also a noted owner of stage properties and businesses, Pinkham was the last owner of the stage line between Augusta and Bangor before the railroad emerged as a strong presence.

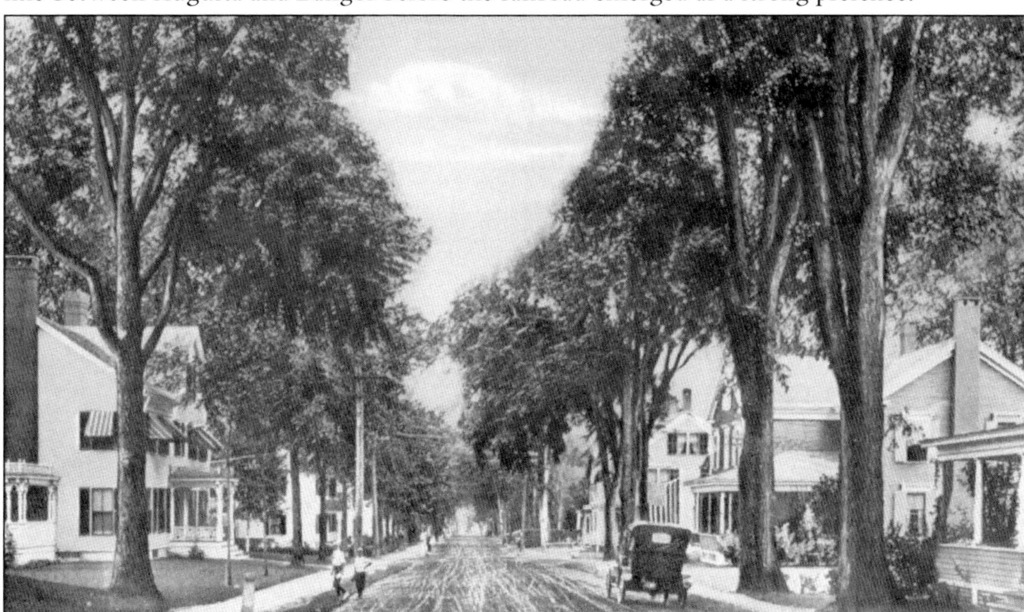

The Honorable Leslie C. Cornish, 12th chief justice of the Maine Supreme Judicial Court from 1917 to 1925, and his wife, Fannie Woodman Cornish, made a home in the 1835 Colonial-style house seen on the left, at the intersection of Green and Chapel Streets. Across the street is the 1856 home of James E. Fuller and his wife, Emily. James was a local wholesale and retail grocer who operated a store on Water Street.

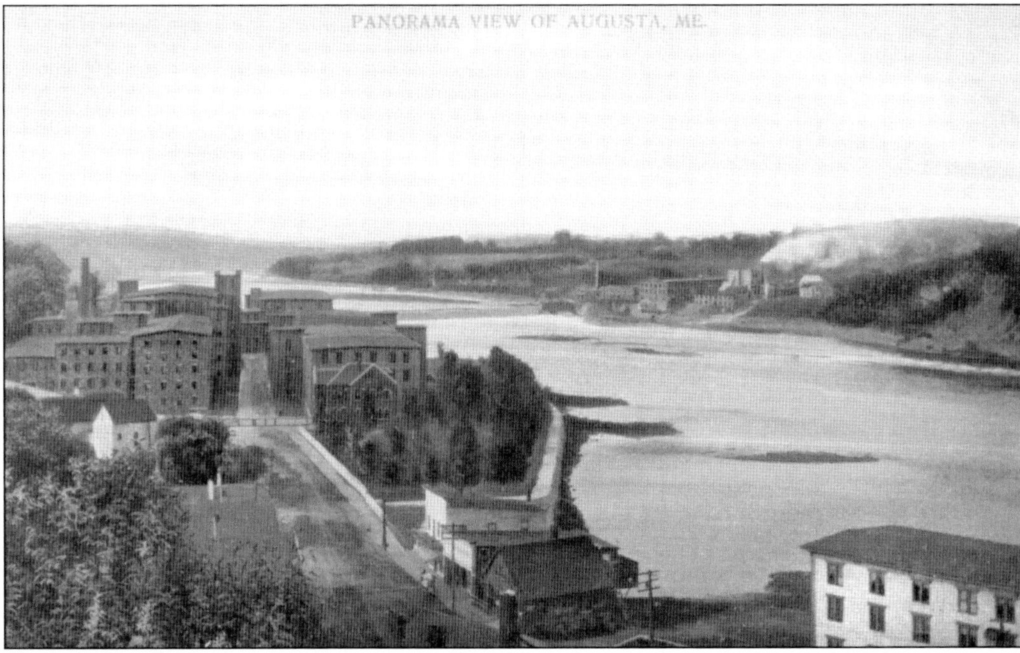

This c. 1907 four-postcard panorama is a rare glimpse at a wide view of Augusta. From the left, the bottom of Northern Avenue leads into the Edwards Mill complex. In the center are barbershops and a grocery store, followed by the north end of the Edwards House. On the other side of the river are the Kennebec Light and Heat Company's pump house and the Cushnoc Pulp and Paper Company.

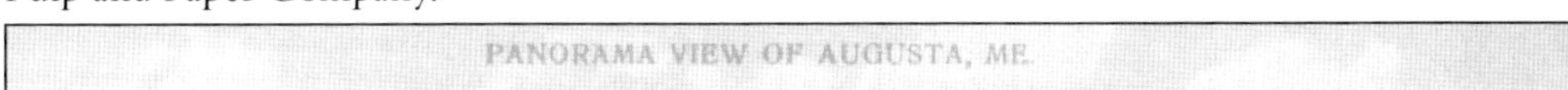

To the right of the Edwards Block is Hides and Wool Print Shop, and on the other side of the train trestle is the Riverside Block. A saloon, clothing store, and sewing machine shop follow, along with the back end of the three-story brick building of the Augusta Real Estate Association. In the background is the brick Gannett Publishing building near the center, with the Augusta City Hall at far right.

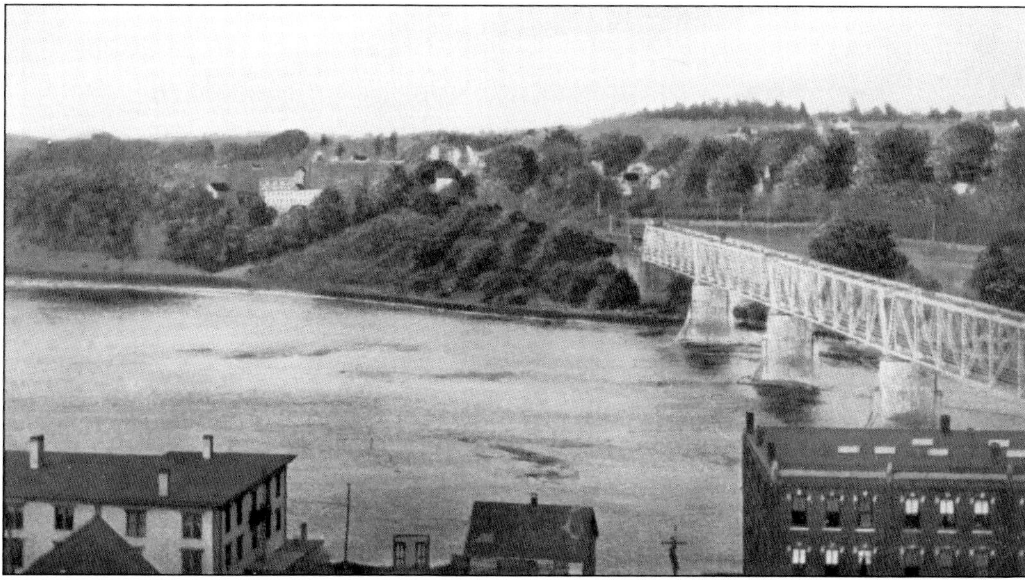

Continuing in the front is the south end of the boardinghouse, a small shed, and one end of the Edwards Block. Crossing the river is the Maine Central Railroad Bridge, with Willow Street winding behind it in the background. Following the railroad tracks from the bridge toward the left is the Lawrence, Newhall & Page Company's window frame and sash factory at the end of Maple Street.

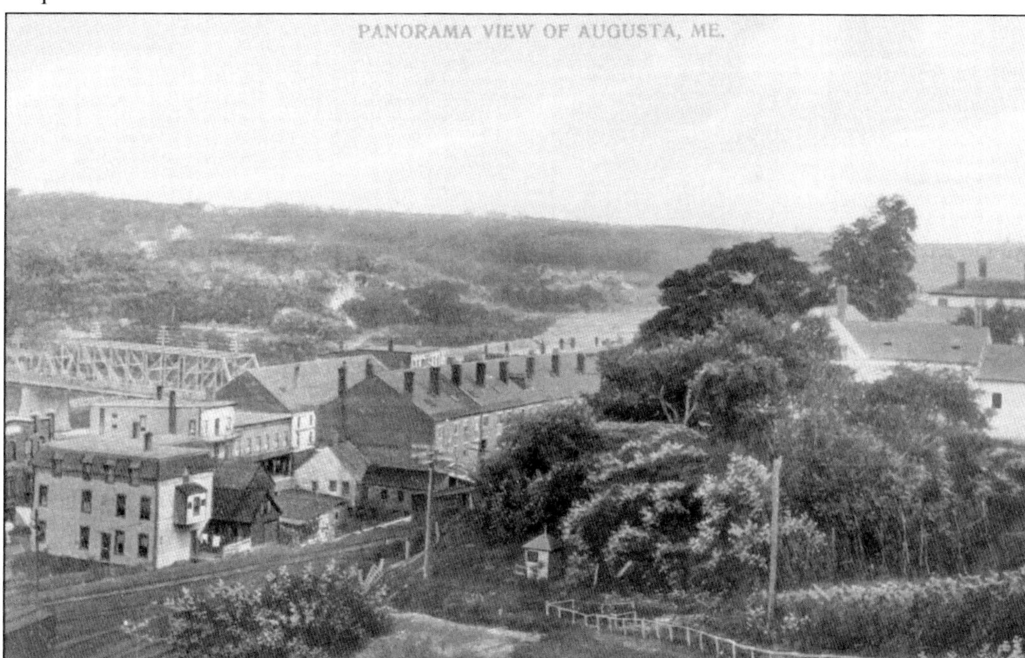

Continuing south from the mansard-roofed structure at the lower left are a millinery, barbershops, laundry, and a dye hall. The buildings with rows of chimneys are part of the Bridges Block, with the Union Block directly across the street. Heading north is the City Hotel, which burned in 1912, destroying much of this neighborhood. The Kennebec River Bridge is in the back, and on the right is the Crosby Street Place neighborhood.

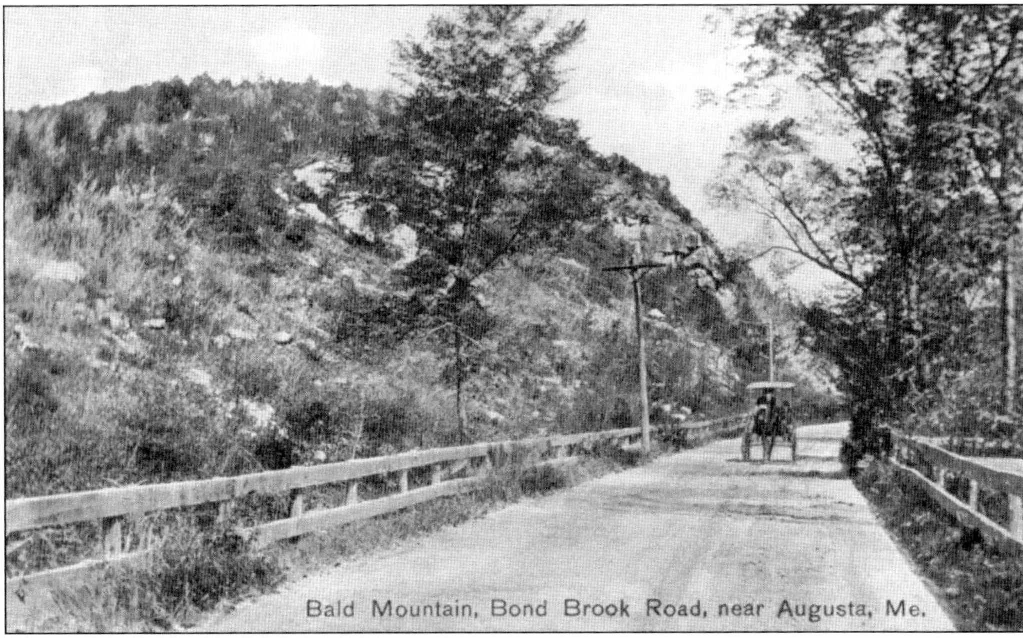

Located a little more than a quarter mile from Mount Vernon Avenue, this mountain is now covered with trees and brush, although the rock faces are still visible. In 1909, Bond Brook Road was little more than a dirt byway. This view is looking toward Augusta, with Bond Brook barely visible on the right. Coombs Mill lies in the opposite direction.

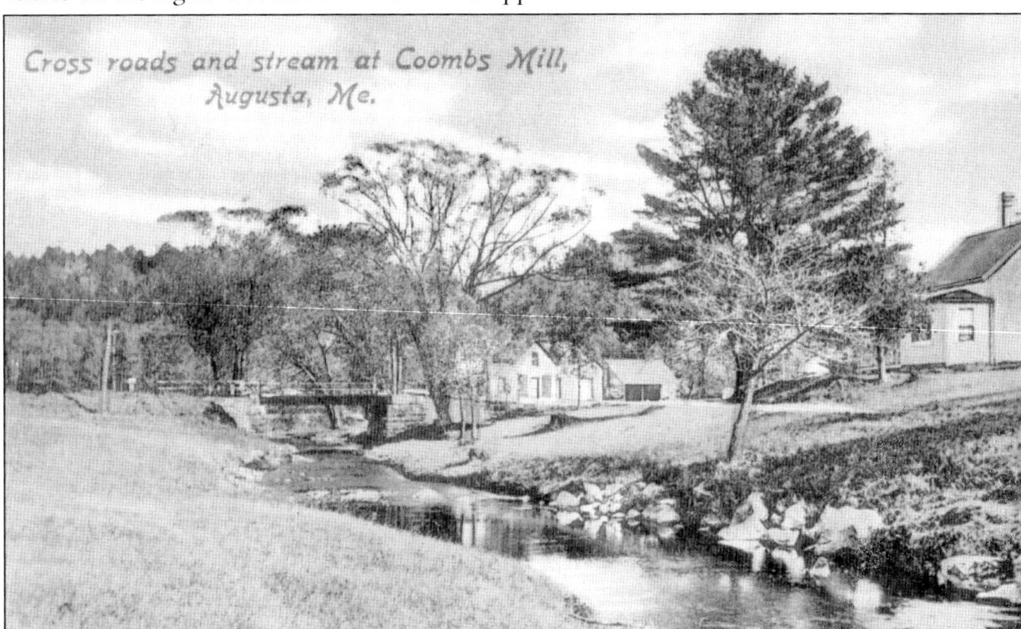

The westerly end of Mount Vernon Avenue, now called the Bond Brook Road, once split into north and south crossroads (across the bridge and off the left edge and to the right in front of the house, respectively) onto the Coombs Mill Road, currently known as the Leighton Road. Coombs Mill is located directly behind the viewer; the Coombs family once owned much of the land in this area.

Ten

Along the Waterfront

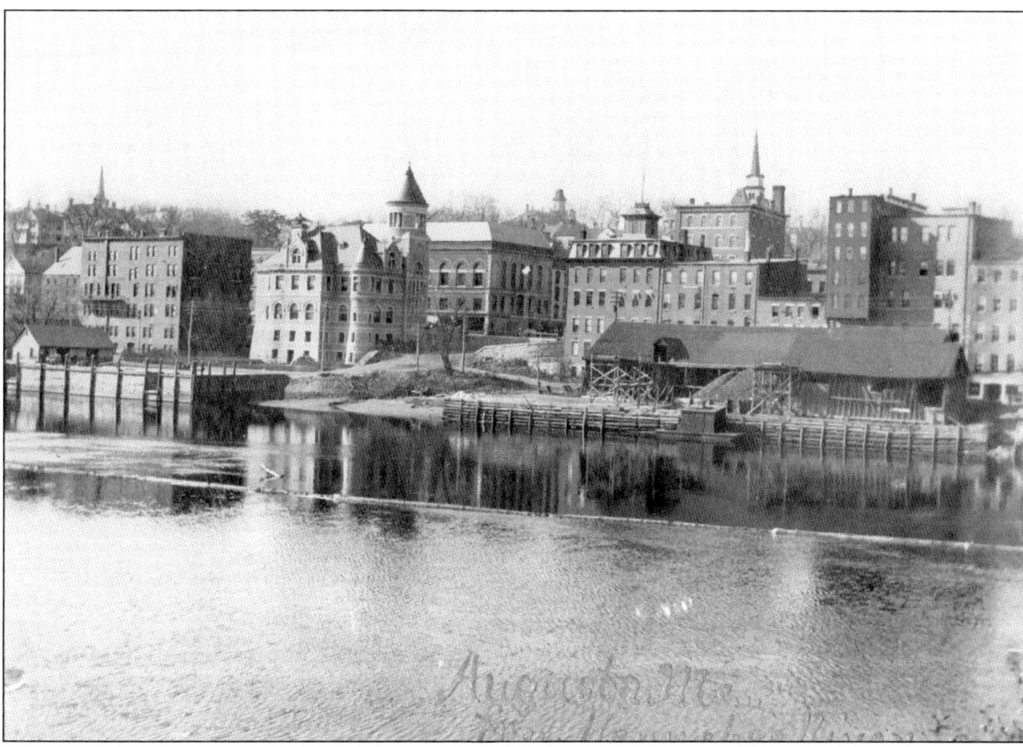

This c. 1895 image offers a rare view of the waterfront without any ships present. Smith's Wharf is at far left, and Central and North wharves are farther upriver, supporting various coal sheds. Winthrop Street winds its way between the post office and the Allen Block, and on to the water's edge. Granite Hall can be seen on the other side of Market Square.

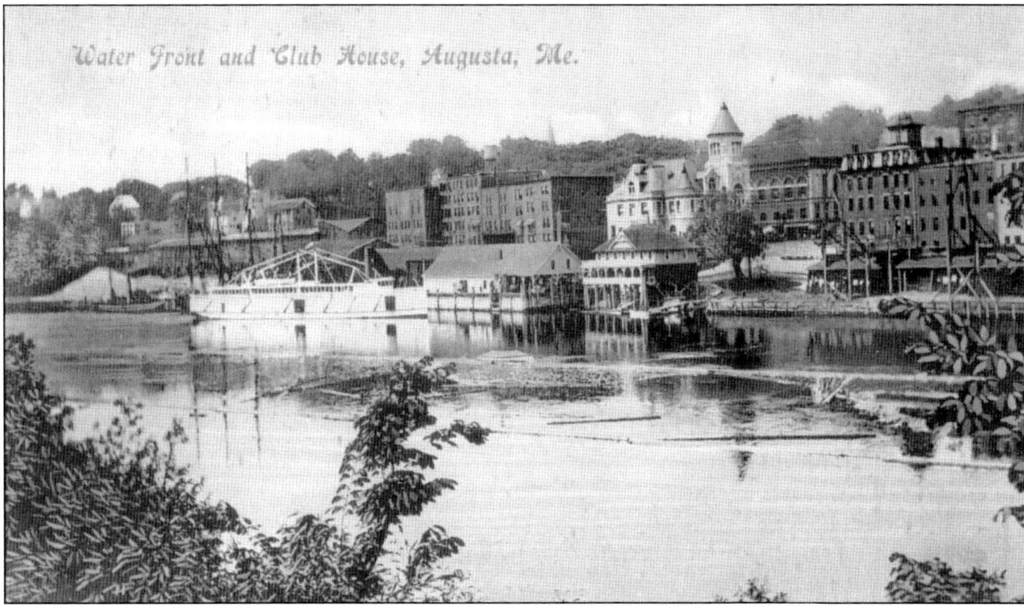

The Kennebec River was once alive with boating and shipping activity. Just in from her return trip from Gardiner, the steamer *City of Augusta* is seen pulling into dock at the Eastern Steamship Company's freight house while a three-mast schooner is off-loading at the Purinton Brothers coal sheds behind her. The recently completed Augusta Yacht Club sits farther upstream, and several more coals sheds are just onshore to the right.

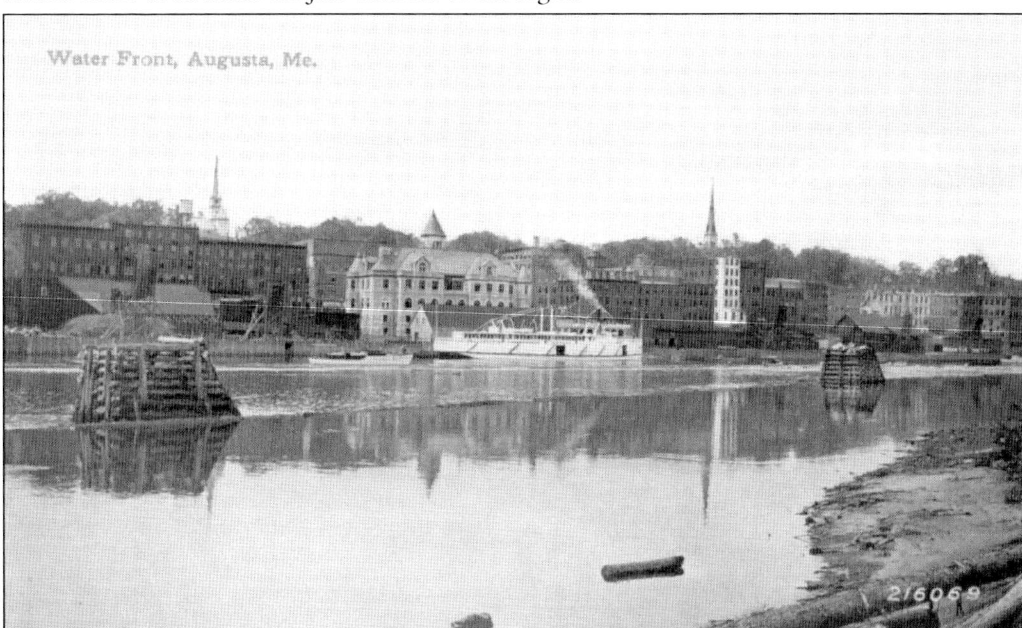

Augusta's business district is seen from the waterfront of roughly where the Augusta Lumber Company was located. The two log boom piers seen here were constructed of logs driven into the riverbed, then surrounded by a cribwork of logs, and finally filled with stone. They were used to anchor log booms for the lumber mills. Now gone, vestiges of the piers can still be seen at low tide.

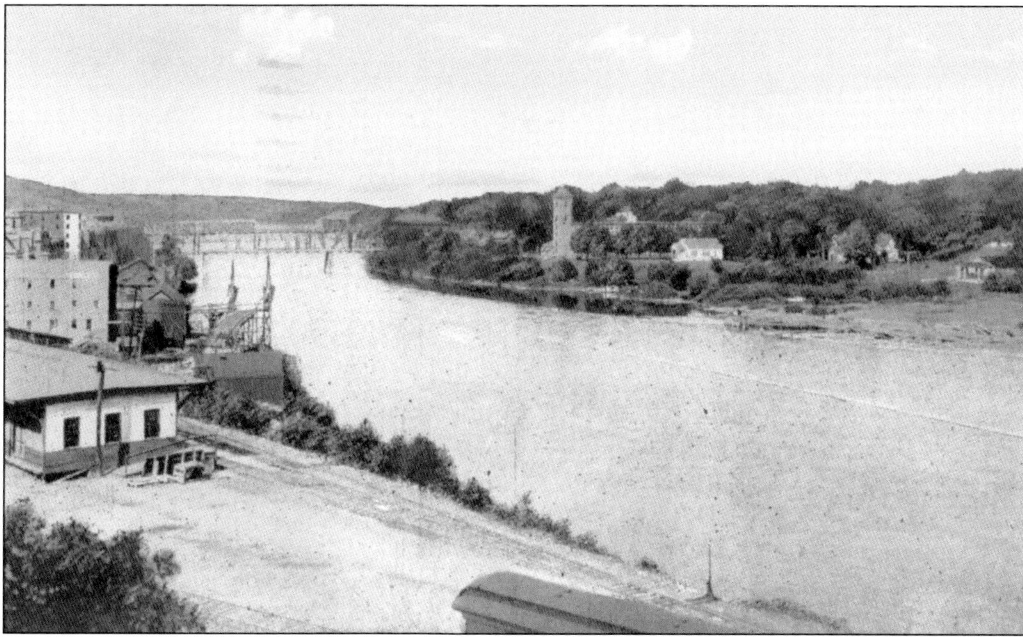

Viewed from the top of Rines Hill, the end of Maine Central Railroad's freight house is seen on the left side. The livery stable and garage are directly behind it, and Purinton Brother's coal sheds line the water's edge. Across the river is the tower of the Crossett Shoe Company, followed by the small light-colored structure of the Christian Science Chapel.

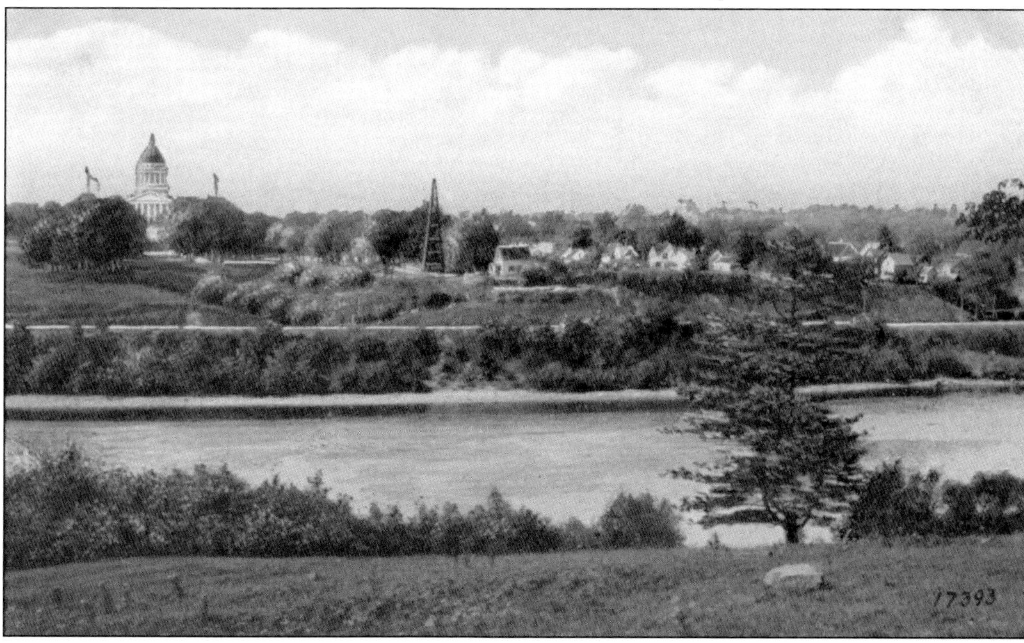

This view toward the capitol was taken from the northern edge of the asylum property. The steel tower, just left of center, was erected at the base of Capitol Street in 1909 and used to hold aloft a seven-eighth-of-an-inch aluminum feed wire for the Augusta, Winthrop & Gardiner Street Railway. The corresponding tower on the near side of the river, out of view, was not far from this site.

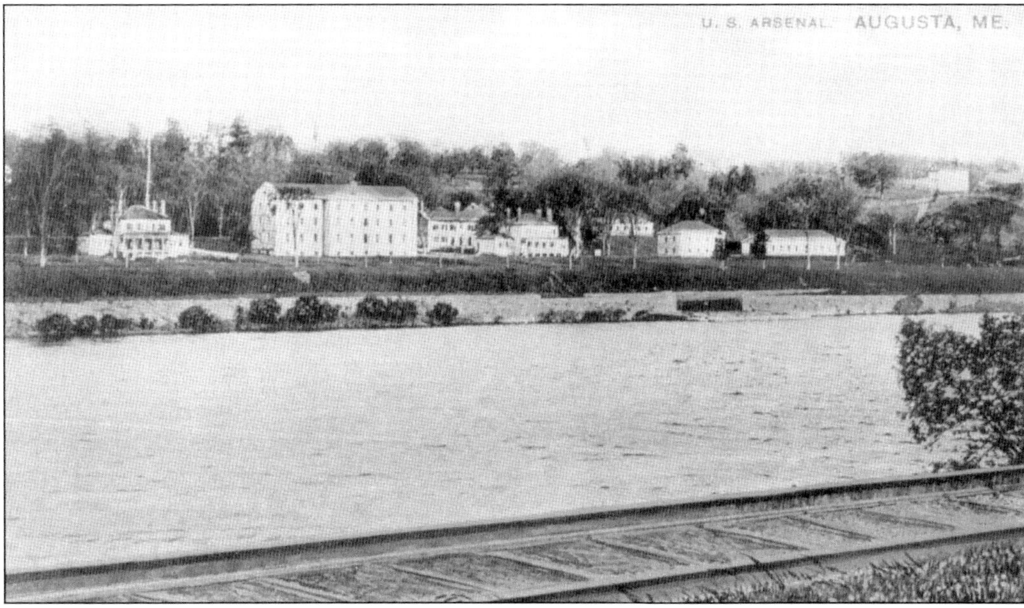

Because of unrest with the British in Canada, the federal government established the Kennebec Arsenal in 1827, when Augusta became the capital. The US Army designed the arsenal in the Federal–Greek Revival style, and the first Hallowell granite stone was laid on the 40-acre lot on July 14, 1828. Over the next decade, 15 additional structures were erected, eight from undressed granite, surrounded by an eight-foot fence.

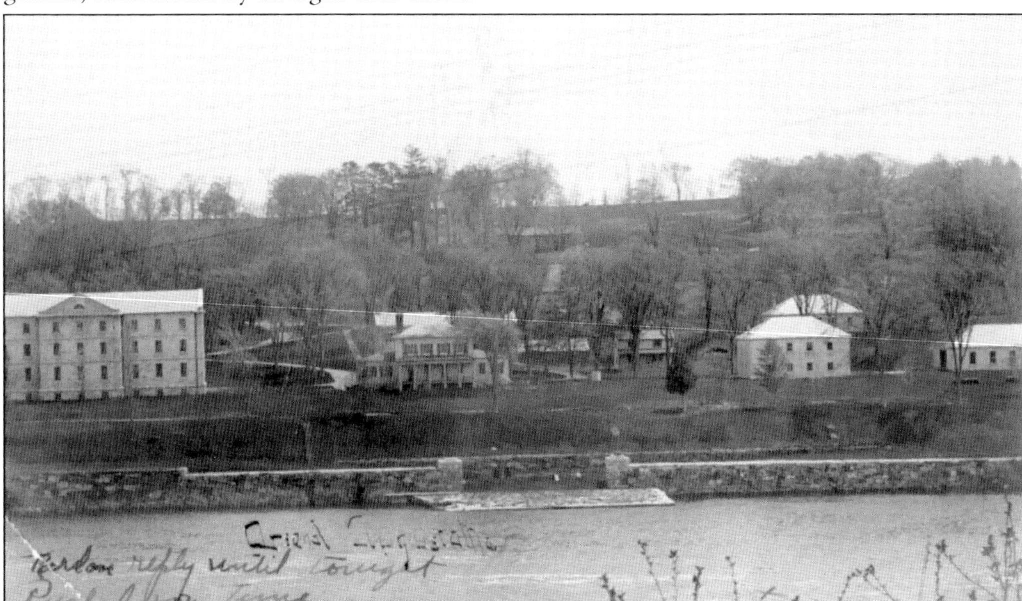

A granite retaining wall and wharf was erected along the riverfront so ships with a 10-foot draft could dock even at low tide. The granite structures are, from left to right, the arsenal building, the No. 3 quarters with the barracks directly behind it, the carpenter's shop with the armory just beyond, and the machine shop. The wooden buildings in the center include a shed and quarters with the laboratory up the hill.

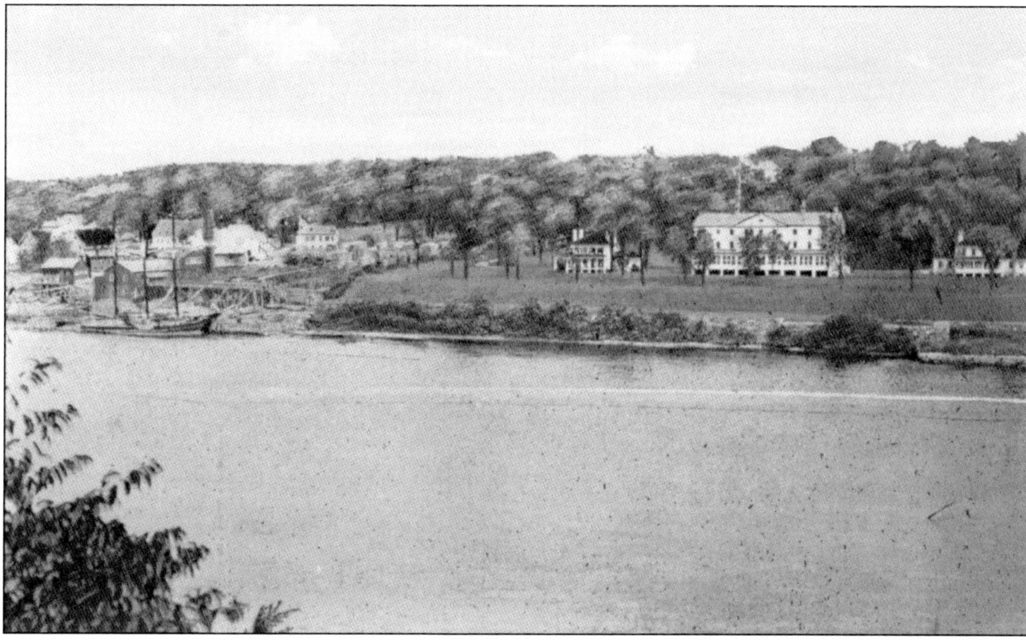

The arsenal was used to manufacture and store vast amounts of ammunition for the Mexican War in 1846, as well as for the Union Army during the Civil War. As national interests pressed westward, the arsenal became less viable, and on September 10, 1901, the last sunset gun was fired. In 1905, the property and buildings were transferred to the Maine Insane Asylum, which they began to occupy the following year.

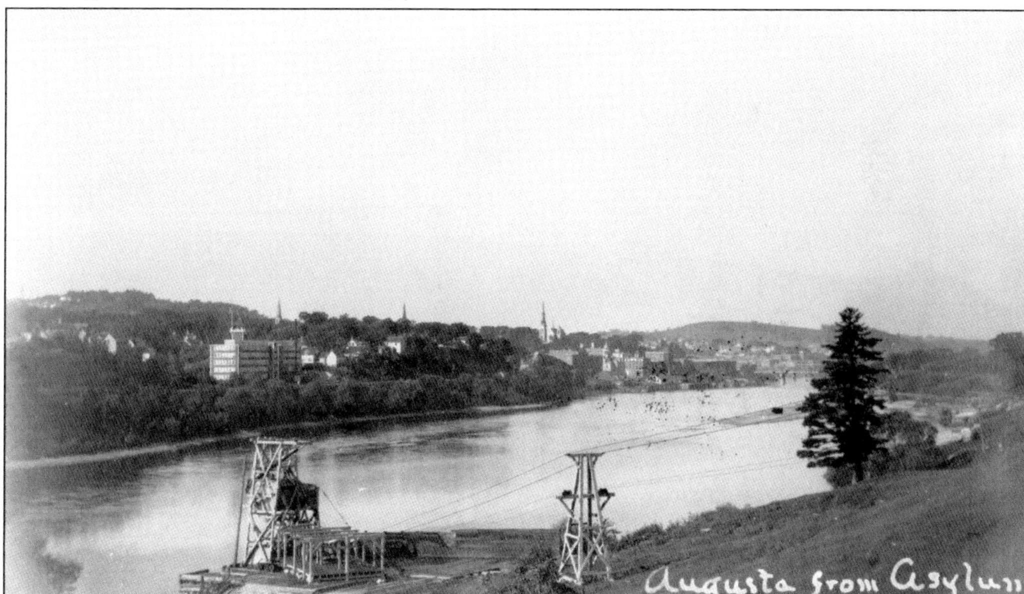

In 1899, the asylum constructed a tramway to off-load coal from a vessel's hold directly into the coal pocket of the engine house. The tramway bucket traveled 1,050 feet each way and lifted the coal 150 feet in elevation. It carried an impressive 30 tons per hour—many times more than the wheelbarrows and carts that it had replaced. Seen here is the loading terminal and retractable dock hoist atop the hospital wharf.

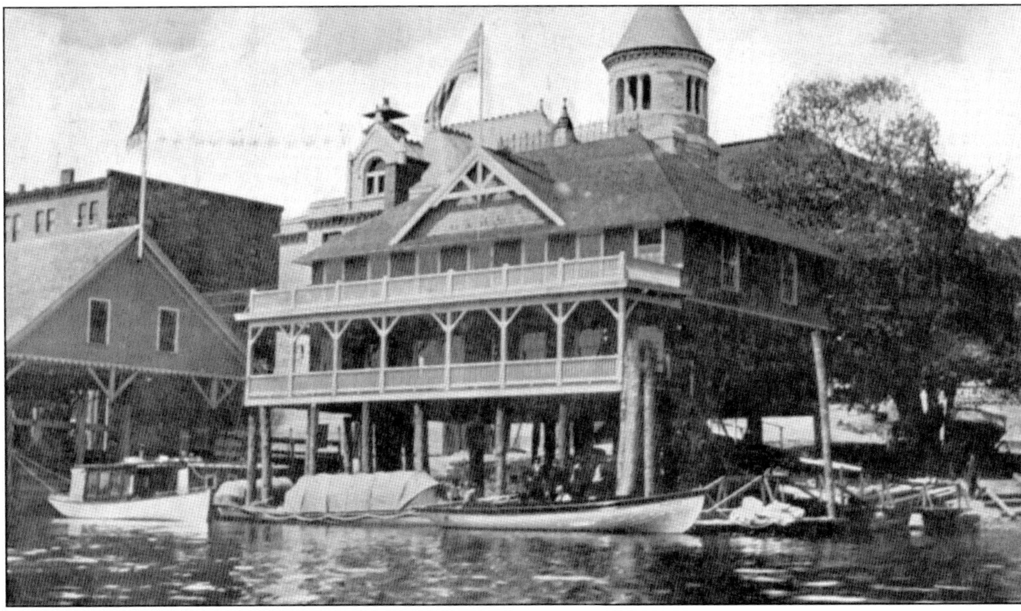

Yachting and sailing became popular during the early 19th century, and lacking adequate facilities, the Augusta Yacht Club erected their clubhouse behind the post office in 1907. Built on pilings 8.5 feet off the water, the two-story structure contained a reading room, locker rooms, and bathrooms on the lower level, while the second floor was a large hall. Broad piazzas skirted each story on the east side.

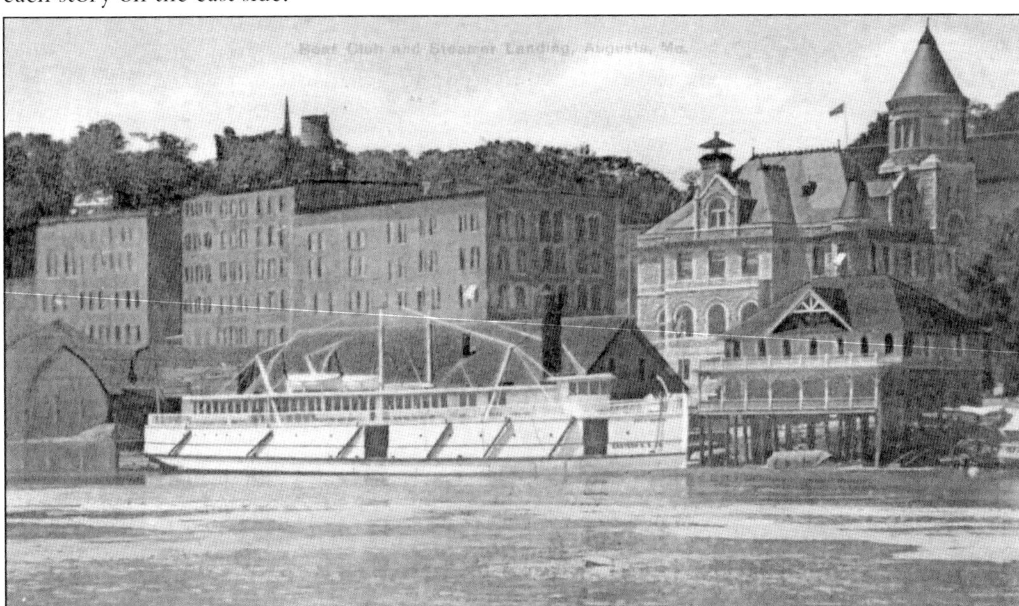

With the construction of the dam decades before, Augusta became the head of navigation and a popular destination for tens of thousands of tourists each year. The steamer *City of Augusta* is seen sitting in her mooring at the Eastern Steamship Company's freight house on this postcard dated 1909. On the right is the Augusta Yacht Club clubhouse that had been built just a few years before.

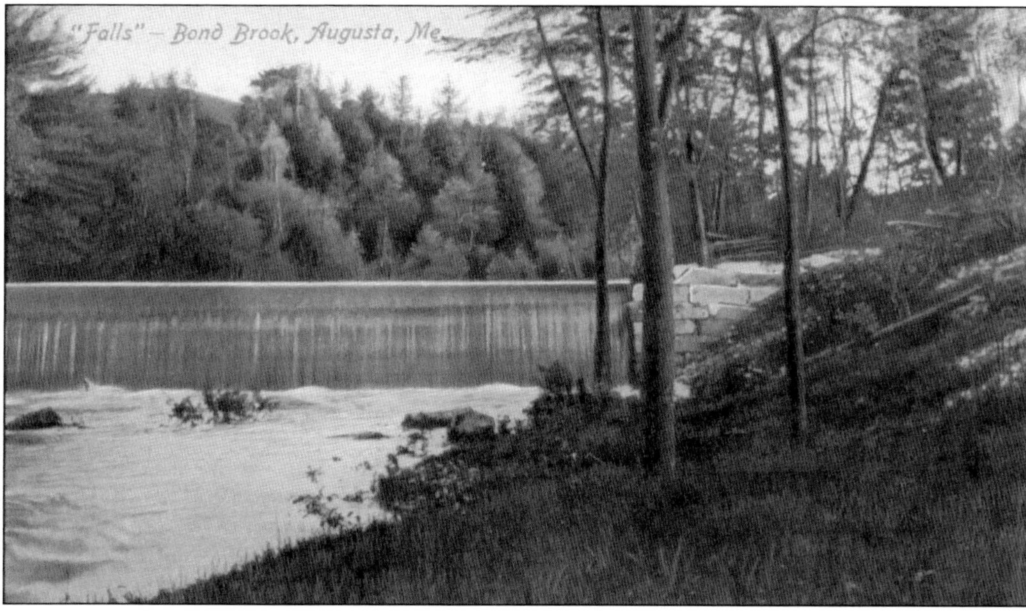

John Jones, later known as "Black" Jones due to his political views, built the first sawmill at Lower Falls in 1773, though he remained there only a short time. Martha Ballard, a midwife and healer whose diaries have achieved international fame, resided at the site of Jones Mill with her family from 1778 to 1791. During her career, Martha delivered 816 babies and cared for countless other patients.

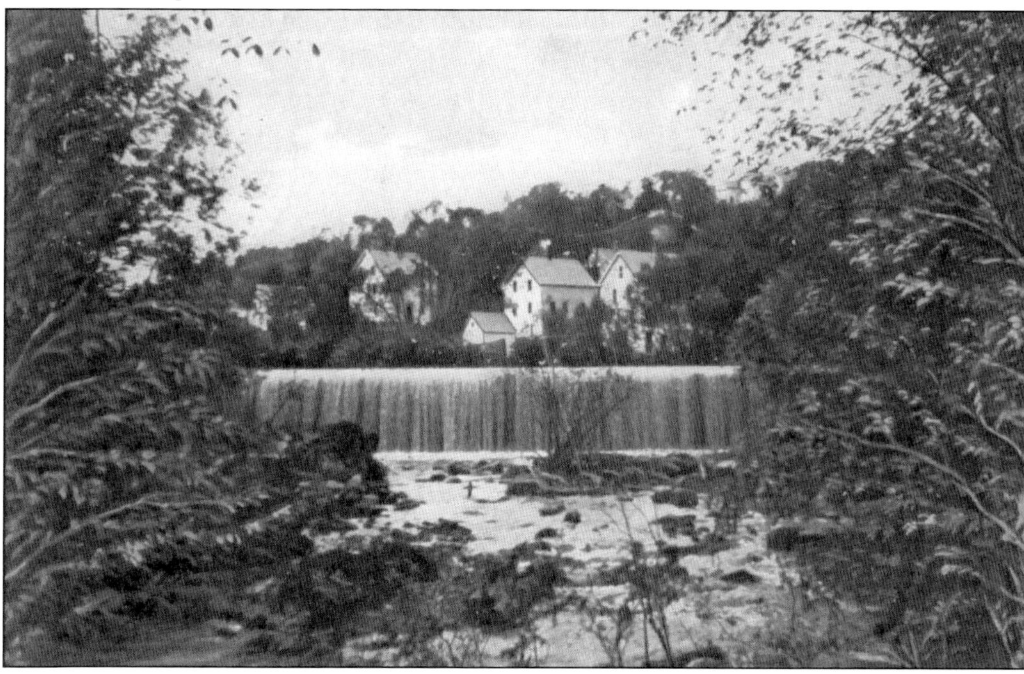

This was the second dam on Bond Brook, sometimes called the Upper Mill Dam. Serving B.F. Parrott's gristmill, it was located at the narrowing of the brook before reaching the peninsula at the Lower Falls. Seen in the background are the homes that line the west side of Mount Vernon Avenue. The dam has long since been breached, and only scattered boulders remain.

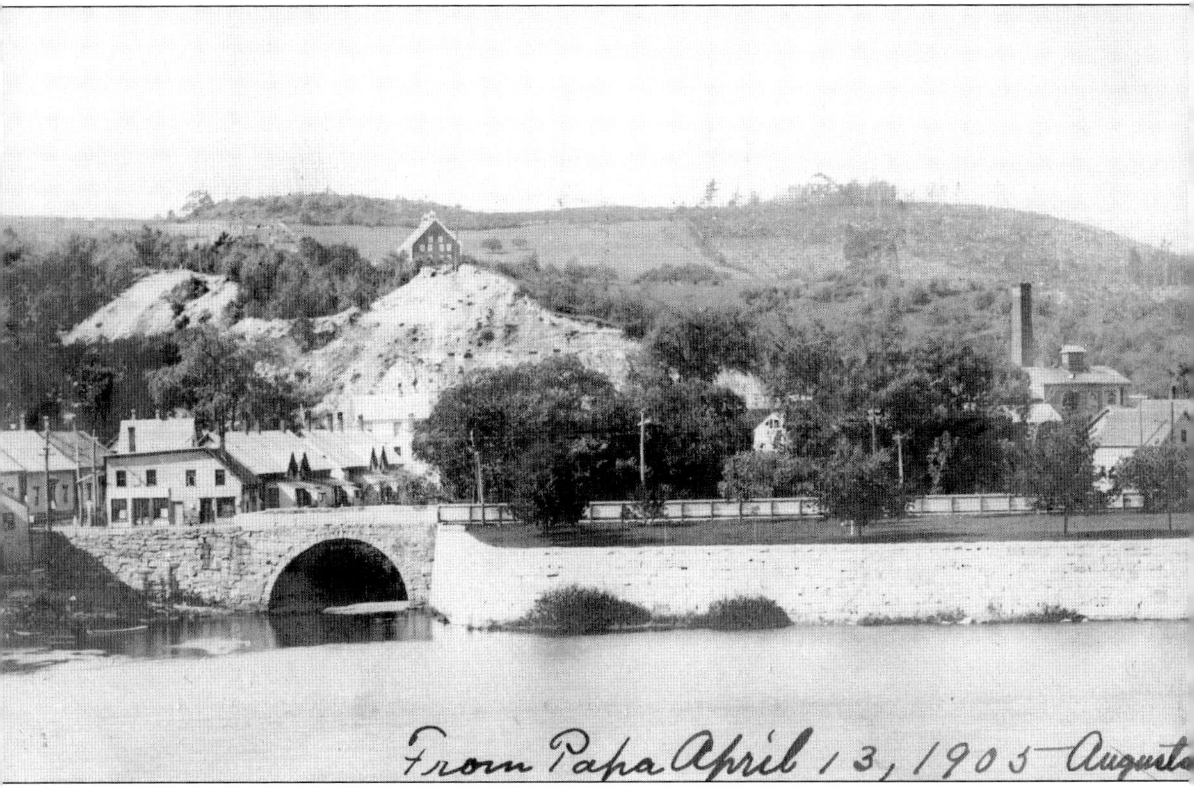

Looking from the east side, and from left to right, a number of tenement duplexes and four-unit buildings can be seen lining either side of Bond Street. Many of these structures were built in 1884 as employee housing for the Edwards Manufacturing Company. The large building, almost directly above the Bond Brook Arch, belonged to the Augusta City Farm. Established in 1805, the poorhouse was a sanctuary for the destitute before the advent of social security programs. Farther along this section of tree-lined Water Street, the north smokestack and cupola of the brick Augusta Gashouse comes into view. Built in 1853, the gas company lit the city of Augusta for the first time on October 26 of that same year. In February 1887, the legislature chartered the Kennebec Light and Heat Company and authorized the sale of the gashouse property and franchise to it.

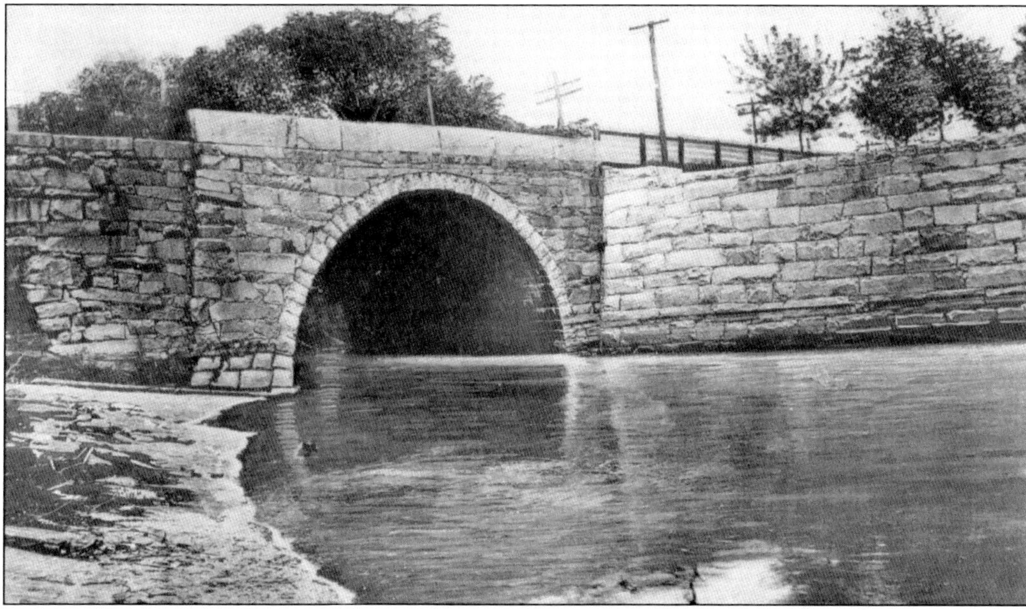

At the 1849 annual town meeting, it was determined that a stone arch would replace the wooden bridge spanning Bond Brook. In ill repair, the bridge had a habit of floating off the abutments during a flood. Ephraim Ballard constructed the arch for just over $6,400. Although it was six feet higher and much wider than the original span, it was still completed in approximately 200 days.

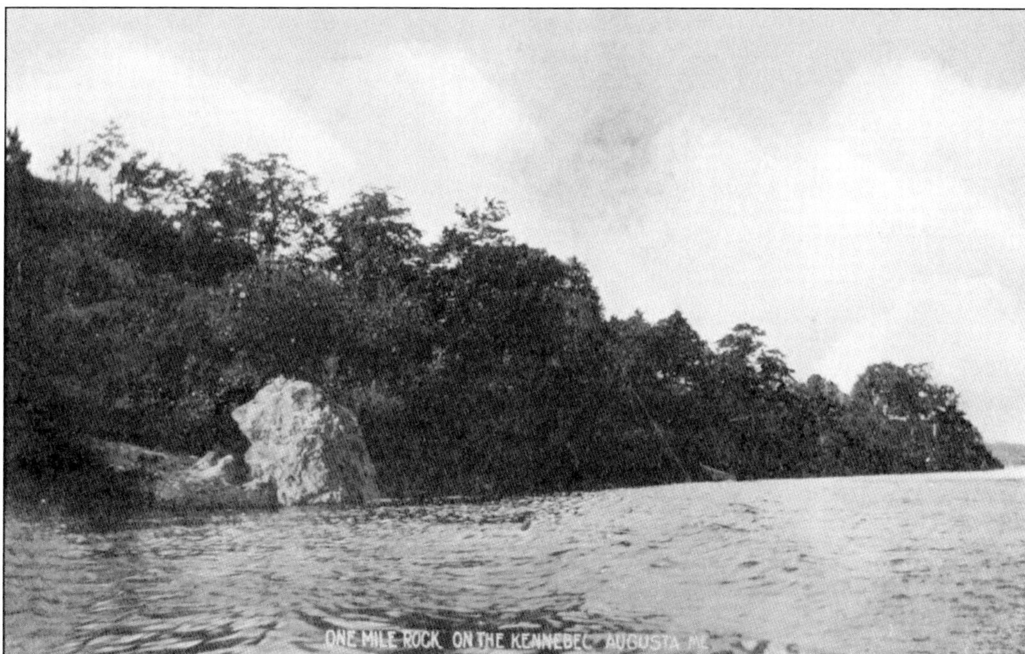

Mile Rock, as its name implies, lies on the west bank of the Kennebec River about one mile south of the Augusta business district. Used as a navigational aid since its earliest days, the rock doubled as a popular swimming hole for kids in the early 20th century and what became known as the "tramp jungle," a congregating place for wayfarers in the 1930s.